DALRYMPLE
CRESCENT
A SNAPSHOT OF
VICTORIAN
EDINBURGH

~

DALRYMPLE CRESCENT
A SNAPSHOT OF VICTORIAN EDINBURGH

~

Joanne Lamb

T & J LAMB

First published in 2011 by

T & J LAMB

9 Dalrymple Crescent

Edinburgh EH9 2NU

www.dcedin.co.uk

ISBN: 978-0-9566713-0-1

British Library Cataloguing-in-Publication Data

A catalogue record for this book is available from the British Library

Designed and typeset by Mark Blackadder

The publisher acknowledges a grant from

THE GRANGE ASSOCIATION

towards the publication of this book

Printed and bound by Bell & Bain Ltd, Glasgow

CONTENTS

FOREWORD

Seen from the perspective of the passing centuries, the history of Dalrymple Crescent is short, certainly by comparison with that of the historic Grange of St Giles and Grange Loan, its ancient thoroughfare, where once upon a time highwaymen lurked and Bonnie Prince Charlie was welcomed as he entered Edinburgh.

However, much has been going on during the life of the street. This book tells the story of each house and its inhabitants. It provides a fascinating social history of those who lived and worked in this part of the Grange when it was being developed in the latter part of the nineteenth century. For them and so many others, as you will discover from its pages, the Grange was their home for most of their lives. This book contains a mine of information and should be of interest not only to those who live in the street, such as myself, but also to those who live further afield.

Joanne Lamb is to be congratulated on her assiduous research and the imaginative way in which she has used it in creating this account.

CULLEN OF WHITEKIRK

DEDICATION

To Dorothy,
who linked the past with the present

PREFACE

Although this is a book about Victorian Edinburgh, it is very much a product of the 21st century. It would not have been possible without the digitisation of official records, and the availability of information on the World Wide Web. I have, of course, also used traditional written material, and a bibliography is given at the end of the book. Electronic sources are divided into two: the general ones, which are described below, and particular ones, which are cited in the notes for each chapter.

The general sources are:

1. The official records come mainly from Scotland's People.[1] These include wills, births, marriage and deaths from both Old Parish Records, and Statuary Records, and census records from 1841 to 1901.

2. A supplementary source is the International Genealogical Index of the Church of the Latter Day Saints site,[2] which gives information on births marriages and deaths from the whole world, but is supplied by volunteers and so is incomplete. It also gives information on the 1881 census from England and Wales, Canada and the USA.

3. Edinburgh City Library[3] provided census data for the city, and also the Post Office Directories for the period.

4. The National Archive of Scotland[4] provided the Sasine records, and also Valuation Rolls for the city. The field books for the Inland Revenue survey of 1912 are also held in the National Archive.

5. *The Scotsman* Archive[5] provided information from advertisements, announcements, articles and letters.

6. English births, marriages and deaths have come from FreeBMD,[6] a project which is transcribing the Civil Registration index of births, marriages and deaths for England and Wales.

7. Unless otherwise stated, more general information has come from Wikipedia[7].

A few words must be said about one particular source: the Inland Revenue survey of 1912. This provided the most contemporary description of the houses in Dalrymple Crescent, but the material is not easy to work with. The National Archive of Scotland holds the field books of the surveyors who carried out the work. Luckily, for Dalrymple Crescent, only two surveyors were used, and their handwriting was quite neat. Nevertheless they used shorthand notation, and Scottish architectural terms, which were not easy to interpret. To help the reader, I have provided a short glossary of architectural terms, with references to more authoritative websites and books.

I have also included a list of the names of the principal people associated with Dalrymple Crescent, and a list of Edinburgh streets mentioned in the text. The latter refers to the two maps on Plates 24a and 24b.

A book like this cannot be written without the help of very many people. First I would like to thank Anja Ansel and Andrew McPherson for encouraging my first faltering attempts to write up what I had discovered. Later, I received invaluable professional advice from Malcolm Cant, and support in my search for a sponsor from Hil Williamson of Edinburgh City Library, and David Hicks of the

Edinburgh World Heritage. I cannot thank these people enough for helping me to see this project through. Special thanks of course go to the Grange Association who have so generously supported the book, and to Tony Reeves who pointed me in the right direction.

My friends and neighbours in Dalrymple Crescent have all been enthusiastic about the project, and I thank them for supplying such useful information. I would particularly like to thank Douglas Cullen, Adam Forsyth, Karine MacIver and Bert Robertson.

In collecting the data, I have had help from all over the world. Here I must mention Professor John Sheets in America, Anne Stewart and her relatives in Canada, and Andrew Carnon and his relatives in Australia. Closer to home I must thank William Mearns and Robert Bartholomew.

The official bodies have also been very supportive. I must particularly acknowledge Edinburgh City Library, the Dictionary of Scottish Architects, the British Geological Survey, the National Archive of Scotland, the National Library of Scotland, the Royal College of Physicians, Edinburgh, The Scotsman Publications and Scotland's People.

Publishing a book has been a new venture for me, so I must give special thanks to those who helped me through the process: to Gillian Cloke, Mark Blackadder and Derek Auld.

Last but not least, my husband Terry, my greatest supporter and my greatest critic. Without his help, this book would never have been published.

DALRYMPLE CRESCENT
EDINBURGH
OCTOBER 2010

LIST OF ILLUSTRATIONS

INTRODUCTION

When we moved into Dalrymple Crescent in 2006, I was intrigued by the information on the seller's schedule which stated that the house had been built circa 1862 by a builder named Samuel Hunter 'along with numbers 7 and 8' and that 'Hunter's daughter was in fact the first occupant'. I started to investigate the history, and was spurred on by receiving the original title deeds from our solicitors, since the deeds were no longer required for legal purposes. What I found was so intriguing that I decided to investigate the whole of Dalrymple Crescent, from its creation in 1862 up to 1901. I drew mainly on the abstract of the Register of Sasines,* which recorded the buying and selling of property, and also the census records for the four decades: 1871, 1881, 1891 and 1901. This information gave such a fascinating glimpse of the people living here in Victorian times that I decided to follow up some of the stories; and this book is the result. In addition to the census records, I used the records of births, marriages and deaths, and *The Scotsman* archives also gave some useful insights. In addition, trawling the Web disclosed other snippets of information, and the Edinburgh and Leith Post Office Directory was an invaluable source. Details of how I went about tracking down the inhabitants of the Crescent are given in the Afterword.

I soon learned many things about Victorian Edinburgh that I had only been vaguely aware of before, and found myself exploring

---

* The Register of Sasines is a register of land titles and property obligations that has been kept in Scotland since the 17th century.

the social and economic life of the city, and discovering that names that meant nothing to me were in fact quite well known in their respective fields. I have tried to capture some of this background information in the first and last chapters.

Dalrymple Crescent is located in an area called the Grange: a conservation area to the south of Edinburgh's city centre. It is a highly sought-after residential area, with good access to the centre, shops and schools. It has many beautiful streets, and Dalrymple Crescent (Plate 1a) is one of its gems. Running between Findhorn Place and Lauder Road, it is a quiet street. The road itself is quite narrow, but the houses are set well back, giving a feeling of spaciousness. The gentle curve of the Crescent seems to pull the houses together, strengthening the feeling of community. All the houses were built in the latter half of the 19th century. Although there have been a number of additions, divisions and conversions, the street retains its Victorian identity. The houses are of different styles and sizes, but the use of similar stone and slate, and the uniform lengths of the gardens give a sense of unity. This then is the street whose history I set out to explore. Who were the Victorians who built the street and lived and worked here?

PART 1

*Building
Dalrymple Crescent*

$\sim$

CHAPTER 1

Dalrymple Crescent
in context

~

THE GROWTH OF EDINBURGH

In his book *The Transformation of Edinburgh*, Professor Richard Rodger[1] states that 'Before the New Town was built, ... medieval merchants would have easily been able to find their way around ... Edinburgh.' However, by the end of the 19th century, the situation had changed. The population of Edinburgh exploded from 67,000 in 1801 to 298,000 in 1901 and the urban area had grown by over 400% in size.

After 1745, the first expansion was to the north, when the Nor' Loch was drained, and the famous New Town was built. South Bridge, over the Cowgate and linking the High Street to the 'six Districts on the south side of the City' was completed in 1788. This was the age of the Scottish Enlightenment (Adam Smith's *Wealth of Nations* was published in 1776), and Edinburgh University was attracting intellectuals and students from all over Europe. In addition it was the headquarters of the legal and religious institutions that remained distinctly Scottish after the Union of Parliaments in 1707. Improvements in transport systems, particularly the coming of the railways in the 1830s made movement to the cities much easier than before. Although Edinburgh did not have a dominant manufacturing industry, as did Glasgow and Dundee, it was a centre for administrative functions and of service industries such as banking and other financial activities. In addition there was a diverse industrial section covering printing and publishing, engineering, food and

3

drink, clothing and textiles. Edinburgh was therefore both attractive to rural workers who had lost their jobs through improvement in farming, and also less subject to cycles of 'boom and bust' than Glasgow or Dundee. It also supported a prosperous middle class who had the means and willingness to move into modern homes.

By the 1830s Edinburgh had expanded again, creating a 'second New Town' to the north, in streets such as Moray Place and Drummond Place. However, the attraction of the southern suburbs was considerable, and houses were built in Newington as early as 1795. Between 1830 and 1851 the property market stagnated, but the potential for profit was obvious, and the owners of land on the fringes of Edinburgh were preparing to sell as soon as the market revived.

Plate 1b shows Edinburgh in 1816 with large estates bordering the city to the south. Princes Street and the New Town can be clearly seen, and the Meadows lie just north of the Grange estate. To the east of the Meadows, three main roads run south. They are (from west to east) Causewayside, the Bridges, and the Dalkeith Road.

FEUING

Feuing was a uniquely Scottish way of disposing of land, somewhere between the English freehold and leasehold systems. The system had its origins in the medieval feudal system, which gave rise to terms like 'superior' and 'vassal', but in Victorian times the system developed to meet the needs of contemporary landowners and developers. In the feuing system, the land is sold outright, and the vendor relinquishes all rights, provided that the feu duty, a fixed annual sum, is paid to the superior, that is, the person who owns the feuing rights. The purchaser or vassal has the right to keep or dispose of the land as he wishes. This means that the risk of the planning blight, which could be associated with a fixed lease, is reduced. From the superior's point of view, he and his heirs obtains a fixed income in perpetuity. The feu duty is fixed at the time of the contract, and cannot be increased after that time. Therefore, it is in the superior's interest to make this duty as high as possible.

The feuing system had a number of repercussions. It was possible for the vassal to sub-feu the land and property on it, and to set his own feu duty. To take an example, the landowner might set a feu duty of £200 per annum. A builder might build several houses, and sell these, setting his own feu duty. If he asked for £100 for each of five houses, this would give him a profit of £300 per annum on the houses he had built. An important feature of the system was that, in the event of death or bankruptcy, the annual feu duties were the first charge on the estate. Therefore banks and individuals were well-disposed to using a feu as security for a loan. This was one way that builders raised cash for their operations.

In feudal times the feu contract had been an exchange of land for services to the landowner (for example, military service), but in the 18th century this was replaced by annual payments of money. Earlier contracts merely recorded the obligation, but in the 19th century the practice arose of putting conditions on the use of the land. In this way the superiors could influence the use of the land that they were feuing, since these conditions (or 'burdens') were legally binding.

THE FEUING OF THE GRANGE

In 1825 Sir Thomas Dick Lauder, by Act of Parliament, obtained permission to feu his lands in the Grange, upon certain conditions that were designed 'to maintain a high standard in the layout of the streets, the design of the houses, the value of the properties, and the exclusion of all development other than for residential use'. A feuing plan was drawn up by Grainger and Miller. However, also in 1825, there was a stock market crash that started in the Bank of England, and, although Scotland was less affected, there was a decline in the rate of property development in Edinburgh. A few houses were built in 1845, but Sir Thomas died in 1848, and it was left to his heir, Sir John Dick Lauder, to implement the enterprise. In 1851 another feuing plan (Plate 2a) was drawn up by David Cousins, based on the 1825 plan, but breaking up the grid pattern by introducing Dalrymple Crescent, St Catherine Place and Tantallon Place as curved streets, softening the geometric layout of the first plans. The plan is oriented with east at the top. Dalrymple Crescent is to the east (above Grange House), between Lauder Road and Findhorn Place. The names of the streets are mostly linked to the Dick Lauder family. Dick Place and Lauder Road are obvious. Dalrymple Crescent was named after Sir John's wife, Lady Anne Dalrymple.

The Scotsman advertised the first feu plots to be sold by auction in 1852, but it was not until 1862 that Dalrymple Crescent was offered for sale. Ninety-three lots were put up for auction in 1852, in Mansion House Road, Dick Place, Lauder Road, Grange Loan, Cumin Place, Grange Road, Tantallon Place and Hatton Place. A further 52 were advertised in 1860, now including Seton Place and Findhorn Place. Then, in January 1862 an advertisement appeared in The Scotsman. There would be 'Exposed to FEU by Public Auction, within the Rooms of Messrs Dowells & Lyon, No 18 George Street, Edinburgh, upon Monday 21st day of March 1862, at Twelve o'clock noon':

> THOSE PORTIONS of the ENTAILED ESTATE of GRANGE consisting of Sixty-six Lots, laid out for Feus, as the same are delineated on a Feuing Plan, prepared by Mr Robert Reid Raeburn, Architect, Edinburgh, and situated in the Roads or Streets called, or to be called, the Mansion-House Road, Dick Place, the Lauder Road, Cumin Place, the Grange Road, Findhorn Place, Seton Place, Tantallon Place, Saint Catherine Place and Dalrymple Crescent.

The architect was now Robert Raeburn, and in his feuing plan of 1864, nine houses had already been built in Dalrymple Crescent.

CHAPTER 2

The feuing of Dalrymple Crescent

~

In March 1862, Sir John Dick Lauder 'Exposed to Feu by Public Auction ... Portions of the Entailed Estate of Grange consisting of Sixty-six Lots to be Let, Granted or Disponed in Feu Farm'.* Nine of these were in Dalrymple Crescent, and they were numbered 176 to 184 (see Plate 2b). The auction was held on 12 March 1862, and all the lots were disposed of. The Feu Contracts were very detailed, running to ten or more foolscap pages. Plate 3 shows the last page of one contract, with Sir John's signature.

The lots numbered 176 to 183, that is, all of the north side of Dalrymple Crescent except the corner site, had to be 'one storey or one storey and a half only'. The plans and elevations had to be approved by Sir John Dick Lauder, and no building could commence 'until the same had been sanctioned'. The front walls of the 'villas or dwelling houses' had to be at least 35 feet from the front wall bounding the feu. The value of the property should be 'at least Five hundred pounds sterling'. The 'dwelling house and offices' should be completed before Whitsun 1863. The boundary walls had to be built of 'stone and lime', and could not exceed eight feet in height. Sir John was building the road, drains and sewer, and each property had to pay him in proportion to the ground occupied. The feuars were bound to keep the street in good repair 'in all time coming'. The road,

---

* Feu Farm was the type of tenure where the 'Vassals' were required to pay a feu duty to the 'Superior' (Scottish Parliament research note 'Abolition of Feudal Tenure' August 1999).

drains and sewer would be certified by Robert Raeburn, and the feuars should accept his certificate. The feuars also had to 'make and keep in repair' the pavement and gutters. The feuars 'should be bound and obliged to lay out' the ground not built on as 'garden ground, grass or shrubbery', and to keep them in a 'neat and ornate manner'. There followed a long list of types of building they could not build, starting with breweries, and ending with 'manufactories of any kind whatsoever'. They were also prohibited from keeping 'shops, warehouses or yards' or 'doing anything ... which could be reckoned a nuisance'. The contract then refers to the Act of Parliament that allowed the Dick Lauders to sell the land.[1]

The feu for the land that was auctioned was calculated at the rate of £25 per acre. There were also extra fees 'at the entry of each heir and singular successor'.

The south side of Dalrymple Crescent was offered in a similar auction on 22 September 1864, and, if anything, the conditions were even more strictly spelled out, with comments about the height of boundary walls, and the rights of adjacent properties that had already been feued. This time 54 pieces of land were auctioned, and those in Dalrymple Crescent were numbered 234 to 243. In all just over 5 acres were feued out, as follows:

North Side

Lot 176, which became house No 1, was 0.250 of an acre.

Lot 177, which became No 2, was 0.225 of an acre.

Lot 178, which became No 3, was 0.400 of an acre.

Lot 179, which became No 4, was 0.269 of an acre.

Lot 180, which became No 5, was 0.199 of an acre.

Lot 181, which became No 6, was 0.120 of an acre.

Lot 182, which became Nos 7, 8 & 9, was 0.369 of an acre.

Lot 183, which became Nos 10 & 11, was 0.402 of an acre.

Lot 184, which became No 12 (25 Findhorn Place in Victorian times), was 0.333 of an acre.

South Side

Lot 234, which became No 30 (later 27), was 0.250 of an acre.
Lot 235, which became No 26, was 0.248 of an acre.
Lot 236, which became No 25, was 0.248 of an acre.
Lot 237, which became No 24, was 0.248 of an acre.
Lot 238, which became Nos 22 & 23, was 0.248 of an acre.
Lot 239, which became Nos 20 & 21, was 0.245 of an acre.
Lot 240, which became Nos 18 & 19, was 0.290 of an acre.
Lot 241, which became Nos 16 & 17, was 0.260 of an acre.
Lot 242, which became Nos 14 & 15, was 0.237 of an acre.
Lot 243, which became No 13, was 0.225 of an acre.

The time taken to complete a feu contract varied significantly. The logistics must have been complicated, since Sir John Dick Lauder signed all of his contracts, and he was living in Aberdeenshire at this time. Moreover, when he died, there was a hiatus until his heir, Sir Thomas North Dick Lauder appointed an agent to act in his place. As we shall see, there were often changes in ownership between the time of the auction and the time the feu contract was drawn up.

THE FIRST OWNERS

The first owners can be grouped into four different types: investors, builders and architects, landlords and owner-occupiers. In this section we will look at the people who owned the plots in Dalrymple Crescent, up to the point where a house was occupied. The fuller stories of the investors and the builders and architects will be told in the next section; the stories of the landlords and owner-occupiers are told in later chapters.

Lot number 176 was bought by Elizabeth Johnston, a widow living in Linlithgow. She had a house built on it, which she rented out. The feu contract was completed in July 1862.

Lot number 177 was bought by two sisters, Elizabeth and Janet Sinclair, who lived in Stirling and rented out the house built on the site. The feu contract was completed in November 1863.

Lot number 178 was bought by Edward Lothian, who lived in the house built on the plot. The feu contract was completed in February 1863.

Lot number 179 was bought by Robert Inglis, who sold the plot to the builder David Rutherford. The feu contract for Robert Inglis was completed in May 1862, and the sale between him and David Rutherford in January 1866. David Rutherford sold the house he built (No 4) to Robert Sinclair Smith in April 1867.

Lots number 180, 181 and 182 were bought by the builder Robert Hunter. He transferred lot 180 to his son James Hunter, and lot 182 to his son Samuel Hunter, and built a house for his own use on lot 181. The feu contracts for 181 and 182 were completed in December 1862, and for 180 in January 1863. James Hunter built No 5 Dalrymple Crescent on lot 180, and sold it to Henry Newcombe in July 1864. Samuel Hunter built three houses on lot 182. The sale of No 7 to Charles Wilson was completed in May 1864; No 8 to George Campbell in January 1865 and No 9 to David Cowan Mudie, also in January 1865.

Lot number 183 was bought by the architects Charles Leadbetter and James Wilson Smith, of the firm of Leadbetter and Smith. The feu contract was completed in July 1862. They built two houses on the plot. The sale of No 10 to Rev. John Duncan was completed in May 1864, and of No 11 to George Tod Bathgate in April 1863.

Lot number 184 was bought by Robert Middlemass, the baker, who lived in the house he had built on the site. The feu contract was completed in May 1862.

On the south side, *lot number 243* was bought by the solicitor Alexander Henderson Chalmers, who had a house built on it.

On 4 January 1865, a newly erected villa, at the east end and south side of Dalrymple Crescent (i.e. on lot 243) was advertised in *The Scotsman*. It consisted of 3 storeys, with 6 rooms on main and upper floors, with bathroom, closets and pantry. The kitchen, washhouse and offices were on the basement floor. The feu duty was £5-12-6d, and the price £900. On 18 January, it was advertised again with the headline of a price reduction (but still £900!). The advertisement stated that it was built under supervision of Mr George Cousin, surveyor, Royal Exchange, and that Mr McKenzie, gardener, at Grange Loan would show the house. It was sold to Rev. Robert Gemmell, and the feu contract was completed by July 1865.

Sir John Dick Lauder died on 23 March 1867, and all the following transactions were completed after his death.

Lots number 234 to 242 were acquired by Robert Paterson, the City Architect, through his solicitor William Marwick. He then transferred the plots to others, before the feu contract was completed.

Lots number 238 to 242 were transferred to the builder George Alexander, who had also acquired a lot in Lauder Road at the same auction. This made for a very complicated feu contract, which was completed in July 1868. It is noteworthy that the houses built in Dalrymple Crescent had to have a value of no less than £500, while the one in Lauder Road had to be at least £1000. George Alexander built ten semi-detached houses on the five lots in Dalrymple Crescent (Nos 14 to 23) and rented them out.

Lot number 234 was transferred to the solicitor Peter Simpson, and the feu contract was completed in December 1868. He in turn transferred the land to the builder and joiner James Hogg, in October 1873. James Hogg built a detached house, which he sold to Camilla More and her siblings in May 1875.

Lots number 235, 236 and 237 were transferred to the architect John Paterson, the feu contract being completed in November 1873. John Paterson died in July 1877, leaving the plot of land to be disposed of by his trustees. Lot number 235 was transferred to Thomas Ogilvie Cownie, who lived in the house built there. The sale was completed in May 1878.

Lots number 236 and 237 were sold to the contractor and quarry master George Stratton, in August 1878. He built a house on the site of lot number 236, and rented it out. Meanwhile he transferred lot number 237 to his father, David Stratton in December 1878. David Stratton in turn transferred it to John Middlemass (the son of Robert Middlemass) in November 1882. John held on to the property for another four years, before transferring it to his father in May 1886. In December of that year, Robert Middlemass eventually sold the land to John Robb Matthew, who lived in the house that he had built.

INVESTORS, BUILDERS AND ARCHITECTS

Robert Inglis

Robert Scott Inglis was a stationer and publisher, with premises in George Street. He was born in Melrose in 1820. He bought the plot in Dalrymple Crescent at the same time as he and his brother William bought adjoining plots in Dick Place. It was here that they built their villas, and Robert sold the land in Dalrymple Crescent to the builder David Rutherford four years later.

In 1871 Robert was living in Orchardson Villa, Dick Place with his wife Eliza. She was 11 years younger than him, and came from Edinburgh. Next door William, who was a bookseller, was living with his extended family. He was a widower, also born in Melrose in 1823.[2] With him were his brother Charles, his sister-in-law Agnes Buchan and his mother-in-law Helen Buchan. Charles was 43 at the time of the 1871 census. He was also born in Melrose, as was Agnes. Helen Buchan was the widow of a factor. She was born in Sorbie, Wigtownshire in 1802. Agnes was aged 27, and unmarried.

In addition there were two cousins either staying or visiting. Grace Paterson was the wife of a clergyman, born in Baldon, Wigtownshire in 1828. With her was her four-year-old son, James, who was born in Aberdeen. The other cousin was Elizabeth Aitken, married, and born in Blacknock, Wigtownshire in 1842. Her position was given as 'gentlewoman'.

Robert was a partner in the firm of Gall and Inglis,[3] who specialised in 'ready reckoner' tables and atlases. His two sons, James and Harry, also entered the business, which survived in the same family until the 1970s.

William died in October 1887, and Robert died in December of the same year.

David Rutherford

David Rutherford and Sons was a building company that was active from the 1860s to 1881. David Rutherford died in 1874, but the business continued, and in 1881 was based at 4 Merchiston Crescent.

The firm bought Lot 179 from Robert Inglis, and built a house, which was sold to Robert Sinclair Smith.

The Hunters

Robert Hunter was a builder who had been born in Roxburghshire in 1797 or 1798. His father, William, was a gardener, and his mother was Helen, née Oliver. He married Marion Sinclair, who came from Dumfries and was born in 1799 or 1800. They had ten children: William, born in 1821; Elizabeth, born in Jedburgh in 1822 (the only child not born in Edinburgh); Robert Junior, born in 1826; Antony in 1828; Marion Junior in 1831; Samuel in 1832; James in 1833; David in 1836; John in 1838; and Wilhemina in 1840.

It was a family business; the Hunters bought land, mainly in Newington, and built tenements and houses, which they sold or rented out. In 1841 they were living in the South Back of Canongate, in the Old Town, with all ten children. Robert is described as a stone mason. In the 1851 census, Robert is described as a builder, Robert junior as a journeyman mason, and Samuel and James as apprentice masons. Ten years, later, in 1861, the family was living at 4 Lord Russell Place, Newington. Robert and James had left home. Samuel is described as a sculptor, and David and John were masons. In 1863 Samuel married Agnes Thomson, who was born in Edinburgh in 1842. Their daughter Agnes Hardie Hunter was born in 1864. As we have seen, the family bought three lots at the auction of March 1862. Robert built No 6 for himself and his family, while James and Samuel built houses to sell. The brothers advertised their property in 1864. James built No 5 and advertised it in *The Scotsman* in February 1864, describing it as a 'detached villa now finishing' with 'eight apartments, a bathroom with hot & cold water and other conveniences'. The advertised price was £900. The sale was completed in July 1864, although as we have seen from the feu contract for Lot 182, there could be some delay between the sale and the finalising of the contract. Also in February Samuel advertised two of his houses, Nos 7 and 8, describing them as 'two semi-detached villas now finishing'. They each had six rooms, a bathroom, a washhouse, a kitchen, a servant's room, and 'Closets etc'. The feu duty was £2. He appears to have had some difficulty in selling, as the advertisement was repeated several times in February and March. The first was sold in May 1864, but the second was re-advertised in August and November 1864.

> TO BE SOLD OR LET. Entry Immediately, that NEW SEMI-DETACHED VILLA, No. 8 DALRYMPLE CRESCENT, GRANGE. Apply to SAMUEL HUNTER, Builder, No. 6 Dalrymple Crescent.

It was finally sold in January 1865. No 9 is a detached house, and it was sold in May 1864.

The family appeared to be prospering, with Robert, now 67, living at No 6, with his wife Marion, daughter Elizabeth, and younger sons John and David. Young Marion (also called Mary Ann) was keeping house for James at 3 Grange Road. Samuel had a number of addresses. In the feu contract of 1862 his address is given as Bellevue, Broughton. Between then and 1865 his address is sometimes given as Oxford Street (where he was building a tenement) and sometimes Dalrymple Crescent. He may have lived in No 9 briefly, or he may have been staying with his father.

Then in October 1865, a tragedy struck the family. John, the youngest son, who had always been 'erratic in disposition',[4] murdered his mother Marion and sister Elizabeth. Normally he was kept 'in close confinement in his father's house' but he had tried to leave; his mother and sister had attempted to stop him, and he turned on them. He was tried on 27 November 1865 at the High Court in Edinburgh. The trial was adjourned, John was found to be insane, and was 'To be kept in strict custody in the prison of Edinburgh, awaiting Her Majesty's pleasure'.[5] The beginning of *The Scotsman* article reporting the tragedy can be seen in Plate 4a.

Following that, in January 1866 James was declared bankrupt. This was not an unusual situation for the time, when builders and investors were continually borrowing money to fund their activities. According to the account in *The Scotsman*, there had been a fire at his woodyard in St Leonards in April 1865, and he had lost goods to

the value of about £550. There had been another fire in his
woodyard in Victoria Place the preceding January, but on that
occasion insurance had covered his losses. However the second fire
had left him with 'but two carts, two cart-horses and a gig-horse'.
These he sold to Samuel, and used the money to pay his workmen's
wages. He had no business books, as they were all burnt in the St
Leonard's Street fire.

> In October last I resided at number 3 Grange Road. All the
> furniture had been taken from there to my sister's home in
> Dalrymple Crescent, her father's house. My sister Mary-
> Ann lived with me in No 3 Grange Road, keeping house for
> me. She had kept house for seven years, and I thought it
> right to hand over all my furniture to her fourteen months
> ago.

He goes on to say that he can identify the furniture that was previously his. Similarly he explains that he had owned houses in Victoria
Place next to the building yard, but that he had sold them and used
the money to pay off a heritable bond, and to pay wages. In October
he had called a meeting of his creditors to explain that he could not
pay the money owed. When he was cross-examined, further transactions of buying, selling, building and borrowing were identified, but
the hearing was adjourned without a conclusion being reached.

It is difficult to know how the murder affected James' business
activities. The fire in St Leonards had been in the April previously,
and he was obviously sailing close to the wind. However the meeting
with creditors was in the same month as the murder, so it is possible
that his family affairs had overwhelmed him at a time when his
finances were at a critical state.

After the tragedy Robert sold No 6 in December 1865. In 1871 he
was living at 7 Grange Road, with a new wife, Ann (née Watt). In the
census of that year his age is given as 63 (he was in fact 73) and hers
as 32. They had two daughters, Margaret who was two years old, and
Robina who was two months. Mary Ann was also living with them,
and was described as a dressmaker.

Anne (or Annie) died in September 1871 of a 'disease of the right lung'. In her death certificate, her age is given as 30, making her two years younger than the census reported. Her father was a joiner, John Watt, and her mother had been born Margaret Hislop. Robert died in June 1877, when he was living in Grange Loan. He was 79. His death certificate described the cause as 'general failure due to old age', but the immediate cause was bronchitis, which he had for 8 days before he died. Samuel reported his death.

Mary Anne was left to bring up her two half-sisters, and in 1881 she was living with them at 9 Grange Loan. She was 50 and an annuitant – someone living on an annuity. Her sisters are described as her nieces. Ten years later they were living at No 8 Grange Road. She was 60, and described as living on private means. Margaret and Robina were now 21 and 19 and described as sisters. Margaret was a dressmaker, but no occupation was given for Robina. Finally, in 1901, Mary Anne was still living at 8 Grange Road, just with Robina, this time described as her half-sister.

Samuel meanwhile continued to develop land in the Grange and Newington areas. In 1881 he was living at 323 Leith Walk. With him were his wife Agnes, his daughter, young Agnes, and another daughter, Marion, born in 1866. He continued to work as a builder and sculptor (see Plate 4b), and was still building in 1891 when he bought a portion of land in what was to become Pilrig Street. It was bought from John Mackintosh Balfour Melville of Pilrig and Strathkinness who was feuing part of his estates. The plot had a frontage of 54 feet and was 140 feet in depth. Samuel died in 1893, aged 62, at 62 Pilrig Street, and his daughter Agnes reported his death from heart disease.

Leadbetter and Smith

Charles Leadbetter and James Wilson Smith formed the partnership of Leadbetter and Smith, a firm of architects practicing at 38 Hanover Street. They bought Lot 183 and built Nos 10 and 11 on the site. Their partnership was brief, lasting from about 1861 to the mid 1860s when James left to set up his own practice.

Charles Leadbetter

Charles Leadbetter was born at Innerleithen, the son of Alexander Leadbetter and his wife Margaret Brunton, and baptised on 10 May 1813. He was one of seven children. He married Catherine Burnet in Edinburgh in October 1846. She was born in 1825. They had at least three children: Margaret, born in 1848, Catherine in 1852 and Jessie in 1855.

In 1881 he was living at 12 St Andrews Place, with Catherine and Jessie, who was unmarried, and whose occupation was given as Assistant Housekeeper. Jessie died in June 1881 at the age of 26. Charles died on 26 February 1888, aged 74.

He was involved in a number of notable buildings around Edinburgh and the Borders, including: 80–86 High Street, Peebles in 1855; The Reformed Presbyterian Church, 26 George IV Bridge, Edinburgh (now the Frankenstein Pub) in 1859; 10 John Street, Portobello in 1860 and 1877; 67 the Promenade, Portobello in 1863 and 1873 and The Royal Blind Asylum, Craigmillar Park, Edinburgh in 1874.

He was also responsible for the design of the villa, Rathan, when Robert Middlemass extended his property at 25 Findhorn Place (later 12 Dalrymple Crescent) in 1876.[6]

James Wilson Smith

James Wilson Smith was born in 1836 or 1837, the son of John Smith and his wife Margaret. In 1841 he was staying at the 'Gaol & Bridewell' of Edinburgh, where his father was governor. His mother's maiden name was probably Wilson, since a Margaret Wilson, aged about 60, was living with them at the time. (James' mother, Margaret Smith, was about 30). According to the 1841 census there were five children: Margaret aged eight, James aged six, Isabella aged four, Mary aged two and Jessie, three months old.

James was a pupil of the architect David Rhind, and when he was eighteen Rhind recommended him to the Trustees' Academy School of Art in Edinburgh. He entered the Academy on 15 October 1853 and left on 12 July 1855. In 1871 he was still living with his parents and his father was still the prison governor. From 1870 to 1872 his business address is given as 13 Frederick Street, but there are no entries in the directories from 1873 onward. John Smith died in 1875, and in 1881 James was lodging with a railway porter and his family at 7 Calton Hill. The porter was William Cameron, aged 27, his wife was Helen, and they had a daughter, Jessie, who was one year old. James W. Smith's occupation is given as architect.

Professionally he worked with Charles Leadbetter on 10 John Street, as well as the houses in Dalrymple Crescent, and is also associated with adding a new wing to Queensberry Lodge, Canongate, Edinburgh in 1865, and with the designs of the Congregational Church, Dalkeith in 1868 and of Liberton Free Church, Gilmerton Road, in 1869.[7]

Alexander Henderson Chalmers

Alexander Henderson Chalmers bought the land on the southeast corner of the Crescent from Robert Paterson. He commissioned George Cousin to supervise the building of No 13, but he never lived there. We know that he was a Writer to the Signet,* and that he died in March 1872, when he was living at Ruby Cottage in Aberdeen.

George Cousin

George Cousin, who supervised the building of No 13, was the brother of David Cousin, who had drawn up the 1851 feu plan of the Grange. David was one of the most outstanding architects of his generation, but unfortunately was dogged by ill health. George was born in 1807 or 1808, and practiced as an ordained surveyor from about 1840. He also did architectural design. In 1841 he was living in Johnston Place with his wife, Wilhelmina, who was about the same age as him. By 1864 he had been joined by William Ormiston, although the practice title of Cousin & Ormiston was not adopted

---

* The Society of Writers to Her Majesty's Signet is an independent, non-regulatory association of solicitors, most of whom are based in Edinburgh. Members of the Society are called Writers to the Signet.

until about 1877. He was the architect of Grange Publishing Works, which was built in Causewayside in about 1880 for the Banks family (Henry Haig Banks lived in No 11 Dalrymple Crescent). In 1881 he and Wilhelmina were living at 5 Bruntsfield Terrace, when they were both aged 73. His occupation was given as 'Surveyor and Valuer of Household Property'. George Cousin died on 17 September 1890 but Ormiston, who became Lord Dean of Guild, continued to practise under the firm's name.[8] George Cousin was also a Town Councillor, and 'an ardent social reformer'.[9]

Robert Paterson

Robert Paterson was an architect who was heavily involved in the development of the Grange. Between 1865 and 1871 he was involved in 20 feu contracts from Sir John Dick Lauder or Sir Thomas North Dick Lauder. Robert Paterson was the son of Robert Paterson, a surveyor. His mother Margaret had been a Paterson before her marriage. He was born in Edinburgh in 1825, and designed a number of distinctive buildings in Edinburgh, including the Café Royal in 1863, several United Presbyterian Churches, and villas at 59 Dick Place and 3A Chalmers Crescent. He also worked on a number of tenement buildings, and Warrender Baths.

In 1881 he was living at 47 Grange Road with his wife Margaret (née Wyllie), aged 52, his daughter, Elizabeth and three sons. Elizabeth was 31 and unmarried. James, aged 29, was a master plumber, John, 25, was a general clerk, and George, 21, was an apprentice surveyor. Robert Paterson became City Assessor for Edinburgh. He died of apoplexy at 47 Grange Road in October 1889, aged 66 and is buried in Grange Cemetery. His son Robert reported the death.[10]

George Alexander

George Alexander was born in Liberton, near Edinburgh, in November 1818 to John Alexander and Euphans Dow. He had two brothers, Andrew and John, and a sister, Helen. In December 1846 he married Ann Murray, who was born in Perth in 1828. They had at least 11 children, all born in Edinburgh: Christiana, born in 1847, George Murray in 1851, Thomas in 1853, Annie in 1856, Euphemia in 1857, Mary in 1859, Jessie in 1860, John in 1863, James in 1864, Robert in 1868, and Edward William (or William Edward) in 1872.

From the census data we know that in 1861 the family were living in a tenement at 9 Grange Loan: Christiana, George Murray, Thomas, Annie, Euphemia, Mary and Jessie were at home. James was born at No 8 Grange Loan in 1864. In 1871 they had moved to 18 Grange Loan: Christiana, George Murray, Thomas, Annie and Euphemia were living at home. Then in 1881, they were at 46 Grange Loan: Thomas, Euphemia, Mary, Jessie, John, Robert and William were living at home. Annie was already married, but was visiting.

The family carried out its business from 1 Fountainhall Road and, throughout the latter part of the 19th century period, advertised villas for rent in Dalrymple Crescent, Findhorn Place, and other areas of the Grange. When George died, James carried on the family business, but the other members still kept a financial interest in the business.

George died in August 1892, aged 73 leaving a considerable estate. In addition to the properties in Dalrymple Crescent, he owned: Nos 84, 88 and 90 Findhorn Place; Nos 1, 9, 40, 42, 44 and 46 Fountainhall Road; Nos 2, 3, 5, 7, 9, 20, 22 and 24 Grange Loan; Nos 2, 4, 6, 14 and 16 Mayfield Road; Nos 252, 254, 256, 258, 260 and 262 Causewayside and the family home at 46 Grange Loan.

The first Sasine record after his death is in November 1893, and it records that the trustees of his estate have set up a bond to provide for widows. In 1896, the trustees made over the estate to his heirs. His wife Anne and daughter Euphemia had died before 1893, and Jessie Alexander received 1/11th of the estate. The remaining heirs acted together as a syndicate, and collectively or individually borrowed against their shared estate. From these transactions we get a glimpse of the activities and whereabouts of George's children. In May 1896:

1. Annie had married Rev. William Agnew, a Free Church minister and was living in Galltoun, Kirkcaldy.
2. Edward was living in Cairnton of Boyndie, Portsoy, Banffshire.

3. Christiana was a widow, living in Port Dover, Ontario, Canada. Her married name was Williams.
4. John was also living in Port Dover.
5. George Murray was an architect living in Cape Town.
6. James was a builder who had taken over the builders yard at 1 Fountainhall Road.
7. Mary had married William Wood Roger and was living at 21 Princes Square, Strathbungo, Glasgow.
8. Robert was living at Reidsville, Albany County, New York.
9. Thomas was also living at Reidsville.

Also in May 1896 Edward borrowed against his share, and repaid it in August 1898. At that time he was described as a farmer at Keithney, Inverurie.

In May 1899 four of the syndicate borrowed against their share in the estate. They were James, Mary, William Agnew and Robert. James was now living at 6 Mayfield Road. Mary was widowed and still living in Princes Square. William Agnew was now secretary of the Drummond Institute, Stirling.

In January 1901, the heirs are again mentioned. Anne and William Agnew were now living at 26 Snowdon Place, Stirling, and William was Editor at the Drummond Institute. Christine was now living at 198 Elm Street, Albany, as was Robert. John was still at Port Dover, and Thomas in Reidsville. Jessie had married a Canadian teacher, Frank Riddell, and was now living in Canada.

The 1901 census shows that James was living at 32 Grange Loan. He was then 36, and his occupation was 'builder'. His wife, Jessie was born in New Zealand in 1869. They had two children, George, aged seven and Alice, aged three, both born in Edinburgh.

John Paterson

John Paterson was the son of Thomas Paterson, a clerk of works, and Margaret Deans Instant. He was born in Hamilton, Lanarkshire, in January 1832. He was the eldest of six children. His brothers were

George, Robert and Thomas, and his sisters, Jane and Margaret, all of whom were born between 1837 and 1846. He married twice, to Jane Naismith in Hamilton in 1856, and later to Margaret Tolmie.

He set up his architectural practice at 27 Cockburn Street, Edinburgh in about 1863, in partnership with Robert Thornton Shiells. The partnership lasted until about 1867, when Paterson set up office at 21 St Andrew Square and Shiells at 62 George Street.

John Paterson was responsible for three double villas in Lauder Road (Nos 41, 43, 45, 47, 49 and 51). He also worked on the Beehive Inn in the Grassmarket, the corner between Chambers Street and South Bridge, and several United Presbyterian Churches.

In 1877 he was living at 3 Morningside Park, with his office at 21 St Andrews Square. He died of pneumonia in July of that year, and is buried in Grange Cemetery. He was 45 years old, and his brother Robert reported his death.[11]

Peter Simpson

In 1881 Peter Simpson was living at 23 Nelson Street. He was 52, and had been born in Perth. He was a Solicitor to the Supreme Court (SSC)*. His wife, Elizabeth Peebles, was two years younger. She came from Anstruther in Fife. They had three talented daughters – Jessie, 20 was an authoress, Margaret, 17, was a composer of music and Lizzie, 14, was an artist – and their son, Patrick, aged 12, was at school. Jessie was born in Pittenweem in Fife, and the other children in Edinburgh. Elizabeth's death was announced in *The Scotsman* on 12 November 1895.

James Hogg

James Hogg was a builder and joiner. In 1881 he was living at 14 Blackwood Crescent, and employed 11 men and a boy. He was born

---

* SSC denotes a member of The Society of Solicitors in the Supreme Courts of Scotland, representing lawyers who practice in and around the College of Justice, which comprises Scotland's Supreme Courts.

in Hume in Berwickshire in 1840. His wife Marion (née Edgar) was born in Moffat, Dumfriesshire in 1843. They had three children, all born in Edinburgh: Marion, born in 1878, Isabella in 1880, and Christina in February 1881. At the time of the 1881 census, Marion's unmarried sister, Christina was staying with them. She was also born in Moffat, in 1850.

David and George Stratton

David was born in the parish of Caputh in Perthshire in 1823, and his wife, Agnes Gairns, was born in the parish of Methven, also in Perthshire in 1821. They had three children, George and James (or John) William and a daughter, Agnes. George was born in 1853, James in 1851 and Agnes in 1849. All were born in New Monkland in Lanarkshire. David Stratton was the surveyor of roads for Midlothian.

In 1877 the firm of J. W. & G. Stratton had premises at 7 West Mayfield and 13 Middleby Street. They were described as contractors and quarry masters, and had quarries at Barton Mount, Ratho and Ravelrig. In 1881 George was living at 13 Seton Place with his wife and four children. His wife, Marion, was a year younger than him, and came from Coatbridge. His children were all born in Edinburgh. They were Marion, aged five, David aged three, John aged one and George aged eight months. In 1890 *The Scotsman* reported a case in which a gas company claimed that a mineral company had 'injured (some gas pipes) through mineral workings'. The Sheriff ordered the latter company to repair the damage 'to the satisfaction of Mr George Stratton, contractor'.

In 1891 David was living at 13 Middleby Street, with Agnes and James William. The census reported that James was unmarried, and a building contractor by trade. David died in June 1892, aged 69, and George died in 1897, aged 44, at Holland Lodge, 1 South Gray Street.

PART 2

Living in Dalrymple

CHAPTER 3

The North side

~

The lives of the residents of Dalrymple Crescent are discussed in the next three chapters. In this chapter we look at the people living on the north side of the street, and in the next two chapters those on the south side. In most cases it is possible to look at a family along with the house in which they lived. However, some cases are more complex; sometimes a family lived in more than one house during the time, and in other cases more than one member of a family lived in the street. These families are considered in Chapter 6.

As we have seen, the north side of Dalrymple Crescent was developed slightly earlier than the south side, and the houses were of a different character. Most were developed by individual builders or architects, and so each has a different style. The requirements of the feu contracts, however, give them an overall coherence, and most are of a modest height (no more than one and a half storeys). The inhabitants were a mixture of tenants and owner-occupiers, some of whom lived in the street for many years. This chapter tells the story of the houses on the north side, and their owners and occupiers.

In 1912 the Inland Revenue conducted a survey of houses in Scotland, and the National Archives of Scotland have the field workers' note books in their possession. Although slightly later than our period, they offer the best insight into the physical structure of the houses in the late Victorian period. I have therefore drawn on them for the physical descriptions of the houses. In passing, I have noted where the field books give more information about the residents of the Crescent during the period we are interested in.

NO 1 DALRYMPLE CRESCENT

In the 1912 Inland Revenue survey, No 1 Dalrymple Crescent is described as a small detached house, two storeys high, with a slight camp* on the first floor. Like most of the buildings in the street, the walls were of coursed rubble – that is the stones are evenly spaced, but unpolished. It had one bow window, with a polished stone surround. There was a single-storey wing at the back.

In 1912 the entrance was by a wood and glass vestibule on the west gable. It and the hall had tiled flooring. There was a pantry, and a press under the stairs. The lower rooms consisted of a dining room, a sitting room, and a kitchen, with a washhouse out the back. Upstairs there were four bedrooms, and a bathroom.

The house was first owned by Elizabeth Johnston, who lived in Linlithgow and rented out the property. From 1863 to 1867 it was let to William Gorrie. Then Robert William Fraser rented it in 1868.

Elizabeth died in 1869, and on 4 December 1869, the house was advertised for sale in *The Scotsman*. It was described as a villa with seven rooms, 'bathroom, kitchen, etc'. It had a 'washing house' and a large garden well stocked with fruit trees. The advertisement stated that the house was occupied by Rev. Robert Fraser MA, and could be seen on Mondays from 2 to 3. It had been built in 1863, the Feu was £5-6s, and the upset price was £850. Offers would be received until 15 December by Andrew Little, Solicitor, Linlithgow.

It obviously did not sell, since it was re-advertised on 5 January 1870, and then again on the 8th. This time it was sold by auction at Lyon and Turnbull's, and extra information had been added to the advertisement: 'most Grates and Gas brackets belong to the proprietor and as such will be sold with the house.' The house was 'in excellent repair and thoroughly papered and painted'. The rent was £52-10s and the upset had been reduced to £750 'to ensure competition'. It could be seen 'by Card' on Mondays and Wednesdays from 12 to 3.

On 20 January 1870 it was announced in *The Scotsman* that it had

---

* Definitions of architectural terms can be found in the Glossary.

been sold for £795. It had been bought by David Gilmour. Robert Fraser continued to live there until 1873.

Between 1875 and 1881 it was occupied by Mary Ann Philips, and from 1882 until 1901 it was inhabited by Wallace Hicks, who bought the house from David Gilmour in 1893. Wallace Hicks still owed the house at the time of the 1912 survey of buildings. Plate 5a is a postcard of the house as it would have been at the end of the 19th century.

Elizabeth Johnston

Elizabeth Johnston is described as the 'relict of Hugh Nibblie Thomson, innkeeper, Edinburgh'. Hugh died in 1859, aged 45, of 'disease of the lungs'. They were married in August 1839. At that time Hugh was described as a grocer, and he was living in Fountainbridge. Elizabeth (or Eliza) was described as the daughter of the late James Johnston, Spirit Dealer in Liberton, and was living in Hill Place. She was born in Liberton in 1811. Their daughter Agnes was born in February 1840.

At the time of Hugh's death they were living at 91 South Back of Canongate in Edinburgh. His father, John, had been a clerk. When she feued the plot, Elizabeth Johnston was living in Linlithgow. She died in 1869, and the property was inherited by her daughter Agnes, who was also living in Linlithgow and married to Andrew Little, a Writer to the Signet.

William Gorrie

William Gorrie was born in Keltie, Fife in 1828, the son of Daniel (or Reid) Gorrie and Jane Moffat. In 1854 he married Margaret Hall, from Berwick-on-Tweed, who was a year younger than him. In 1861 they were living at No 3 South Gray Street. They had five children, all born in Edinburgh: Margaret aged six, Daniel aged five, Sara aged three, Mary aged two, and Robert aged one. Margaret's widowed mother, who was born in Berwick in 1793, was also living with them. A daughter, Elizabeth, was born in July 1861.

In April 1862, William Gorrie set up a clothier business with William Anderson, both having previously worked for the firm of Marshall and Aitken, clothiers. The firm of Gorrie and Anderson was situated in 62 North Bridge.

In 1863 another daughter, Isabella Agnes Gorrie was born prematurely, but she only lived for six weeks. Her death was announced in *The Scotsman* on 23 April. The following year a son was born in April, but he died in January of the following year. Again the death was announced in *The Scotsman*. However, in May of 1865 another son, called William, was born, and he did survive.

The firm of Gorrie and Anderson did not prosper. In October 1869, William Anderson & Sons, tailors and clothiers were advertising in *The Scotsman*, pointing out that Mr Anderson senior had been in the 'Late Firm of Gorrie & Anderson'. Soon after, in November, Messrs Anderson and Gorrie were declared bankrupt, and in November 1871, their creditors were informed that they would receive 'a dividend'.

William Gorrie is reported as living at 59 Grange Road in 1868 and 1869. Subsequently the family emigrated to Canada, and is reported in the 1881 census, when they were living in Guelph, Wellington South, Ontario, and William's occupation is given as 'clerk'. Living with him were his wife Margaret, daughters Mary and Elizabeth, and young William.

David Gilmour

David Gilmour was born in Edinburgh in 1846. In 1871 he was living with his mother, Agnes, at 11 Lothian Street. She was also born in Edinburgh, in 1806, and was widowed. David was a 'Grocer's shopman'. In 1881 he was living at 13 West Newington Terrace. He was described as a grocer and wine merchant. By 1893 when he sold No 1, he had moved to 19 Howe Street.

Robert William Fraser

Robert Fraser rented the house between 1868 and 1873. The 1871 census records that he was a Church of Scotland minister, of St John's Parish. According to the New Statistical Account of Scotland (1841), St John's 'was erected in 1838 for the accommodation of the population of the Cowgate'.[1] Robert Fraser was born in Perth in 1811, and was married to Margaret, who was a year older and came from Ireland. Their unmarried daughter, Mary Gertrude was living with them, as was Robert's sister Mary Ann. Mary Gertrude was 30 and born in England. Mary Ann was 58, and born in Edinburgh. They had one servant, Helen Norris, 33, from Inverkeithing.

In February 1872 *The Scotsman* recorded that Robert Fraser performed a marriage ceremony at the house. The bride and groom were George Cairns and Janet Low Moffat, the daughter of a spirit merchant.

In 1876 he was living at 19 Lauriston Street, and he died in September of that year, aged 66. The notice in *The Scotsman* described him as the son of the late Captain Fraser.

Mary Ann Philips

Mary Ann Phillips was born in Aberdeen in November 1831 to Charles Philip and Mary Ann Sim. In 1851, aged 19, she was working as a governess to the family of Rev. Robert Meiklejohn, minister at Strathdon, in Aberdeenshire. She did not marry, and lived at No 1 between 1875 and 1881, supported by 'interest and boarders'. In 1881 an unmarried cousin, John B. Walker, who was 21 and came from Fintray in Aberdeenshire was staying with her. He was related on his mother's side, as his mother, Jessie Ann Boyd, was the daughter of an Elizabeth Sim. There was one servant, Margaret Munro, aged 17, from Keith in Banffshire.

Wallace Hicks

Wallace Hicks was born in November 1850, the fifth youngest of 13 children born to George Hicks and Margaret King, all born in Rothesay on the Isle of Bute. His father was a chemist, born in Northamptonshire, and his mother came from Lochwinnoch in

Ayrshire. In 1841 two children had been born: Emily (or Emilia) and John Sibley.

In 1883 John's son George Sibley Hicks was a first-year medical student and living with his uncle Wallace at No 1. We know this because *The Scotsman* reported that he was one of the students involved in a 'disturbance' at the Theatre Royal on 28 June of that year. During the performance of 'My Sweetheart' by 'Miss Millie Palmer and her company', a gang of youths in the gallery started mimicking the performers and singing at the top of their voices. At the start of the second act they started to throw 'peas and gravel' onto the people sitting in the dress circle. There was then a fight between the youths and the other theatre-goers in the gallery until the manager and some of his helpers managed to hand the ring-leaders over to the police. The disturbance was a premeditated affair, since a notice had appeared in the University advertising the evening as a 'students' night at the theatre'. Nine ring-leaders were arrested and tried the following day after a night in the cells. It appeared that a piece of paper was found in the theatre saying 'Go to the Theatre-Royal and see My Sweetheart Minnie Palmer. Grand student night on 28th inst. It is supposed that this will be the greatest students' night of the summer 1883. Come one, come all and bring sticks and pease. Admission 6d 7pm'. On the back of the paper was written 'prepare for a row'. The nine were charged with having 'conducted themselves in a riotous, outrageous and disorderly manner and shouted and bawled and made a great noise, whereby the lieges were annoyed and disturbed and a breach of the peace was committed'. Two of them were further charged with assault. Most pleaded guilty, and were fined £5. However, they were also rusticated by the University: the two ringleaders until the end of the winter session, and the rest, including George Hicks, for the remainder of the summer session.

This was not an isolated incident of student rowdiness. In their history of Edinburgh University, Anderson, Lynch and Phillipson[2] stated that 'well into the twentieth century there were "students' nights" at popular shows when students filled most of the seats and accompanied the performance with raucous singing and shouting.'

In another recorded incident a student described the installation of Sir William Stirling Maxwell as Rector in 1872 as follows.

> I can safely say I did not hear a single word. Tambourines, Jews harps, whistles and many other obscene and undefinable instruments of torture were in great requisition; and as the time wore on, the fury increased and the actors passed from simple noise-making to more decided demon-stration. The first indication of this was a shower of peas thrown in the direction of the platform, and from this small spark of a beginning, sprang the great fire of missiles which shortly appeared. Peas were for a time the staple commodity of this trade, but soon enterprising students improved on the traditional projectiles and employed bits of biscuit, slices of orange and the like.[3]

George's father, John Sibley Hicks, was born in 1839, and died in Toxteth Park, Lancashire in 1907. He studied at the medical school of Glasgow University and worked as medical officer on a liner between Liverpool and America. He married in 1864 and George Sibley Hicks was born the following year in West Derby, Lancashire. John then worked as a GP in Liverpool for about forty years. In 1871 he was made a Fellow of the Royal College of Surgeons of Edinburgh. In June 1907 the *British Medical Journal* published a brief obituary.[4]

Wallace Hicks did not marry, and in 1891 he was living at No 1 with his sister Emilia, also unmarried, who was twelve years older than him. There was also a servant, Margaret Foulie, who was 49 and came from Tyrie in Aberdeenshire. He was an agent for a lace manufacturer. In 1901, Wallace, now a 'manager for fancy drapery' was still living at No 1, with a servant, Jessie Brown, aged 32 from Howford, Peebleshire. He and his sister continued to live there well into the 20th century. The postcard shown in Plate 5a was posted in 1908, sent by Emilia Hicks to a Mrs McCulloch, East End, Kingussie. She says that she 'did not get home till 7.30pm, a very weary journey', with 'not one egg broken'![5]

Meanwhile, George did graduate as a doctor. He took over the

practice of Eyam in Derbyshire about 1888, and married Mary Louisa
Gallagher in 1891. A son, another John Sibley Hicks was born in 1893.
However a year later, George died in tragic circumstances of an
overdose of laudanum. Because there was an inquest reported in
local newspaper, the *Sheffield Independent*, we have a detailed
account of the event.[6]

On the evening of Wednesday 19 December 1894, having been
visiting patients both in the morning and evening, Dr Hicks returned
home about seven o'clock and had a cup of tea. He then went out to
get an evening paper and returned just after ten. The servant said
that she thought that he had had something to drink. He had some
supper, and then told his wife that he would take something to make
him sleep. He did so, and then spat some out, and his wife said that
'he looked curious'. She sent for the chemist in the village, Mr
Froggatt, who arrived about 10.45. Mr Froggatt gave him mustard
and warm water and other emetics, 'but as he did not recover he sent
him to Tideswell to Dr Parks'. Tideswell is about 5 miles from Eyam,
and John Marples, who drove Dr Hicks to Dr Parks's surgery, said
that they arrived there about twelve o'clock. According to the newspaper 'all that science and skill could do was done by Dr J. L. Parks,
Dr T. H. Parks and Dr Hall their assistant, for some six or seven
hours, but the poor fellow never regained consciousness' and he died
about nine o'clock on Thursday morning. The verdict at the inquest
was that he had 'died from the effects of an overdose of laudanum
taken to produce sleep' and 'a vote of condolence was passed to Mrs
Hicks on her bereavement, and expression of sorrow and regret at
the great loss the village had sustained by Dr Hick's death.'

NO 2 DALRYMPLE CRESCENT

No 2 Dalrymple Crescent was a cottage with six main rooms. It has
been considerably enlarged since Victorian times, but the original
building can still be easily discerned. It was first owned by Elizabeth
and Janet Sinclair, who rented it out. The first tenant was Alexander
Aitken, who lived there from 1864 to 1865. Then John Watt rented it

between 1867 and 1869. John Crosbie Paterson was in residence from 1870 to 1882. The Sinclair sisters returned to the house in 1884. Elizabeth died in 1888, but Janet continued to live there until 1894, when the house was sold to John Stewart, who was still living there in 1901.

Elizabeth and Janet Sinclair

Elizabeth and Janet Sinclair were spinster sisters from Halkirk in Caithness, two of eight children born to James Sinclair and Johanna Mackay.[7] Elizabeth was born in May 1817, and Janet in October 1818. At the time of their birth, the village of Halkirk was very new, since in 1803 Sir John Sinclair drew up plans for the village to be built on land that was unsuitable for ploughing. Every one-acre plot had a cottage in its corner. Halkirk was one of Scotland's first planned villages.

In 1881 the Sinclair sisters were living at 14 Drummond Place, Stirling with an unmarried niece, Sonish Sinclair, aged 32. She was probably the daughter of their brother William. However the two sisters moved into No 2 themselves in 1884, and Elizabeth died in 1888. Janet was living in the house in 1891 with two servants: a cook, Mary Blanche, aged 53 and a domestic servant, Mary Nicol, aged 19. At the time of the 1891 census she had a visitor, Mary McKerrow aged 45 from Perthshire, and Janet was reported to be living on private means.

Alexander Aitken

Alexander Aitken worked for the firm of D. Mason & Co, who were tea and coffee merchants based at 88 South Bridge. From Dalrymple Crescent he moved to 13 Chalmers Crescent where he lived until he died in March 1900 at the age of 82. He was born in Paisley, and in the 1871 census he reported that he was a tea dealer employing five people. His wife Elizabeth McLelland was some 14 years younger than him. She was born in Wigtown, as were the five eldest of his eight children. The children were: Margaret, born in 1855, William in

1856, Jessie in 1858, Susan in 1862, Grace in 1864, Bessie in 1867, Alexander in 1869, and Helen in 1870. The youngest three were born in Edinburgh, so the family must have moved to Edinburgh soon after Grace was born.

John Watt

John Watt lived in No 2 from 1867 to 1869. He was a teller with the Commercial Bank of Scotland. *The Scotsman* reported the birth of a son in December 1869, but by 1871 he was living at 10 Dryden Place with his wife, four children and two servants. In the census he gave his occupation as 'Banker'. He was born in Grangemouth in 1833, and his wife, Jessie, who also came from Grangemouth, was some 11 years younger. His children were Alexander aged five, James aged four, Martin aged two, and Mary, who was one month old at the time of the census.

John Crosbie Paterson

John Crosbie Paterson was a clerk with the Inland Revenue, born in 1823 in Edrom, Berwickshire to George Paterson and Jane Mason. His wife, Agnes Ness Paterson was the same age, and came from Kirkcaldy in Fife. They had one son, John George, born in Edinburgh around 1866. They lived at No 2 from 1871 to 1882. In the 1871 census they had one servant, Christiane Ann McAdie, aged 21, from Edinburgh and in 1881, they had a servant named Catherine Howie, aged 25, from Duns in Berwickshire.

John Stewart

John Stewart was a cloth shrinker born in Innerleithen in 1851. He had his own business at 63 Mayfield Road, and lived at 15 West Mayfield until he bought No 2 Dalrymple Crescent in 1894. His wife, Mary A. Stewart, was five years younger and came from Stow in Midlothian. In 1901 they had two children: Jane, born in 1881 and Cranston born in 1890, and they had no living-in servant.

NO 3 DALRYMPLE CRESCENT

No 3 Dalrymple Crescent was owned by Edward Lothian, who lived there from 1863 to 1877. He sold the house to Duncan Fraser Stewart in April 1878. We have a description of the cottage, as given in *The Scotsman* when the property was advertised in February 1878. It contained a dining room, drawing room, three bedrooms, kitchen washing house, etc. The grounds were 'laid out with much taste' and there was a large conservatory and small forcing house. Duncan Stewart lived in the house until 1884, when he rented it out. The first tenant was David Noble Bertram, who lived there from 1886 to 1889. The house was empty at the time of the 1891 census, but James Bett died there in September 1891 and between 1892 and 1894 his daughter, Mrs John Willison, was living there. In December of that year Duncan Stewart transferred the property to his wife, Mary Catherine Divine.

Sometime between 1881 and 1885 the house was altered, and a new storey was built onto the original cottage, and a tower was added. The 1881 census reported that it had five rooms, but by the time of the 1901 census it had ten rooms. In 1875 the Valuation Roles put its rentable value at £50, and ten years later the value was £125, by far the highest value in the street. Most other houses had not changed their value in this period. Also, we have an advertisement from *The Scotsman* from March 1895 when the house is described as having three public rooms, six bedrooms, a bathroom, dressing room, etc. The rent was £120 a year. From 1895 to 1901 it was occupied by Richard Gibson and his family.

The 1912 building survey describes it as a detached house of two storeys. The upper floor had camp ceilings. The walls were of coursed rubble with droved dressings, and several bow windows. The report remarks that the house seems to have been added to, as the third floor of the tower was more ornamented than the lower part, with heavy cornices. The house had gas lighting.

The accommodation was on three floors. On the ground floor was the drawing room with 'white marble old grate' in 'fair order'. The library had 'white marble old grate', and the dining room had a large heavy wooden mantle with an old grate and tiled hearth. There was a small pantry off it that gave access to the kitchen. In addition there was a cloakroom with a basin and WC, a small bedroom, a pantry with a sink, a larder and the kitchen. There was also a stone washhouse with a brick floor and two wooden tubs, with a servant's room off it.

The upper floor had four bedrooms, two of which were small, and one had no fireplace. The bathroom had a cast-iron enamelled bath, a WC and a basin in moderate condition. There was a small box room in the tower with small wood stairs to room above it, a large bedroom with 'grey marble old grate'.

Mrs Stewart still owned the house in 1912, when it was let to Mrs Edith R. Ransome, the mother of the author Arthur Ransome.

Edward Lothian

Edward Lothian was born in Govan in January 1824. He was the youngest of three children born to George and Margaret Lothian. In 1841 he was living with a family called Mason, in Clarence Street in Edinburgh. The census does not give an occupation, but William Mason, who was about the same age (15), was a banker's apprentice. Edward later worked as an accountant with the Bank of Scotland. He never married, and in 1871 he was living alone with two servants: Margaret Sommerville, a widow of 58 and her daughter Anne, aged 23. He sold No 3 in 1878, and moved to Brae Lodge on the Glasgow Road. In 1881 he was described as a retired banker and again was living alone with two (different) servants. He died on 18 May 1881, aged 57.

Duncan Francis Stewart

Duncan Francis Stewart was born in Edinburgh in January 1846, to James and Margaret Stewart. In 1875 he married Mary Catherine Divine at Pancras in London. His father, James Stewart, died in October 1880 at No 3 Dalrymple Crescent. He was described as having previously lived at Stewartfield Lodge, Peebles. In 1881 Duncan Stewart was living in the house alone, with just one servant, Sarah

Howden, aged 53, from Edinburgh. Although he was only 35, his occupation was given as retired warehouseman. From 1885 to 1891 he lived at 151 Eldon Street, Greenock. In 1894 he transferred the property to his wife, and in the Valuation Roll of 1898 her address is given as 51 Morningside Road. Duncan Stewart died in Renfrewshire in 1921.

David Noble Bertram

David Noble Bertram was the son of George Bertram and Eliza Noble. He was born in Edinburgh in December 1852. George Bertram was one of the founders of the engineering company Bertram of Sciennes. He and his brother came from an engineering and paper-making background. Their grandfather had been a mechanic at the old Esk Mills at Penicuik, and their father was a paper-maker and engineer at Springfield Mill, Polton. The factory was established at Sciennes in 1821, and remained on that site until the 1980s. It was long recognised as one of the leading designers and manufacturers of quality paper and board machinery.[8]

In the 1871 census George Bertram was living in Sciennes Hill House with his wife, four children and a niece, but David, who would have been about 20, was not listed in the record. He rented No 3 between 1885 and 1888, so he would have been the first tenant to occupy the house, after it had been extended. At the time of the 1881 census he had been living at 1 Burgess Terrace. His occupation is given as mechanical engineer, and he was working at the Sciennes factory. He was married to Mary, who was about the same age as him, and was born in Denmark. They had two sons: George aged four, and Norman who was one year old. He subsequently moved to 13 Cumin Place.

It was very much a family business. As well as David, two of George's other sons Andrew and John were in the paper-making business. Andrew was based at Milngavie, and John worked at the Sciennes factory.

George Bertram had four sons and three daughters. The eldest daughter, Margaret Spalding Bertram married David Hogg Crouch, whose story is told in Chapter 6.

George Bertram died in 1881, at his house in Ravenswood, Oswald Road. Eliza first moved to Stirlingshire to live with Andrew, and then to No 1 Burgess Terrace, to live with David. She died in August 1886, at the age of 65. Her sons were all quite young when they died. Andrew died in 1894, aged 38, John in 1897, aged 39, and David in 1907, at the age of 54.

James Bett

James Bett was born in Buttergask, Perthshire in 1825. He married Elizabeth Hunter, who was born in 1832 in Lundie, Forfarshire. They had at least four children. The eldest three were born in Kilmallie, Inverness-shire: Jessie Anne, in 1853, Thomas in 1857 and Patrick Hunter in 1861. The youngest, Louisa, was born in the parish of Kilbrandon and Kilchattan, Argyllshire in 1863. In the 1881 census, James was living at Bolfracks House, Fortingall, in Perthshire. Patrick and Thomas were living at home. James was a land agent, Thomas an assistant land agent, and Patrick was studying medicine. Later, James and Elizabeth moved to Bathgate, where Elizabeth died in 1888, aged 57. Two years later, in Bathgate, Louisa married Alexander Inglis, a farmer and estate agent from Greenlaw in Berwickshire.

Meanwhile Jessie Ann had married John Willison[9] in November 1872. In the 1881 census they were living at Acharn Farm House near Killin, Perthshire. John was a farmer who had been born in Douglas, Lanarkshire in 1844. They had four sons and a daughter. Ella was six, John junior was four, James was three, Campbell was one and Douglas was two months old. They also had two of John's aunts, Agnes and Jane Campbell staying with them. They were unmarried, in their sixties, and had been born in Stranraer.

John Willison died in December 1889 at Acharn. He was 45 years old. Jessie Anne was still at the Farm at the time of the 1891 census, and James was still in Bathgate. However he must have moved to Dalrymple Crescent soon after, and died there on 4 September 1891. *The Scotsman* described him as 'sometime residing at Kaim Park, Bathgate, latterly at 3 Dalrymple Crescent'. The announcement also stated that he was 66, and that the funeral would be proceeding to

Bathgate by the 2.20 train from Waverley Station. The house was rented by Jessie Anne until 1894, while Douglas and Campbell attended George Watson's school.* In 1893 Louisa was staying in the house, and in September she gave birth to a baby boy, Louis Alexander Bett Inglis. By 1901 Jessie Anne was back at Acharn Farm House, and in the census she is described as a farmer (widowed). Campbell and Douglas were living with her, and also two younger daughters, Jenny, born in 1882, and Ida, born in 1884.

Plate 5b is a portrait of Jessie Ann Bett on her own, and Plate 6a is taken at the farm with John and their children.

Richard R. Gibson

Richard Ross Gibson was a partner in Sutherland, Cargey & Gibson, stockbrokers, of 13 George Street. He was born in Edinburgh in June 1870 to John Gibson and Jane Ross. His wife, Jane, was born a month later, in Polmont, Stirlingshire. *The Scotsman* reported that they married at the Roxburghe Hotel, Charlotte Square, Edinburgh, on 25 June 1895. Jane is described as 'Jane Hosie, only daughter of Thomas Jones, Esq., Compt Hall Polmont.' It was stated that they would be at home at 3 Dalrymple Crescent after 1 September.

By the time of the 1901 census they had two children: a daughter, Jane, aged four and son, John, aged two. In addition Jane's mother, Jane Jones and nephew Thomas Jones were staying with them. Mrs Jones (née Johnston) was a widow of 68 who came from Edinburgh, and Thomas, aged 16 was born in Natal. There were two servants: a nurse and a cook. The nurse was Mary E. Rankin, aged 31, from Montrose, and the cook was Janet R. Gibb, age 21, from Falkirk.

NO 4 DALRYMPLE CRESCENT

No 4 is described in the 1912 survey as a single-storey detached house. The front walls were of polished ashlars, with a front bow window

---

* Personal communication from Douglas's daughter

and an attic window. The side and back walls were of coursed rubble.
There was a wing to the east, and an outhouse to the back. Since then
a more modern extension has been built on it, but the original house
is still discernible.

In January 1866 Robert Inglis transferred the feu for the lot to
David Rutherford, a builder. Then in April 1867, the house was
bought by Robert Sinclair Smith who lived there until 1869. He sold
the house to James Sinclair in May 1869, and James lived there until
1886. He and his family then rented No 4 to David Graham from 1887
to 1895, and to the Buist family from 1896 to 1901.

In 1912 the owner was Martha Stevenson, the daughter of James
Sinclair. The description of the accommodation notes that the attic
had two rooms, each with a fireplace and window, and there was a
small room with roof light in a bad state of repair. On the ground
floor there was a bathroom with an enamelled cast iron bath, a WC
and a basin in moderate condition. The bedroom had a white
marble fireplace, with an old grate in poor condition. There was a
small parlour to the back with an old grate. The library had a grey
marble mantel and an old grate. The bedroom had a white marble
mantel and an old grate. In the kitchen there was an old range, a
press, a WC and a larder. Outside there was a large washhouse with
two wooden tubs and a wooden floor, and a coal cellar. The report
noted that the boundary walls required pointing and the house
required a lot of repair.

Robert Sinclair Smith

Robert Sinclair Smith was a surveyor of taxes for the Inland Revenue.
He was born in Bower, Caithness in 1826. In 1861 he was living at 14
West Preston Street with his wife and three children. His wife,
Catherine (née Spence) came from Dunnett in Caithness, and was
born in February 1831. The eldest child, William, was also born in
Dunnett, in 1852. The second, Anne, was born in Inverness in 1858,
and the youngest, Robert in Edinburgh in 1860.

Robert Sinclair Smith was a member of the Queen's City of
Edinburgh Rifle Brigade (Volunteers), and was made a Captain in

January 1868. He bought No 4 in 1867, and sold it in 1869. His youngest child, George, was born in Aberdeen in 1873, and by 1881 the family was living in Monifieth, Forfarshire. They subsequently moved to Dundee, where Robert was appointed Second Lieutenant in the 1st (Dundee) Volunteer Battalion the Black Watch in March 1888. He died in October 1894, when he was living in Grange Terrace, Broughty Ferry.

James Sinclair

James Sinclair was a draper, born in 1807 in Penicuik. He was one of ten children born to James Sinclair and Martha Hartley.[10] His wife Isabella was born in England in 1805. They had one daughter, also Martha, born in Edinburgh in November 1837. In 1857 she married Thomas Stevenson, a trimming manufacturer and wool merchant with premises in Princes Street.

James Sinclair's business premises were at 4 Bank Street, and in 1865 he was living at 38 Rankeillor Street. In the 1871 census, he and Isabella were living in Dalrymple Crescent with one servant, Janet Jamieson, aged 16, from Linlithgow.

In May 1876 James and Isabella placed an advertisement in *The Scotsman* for a general servant: 'Wanted immediately for a quiet place. No Family'. In 1881, now aged 74 and 76, they were still living at No 4. They had one servant, Mary Wilson, 18, from Edinburgh.

Thomas Stevenson died in February 1879, and in 1881 Martha was living at No 28 Lauder Road with two daughters and five sons, two of whom were working. Isabella died in 1887, aged 82 and James moved into 28 Lauder Road. A year after her death, he placed the following announcement in *The Scotsman*:

IN MEMORIAM

In memory of ISABELLA ROBERTSON, the beloved wife of JAMES SINCLAIR, who died at 4 Dalrymple Crescent, Edinburgh, 6th October 1887.

He was still living in Lauder Road with Martha and one of her sons,

StClair Stevenson, at the time of the 1891 census. He died in December 1891, at the age of 84.

David Graham

David Graham was a commercial traveller from England. He was born in 1841, and his wife Sarah, also from England, was born in 1843. At the time of 1891 census they had four daughters living with them: Kate aged 16, Rose aged 15, Jessie aged 13, and Margaret aged 11. All were born in England. They had one servant, Jane Packman from Banffshire, aged 24.

William Fraser Buist

William Fraser Buist was born in Muttra, India in December 1835. His father was Lieutenant George Buist of the 10th Light Cavalry, who had married Isabella Jane Masson in 1829.[11] George was born in August 1807, the son of Rev. George Buist of St Andrews, and his wife, Margaret Fernie. Isabella was the daughter of Thomas Masson, and was born in Deal, Kent, in 1804. Isabella had travelled to India in 1828, and the cost of her passage (£200) had been guaranteed by her father and a William Masson, both described as merchants. George and Isabella had two other children: George William Masson Buist, born in 1831 and Isabella Margaret Fernel Buist born in 1833.

George was killed in action at Jalalabad, Afghanistan during the First Afghan War on 29 July 1842,[12] at the age of 34. Margaret appears to have gone to Canada, and died there in 1852.

We next hear of William in the Argentine Republic where he was an 'estanciero' – a rancher.[13] His wife, Harriette Dry Farnie, was the daughter of James Farnie, ship builder and later Treasurer Superintendent of the Royal Infirmary in Edinburgh. She was born in Burntisland in 1842. They had at least five children. The three eldest, Henry, Frank and James were born in Uruguay, and the younger two, William and Eva, were born in Argentina, but they were all British subjects.

In 1893 Harriet had returned to Scotland, and was staying with her sister, Isabella G. Farnie, at 9 Upper Gray Street. She then moved into 4 Dalrymple Crescent, with her family, from about 1895. William Buist died in 1900, aged 64, and Harriet died a few months later, aged 58.

In the 1901 census, James was the head of household. He was an electrician by trade, aged 28 and unmarried. William and Eva were also living in the house, William, aged 18, was a pharmacy student, and Eva, aged 15, was at school.

In 1889 Henry had married Helen J. White Froggatt, and the marriage is recorded in the 'St Andrew's Scotch Presbyterian Church' in Buenos Aires. Two of their children, Henry junior, aged ten, and Aurora aged eight were staying in No 4 at the time of the census. Another of James' nieces, Rita, aged four, was also staying there. She may also have been Henry's daughter, or possibly Frank's.

There were also two servants: a housemaid, Isabella Bain, 18, and a cook, Catherine Murray, 24, both from Caithness.

NO 5 DALRYMPLE CRESCENT

No 5 is another one and a half storey cottage. Extensive work has been done to the back of the house, but the front is relatively unaltered. In 1912 it was described as an 'almost two'-storey building with a wooden porch to the door. The ground floor consisted of a dining room, drawing room, kitchen and servant's room. There was also a washhouse. Behind there was a one-storey cool house, and also a one-storey wooden room that led into the back of the house.

On the first floor there were two bedrooms, a small room, and 'a good size room' as well as a bathroom with a WC, a basin in good condition, and a bath.

The builder James Hunter sold No 5 to Henry Newcombe in July 1864, who owned the house until his death on 2 October 1898. The house was then put up for auction at Dowell's saleroom in November 1898. The asking price was £1175. A WS from Hill Street offered £1260, but the winning bid was £1275 by William Galloway, SSC, on behalf of James Thomson Grieg, who was still living in the house in 1901.[14] He still owned the house in 1912, but had rented it out.

Henry Newcombe

Henry Newcombe was born in York in 1821 and was first a Member, and later a Fellow, of the Royal College of Surgeons of Edinburgh. He was married to Anne Maria Hill, who was born in Edinburgh in October 1826. Her parents were Peter Hill, a publisher, and Jane McDowall. In 1861, they were living in Blatchinworth, Lancashire, although at the time of the census, Anne Maria was visiting friends in Nottinghamshire. They did not have any children living with them during the time they lived in Dalrymple Crescent. In 1871 they had a visitor from Bedford, Agnes Matilda Rutherford, aged 21. Their servant was Margaret Sommerville, also 21, from Lanarkshire. In 1881 they had one servant, Mary Barclay, 21, from Milnathort in Fife. In 1891, they had two servants, Christine Brebner, 22, from Wick, and Hannah Fraser, 19, from Aberdeen.

Doctor Newcombe was mentioned in *The Scotsman* of 18 February 1870 as being present at a lecture at the Royal College of Surgeons by Dr Watson Wemyss FRCS on 'The Construction of Hospitals for the Sick and Hurt'. He was also present at Dean Ramsay's funeral on 2 January 1873, when he sat in the pews reserved for the Scottish Episcopal Church Society.

Anne Maria Newcombe died of heart failure on 12 April 1898 at No 5, at the age of 70. Henry died in the same year, on 2 October, at Woodhall Spa, Lincoln. The announcement of his death appeared in *The Scotsman* on 4 October, stating that the funeral would be held the following day, leaving 5 Dalrymple Crescent at 2pm and going to Rosebank Cemetery. His trustees were Patrick Hill Normand of Whitehill, Aberdour; Thomas William Leask Spence, Secretary of the General Board of Commissioners in Lunacy for Scotland; and Thomas Shaw McLaren, WS.

James Thomson Grieg

James Thomson Grieg was an accountant from Edinburgh. He had been living at 115 Dalkeith Road when he bought the house. In 1901 he was married, but with no children living at home. He was born in 1849, and his wife Sara (née Stirling), who came from New South

Wales, was born a year later. They had one servant, Annie Robertson, aged 25, from Fyvie in Aberdeenshire.

NO 6 DALRYMPLE CRESCENT

After the tragic events of 1865, Robert Hunter sold No 6 to David Henderson, who lived there from 1866 to 1874. The house was advertised for sale in March 1874, and described as a 'Handsome Cottage' with a dining room, drawing room, five bedrooms, kitchen, scullery, bathroom '(Hot and Cold Water)'. The garden is described in detail: 'about a quarter of an Acre, with Greenhouse, Two Vineries, Boiler &c'. The advertisement states that the house was 'built for proprietor's own occupancy', which would seem to imply that it replaced the house that Robert Hunter originally built. It was bought by James Brechin, who lived there until February 1878, when he sold the house to Isabella Thompson and her two sisters, Helen and Mary. They lived in the house until 1886, when they sold it to John Middlemass. He lived there from 1886 to 1898, and sold it to Elizabeth Ritchie in May 1898. She lived in the house until 1901, when she sold it to Isabella Maclean in March 1901.

In 1912 the house was described as being detached, with one storey and an attic. It had splayed quoins and polished ashlar round the window, moulded cornices and three heavily moulded attic windows. The gable and back wall were of coursed rubble. There was a one-storey wing to the back, and the field worker noted that there were 'no bow windows to this cottage'. The accommodation consisted of a drawing room, a sitting room, a dining room, two small bedrooms, a storeroom, and a 'kitchen with bath'. The attic and the wing to the back contained a bathroom, and two bedrooms, and another store room.

David Henderson

David Henderson was a hat merchant from Edinburgh. He had premises at 46 North Bridge and 64 Leith Street. He was born in South Leith in 1826, and remained a bachelor. His parents were James

Henderson and Margaret Adam. In 1871 he was living with his two unmarried sisters: Agnes, a year older than him, and Margaret, six years younger. Two nephews were also staying with them: William and David Waddell. William was a clothier apprentice born in Kilsyth, Stirlingshire in 1852. David was two years younger. He was an architect's apprentice, and was born in St Margaret's Hope, Orkney. They were the sons of David Henderson's sister, Helen. There was one servant, Jane Berwick, 16, from Midcalder in Midlothian.

David Henderson was a keen amateur horticulturist, being mentioned in *The Scotsman* as having won prizes at the Southern Floral and Agricultural shows: for peaches in September 1868, a 'special prize' for two bunches of grapes in July 1869, and for '6 Dahlia blooms' in September 1869.

In 1873 an advertisement in *The Scotsman* ran 'Servant – Wanted a thorough Good General Servant. Liberal wages. Lady and Gentleman only. 6 Dalrymple Crescent'.

Soon after, in March 1874 the house was put up for sale, and in 1881 he was living at Gracemount, Liberton. This was a large house, with five servants including two 'boys in garden' and a 'boy in stables'. His nephew David Waddell and his sister Agnes were still living with him, as was another sister, Catherine Neil, a widow aged 67.

James Brechin

James Brechin was a butcher whose shop was at 1 West Newington Terrace. Advertisements in the Edinburgh and Leith Post Office Directory describe the shop as 'Brechin Brothers butchers, poulterers and sausage makers'. (See Plate 6b).

James was part of a family of butchers. His father was also James Brechin, and his mother was Agnes Hood Adam. There were nine children in the family – two sisters born in 1836 and 1837, and seven brothers. The two sisters, Agnes and Christian were the eldest. Then came James, William, Hugh, Robert, Malcolm, Matthew and Alexander. Malcolm, Matthew and Alexander were born in Cumbernauld, Dumbartonshire, while the elder children were born in Kilsyth, Stirlingshire. James bought the house in May 1874, and in

1876 six of the brothers had their addresses in the Edinburgh and Leith Post Office Directory, although only two of them lived in Edinburgh. William, Hugh, Robert and Matthew lived in Glasgow, while both James and Malcolm gave their address as 6 Dalrymple Crescent. Hugh subsequently became a Baillie in Glasgow.[15]

James was another keen amateur gardener, and won first prize in at the 1877 autumn show of the Southern Horticultural Society for his greenhouse plants. He also exhibited at the International Horticultural Exhibition at Carlisle, also in September 1877. *The Scotsman* reported on the Scottish prize-winners, and James was listed as a prize-winner for vegetables, and for fruit, he was 'third for green gooseberries, third for red currants, and first for blackcurrants'.

The Scotsman also gave a vivid description of the weather: the morning of the show 'opened with an outlook of the most discouraging kind, rain falling heavily, and the sky being densely overcast'. Before noon the discomfort caused by the incessant downpour became worse: 'Under the tramp of the crowd the ground assumed a sloppiness that became worse and worse every minute. All through the afternoon the rain continued falling, till at five o'clock the whole meadow was a miserable swamp, there being almost impassable lochs in at least one of the tents.'

Malcolm married in 1877 and moved from Dalrymple Crescent to Craigielee, 7 Craigie Terrace. His wife, Mary, came from Edinburgh. In the 1881 census they were still at Craigielee. Mary gave her age as 26 and Malcolm was 39. They had two children; Mary aged two and Agnes, aged one.

James married in 1879, and by the time of the 1881 census he was living at Glencairn, Fountainhall Road. His wife Maggie came from Kincardine. He was 46 and she was 30. Staying with them was an unmarried niece, Agnes Moffat, 18, from Glasgow, and a visitor, Anne Murray, 41, unmarried, from Dirleton.

Isabella Thompson

Isabella Thompson was a spinster living at 44 South Clerk Street, when she bought No 6. By the time of the 1881 census she was living in Dalrymple Crescent with her two unmarried sisters: Helen and Mary. Isabella was 48, Helen was 43 and Mary was 38. They had all been born in Dunblane in Perthshire, to Andrew Thompson and Mary Wilson. Their livelihood was described as 'letting apartments', and the house was divided into three separate households. The Thompson sisters had four rooms. The other occupants are described as lodgers. Joseph Middlemiss (76) and his sister Margaret (70) came from Gunnister in Berwickshire. He was a wine merchant with a business in Leith, and they rented two rooms.

James Wilson was a retired doctor from Douglas, Lanarkshire and lodged in one room. He was 84 and died shortly after the census, on 11 April 1881. The record of his will states that he was a surgeon, formerly of Perth in the county of Lanark, Ontario, Canada, and that he had also lived at 44 South Clerk Street.

The Thompson sisters had moved to 40 Warrender Park Terrace by 1886, and on 31 December 1889 Joseph Middlemiss died at Belmont, Levenhall in Musselburgh.

Eight years later, in December 1897 Isabella died at 1 Taylor Place, having also lived at 10 East Norton Place. She was 67.

John Middlemass

John Middlemass was the son of Robert Middlemass, the biscuit manufacturer, who lived in No 12. Their story is told in Chapter 6.

Elizabeth Ritchie

Elizabeth Ritchie, or Peddie or Colenutt, was born in Edinburgh in 1836. In 1891 she was living at 3 Suffolk Road with her husband, George Colenutt, a commercial agent from England, and her son and daughter by her first marriage: Hugh and Christian Peddie. George died in June 1897, and Elizabeth lived at No 6 from 1898. She did not keep the house long, but sold it in March 1901.

Isabella Maclean

Isabella Mary Maclean (née Balfour) was the wife of Rev. Duncan

Maclean, a retired minister of the (Wee) Free Church of Scotland. She was born in Leuchars, Fife, in 1853. He came from Callendar, Perthshire, and was born in 1847. When they bought the house from Elizabeth Ritchie, they were living at 17 Braid Crescent. The house was in Isabella's name 'with the consent of' her husband.

NO 7 DALRYMPLE CRESCENT

No 7 is a semi-detached house, one of a pair built by Samuel Hunter. The Inland Revenue survey of 1912 merely describes it as being similar to No 8. It has two floors, with dormer windows in the upper floor. In May 1864 Samuel Hunter sold No 7 to Charles Wilson, who lived there with his wife until he died in 1884. His son inherited the property, but his widow lived there until 1894, when the property was sold to Frank Rutherford, who was still living there in 1901. At that time the house was known as Neworth Cottage.

Charles Wilson

Charles Wilson was a retired physician who had lived in Moray Place. His wife, Elizabeth Wilson, neé Dove, was born in Earlston, Berwickshire in 1809. In 1871 they were living in No 7 with one servant, Mary Angus, 23, from Perthshire. In the next census in 1881, their servant was a widow aged 46, from Dull in Perthshire, called Marie Sutherland.

Charles died on 19 March 1884. The obituary in *The Scotsman* gives us quite a bit of information about him. He was born in Kelso in 1804, the son of a banker and solicitor, also Charles Wilson. He studied at Edinburgh University, and completed his studies in Paris. He had a medical practice in Kelso from 1828 until 1854. He was the first secretary of the Tweedside Physical and Antiquarian Society, and was instrumental in establishing a museum in Kelso. He was also secretary of the Border Medical Society. In 1854 he went to Vienna to update his knowledge of medicine, and then practiced in Edinburgh for ten years, where he was instrumental in the founding of the Sick

Children's Hospital. For several years he was honorary librarian to the Royal College of Physicians. After his retirement in 1864 he used his knowledge of several European languages to translate poems and songs, some of which were published in *The Scotsman*. He also published a number of medical articles.

After his death the house passed to their elder son, John Dove Wilson, a lawyer (LLD), who was Sheriff substitute for Aberdeen Kincardine & Banff and had an honorary degree from Aberdeen University. The other son was a retired solicitor in Edinburgh. Elizabeth Wilson continued to live at No 7, having a life-rent, that is, the right to live in the house for as long as she wished. In June 1884, she is recorded as living in Aberdeen, but in 1891, now aged 82, she was again living at No 7, with a visitor Euphemia Martin, and a servant, Jane Anne Laing, aged 21.

Elizabeth Wilson died in November 1893, aged 84, and in December her effects were sold at an auction, advertised in *The Scotsman*:

> To-morrow (Friday), 22nd December, at Eleven o'clock, WITHIN NO 7 DALRYMPLE CRESCENT, GRANGE. HOUSEHOLD FURNITURE AND OTHER EFFECTS, a residue, including mahogany pedestal side-board, set of dining table, eight chairs in haircloth, oak hat and umbrella stand and tables, brass and iron beds and bedding, chest drawers, washstands and ware. Brussels and other carpets, crimson damask window curtains, dish covers, crockery, utensils &c.

Frank Rutherford

Frank Rutherford was a cashier, who had previously lived at 16 Gladstone Terrace. In 1901 he was living in the house with his wife, Isabelle and their two daughters. Frank was born in 1848 in Edinburgh. His wife was born in 1845 in Jedburgh. The elder daughter, Margaret was born in Govanhill in 1877 and was a teacher. The younger, Isabella was born in Edinburgh in 1880, and was an art student. They did not have a living-in servant.

NO 8 DALRYMPLE CRESCENT

This is the other half of the pair of semi-detached villas built by Samuel Hunter. The survey of 1912 describes No 8 in a rather succinct manner. There was a dining room with an oriel window, and a kitchen with provision for a bed and accommodation for a maid, but no scullery. There was a servant's room and WC, and a coalhouse outside. Upstairs there was a drawing room, and two bedrooms, both in excellent condition. The front wall was of polished ashlar, and the back wall had a course of 'squared snecked rubble'. The gable was of coursed rubble, and the roof of slate.

In January 1865 Samuel Hunter sold the house to George Campbell, who subsequently sold it to William Bell in 1878. William Bell was still living in the house in 1912.

George Campbell

Although he bought No 8, George Campbell does not appear to have lived in the house. He was living in Glasgow when he bought the house, having previously been in Peterburgh, Virginia, USA. When he sold the house in 1878, he was living in London.

He was born in Halkirk, Caithness in July 1834. His father Benjamin Campbell, had been a shoemaker by trade, and had died in Thurso in 1859. His mother Ann was born in Caithness in 1796, and her maiden name was MacDonald. She married Benjamin Campbell in February 1817. They had at least seven children: Catherine, born in 1818, Christian in 1826, William in 1829, Thomas in 1832, George in 1834, Barbara in 1836 and Murray in 1838.

Something of Ann's early life can be gleaned from the records. Her first daughter, Catherine, was born in 1818 in Halkirk. The next two children were born in Reay, in Caithness, in the 1820s. The four youngest children were born in Halkirk in the 1830s. In the 1841 census Ann was living at Watten, in Caithness with Christian, George, Barbara and Murray. Benjamin was working as a drover and on census night he was staying at an inn at Rosskeen in Ross and Cromarty. In 1851 he was working as a shoe maker, and was visiting a farmer in Halkirk, but it is not known where Ann was at this time.

Two of their children died young: Murray at the age of four, and William when he was 17 years old.

In 1861, after Benjamin's death, Anne was living in Thurso with her ten-year-old grandson, also Benjamin Campbell. He was the son of another of Anne's children, John, whose birth is not recorded. However he married Margaret Walters in 1845, and Benjamin was born in 1852. Another son David was born in 1858.

Ten years later, in the 1871 census, Ann was the head of the household at No 8. Barbara was also living at No 8 with her husband, Robert Sutherland. Robert was a tobacconist, born in Latheron, Caithness in 1835. No 8 was given as Robert's home address between 1871 and 1874.

Christian also married a Sutherland. His name was Francis Sutherland, and they were married on 31 May 1850 at Olrig, in Caithness. Their daughter, Jane was born in Thurso on 1 December 1850, and in 1871 she was staying with her grandmother at No 8, and working as a general servant.

Benjamin Campbell was still staying with Ann in 1871. He was now 20, and his occupation is given as clothier shopman. It has not been possible to trace Ann Campbell after the house was sold, but by 1881 Benjamin had married, and was living at 24 Calton Hill, Edinburgh with his wife and two children.

An inscription at the Westfield graveyard of St Trostan's church in Halkirk gives a final note to the story. It reads

Thomas and George Campbell, London, in memory of their father Benjamin Campbell born Forsie 1796, died Thurso 1859, brother William born in Bruptster 1829, died Swordale 1846, sister Murray born Achchattar 1838, died Thurso 1849, [something undecipherable] his wife Mary Campbell 18 Sept. 1898, their son George 5 Nov 1898; David Waters Campbell 29 Nov 1875 age 17 years.[16]

William Bell

In the 1881 census William Bell is described as a publisher's clerk. He was married to Agnes, and had two sons and a daughter living at home. William was born in Edinburgh in 1835, and Agnes (née Brown) who also came from Edinburgh, was about five years younger. William junior, 17, and daughter Jessie, 15, are described as pupil teachers, while the youngest, Robert, aged 12 was a 'scholar'. All the children were born in Edinburgh. They also had a lodger, Percival Cooper, 22, who was a bank clerk and came from England. They had no servants. In 1891 William junior had left home, and William was now a teacher of music. In this census Agnes, Jessie and Robert have Currie (near Edinburgh) as their place of birth. Robert was a bank clerk. Jessie married Alexander McDiarmid in 1895, and in 1901 William had retired, and only Robert was living at home. He was now a teller at the Bank of Scotland. Agnes' place of birth this time is given as Riccarton (near Currie).

NO 9 DALRYMPLE CRESCENT

In the Inland Revenue survey, No 9 is described as a one and a half storey cottage of rubble walls with polished stone surrounding the windows, and two small gables. The front was covered in ivy, and there was a wing to the back. The accommodation consisted of a drawing room with a white marble fire surround, a dining room, with a press which went right back under the landing of the stairs. On the ground floor there was also a bathroom and kitchen. The upper floor had three bedrooms. Off one was a small closet 'not large enough for a room', but it had a roof light. There was a small dressing room with a window between the other two bedrooms. The general structure of the house has not changed much since it was built.

In January 1865 Samuel Hunter sold it to David Cowan Mudie, who lived here until 1871, when he bought No 10, and moved into it. No 9 was rented out, first to Andrew Henderson, from 1872 to 1877, and them to Andrew William Usher, from 1878 to 1888. From 1889 to 1897 it was occupied by Robert Paterson and his son, Andrew. Then from 1898 to 1901 it was rented by George R. Jamieson. A photograph of No 9 today is shown in Plate 7a.

David Cowan Mudie

David Cowan Mudie bought No 9 in 1865 and lived in it until 1871. His story is told in Chapter 6.

Andrew Henderson

Andrew Henderson was born in Edinburgh on 1 January 1835. His parents were Andrew Henderson and Margaret Paterson. He married Agnes Lawrie, and in 1871 they were living at 20 Annandale Street with four children: Agnes, born in August 1863, James, born in 1865, Margaret, born in 1868 and Mary born in 1870.

Andrew was clerk to Lord Gifford, a well-known law lord. Gifford had been nominated a judge in January 1870, and was known to make up his mind quickly and to act independently and fairly. He experienced symptoms of paralysis in 1872, but worked on until January 1881 when he resigned. He died six years later, but left a bequest to the universities of Edinburgh, Glasgow, St Andrews and Aberdeen for a series of lectures, the Gifford Lectures. These lectures still continue today, with each of the four universities hosting an annual lecture on Natural Theology.[17]

Andrew Henderson and his family lived at No 9 for five years. In the 1881 census they were living at 79 Gilmore Place. Although he was only 46, his occupation was given as retired clerk. He also had two more children, who were born while he was living in Dalrymple Crescent: Andrew junior was born in 1873, and Jane in 1875.

Andrew William Usher

Andrew Usher was not the only member of the Usher family to live in Dalrymple Crescent, so his story is told in Chapter 6.

Robert Paterson

Robert Paterson was a tailor and clothier from Edinburgh, born in 1830. His business was at 91 South Bridge. In 1854 he married Fanny Sutherland, and their son, Andrew, was born in 1858. Fanny was born in South Leith in 1825 to Andrew Sutherland and Barbara Simpson. In 1881 they were living at 22 Melville Terrace, but Fanny was not at home. Andrew was a commercial traveller for the London-based firm of Pawson & Co, whose Edinburgh base was at 16 Princes Street. They moved to No 9 in 1889, but Fanny was again absent from home at the time of the 1891 census. In 1891 they had one servant, Annie Porteus, aged 28, from Corstorphine. They left No 9 in 1897, and moved to 16 Lygon Road, and by this time Robert had retired.

George R. Jamieson

George Robert Jamieson was a merchant who had been born in Shetland in 1867.[18] He was a partner in G. R. & W. Jamieson, wholesale egg and butter merchants, with premises at 10 Jeffrey Street and 5 & 7 Cranston Street. His father was William Jamieson and his mother's name was Agnes Black. The 'W' in the business name could have been his father (although he died in 1887) or his brother William. George married Barbara, also from Shetland, and her maiden name was also Jamieson. They married in Edinburgh about 1890, and had eight children, all born in Edinburgh: Jean, born in 1891, Agnes in 1893, William in 1894, Lydia in 1896, Thomas in 1898, George in 1900, Norman in 1902, and Isobel in 1905.

In 1899 and 1900 they also had Barbara's brother staying with them. He was Rev. Thomas William Jamieson, a Wesleyan Methodist minister. In September 1899, he placed the following advertisement in *The Scotsman*:

> Any lady who can recommend experienced general servant kindly communicate Rev. T. W. Jamieson, 9 Dalrymple Crescent.

In the 1901 census Thomas was no longer staying at the house. There

were two servants: Agnes Gordon aged 24 and Rosalinda Young aged
22. Both came from Shetland, and Rosalinda was a domestic nurse.
George R. Jamieson died in Edinburgh in 1913 and is buried at
Sandwick in Shetland.

NO 10 DALRYMPLE CRESCENT

No 10 is a substantial detached house, which Rev. John Duncan
bought from Leadbetter and Smith in May 1864. He died in February
1870 and his trustees appear to have rented No 10 to Rev. Harry
Anderson and his sisters Helen and Susan Anderson. In April 1872
the trustees sold the house to David Cowan Mudie, who lived there
until his death in 1893. The house was then rented out, to Harry
Lawrence Usher from 1896 to 1898, and to Robert S. Gracie in 1900
and 1901. A sketch of No 10, drawn in 1991, is shown in Plate 7b.

Professor John Duncan

In May 1864 when Rev. John Duncan bought No 10 he was Professor
of Hebrew and Oriental Languages at New College, Edinburgh. He
was born in 1796, in Aberdeenshire, to John Duncan, a shoemaker,
and Anne (née Welch). He married Janet Tower in 1837, but she died
two years later, giving birth to their second child. His second wife was
a widow, Janet Torrance (née Douglas), by whom he had two
daughters. He was working as a minister in Glasgow, when he was
asked to go to Pesth in Hungary as leader of the first Missionary to
the Jews from the Church of Scotland. He was a respected scholar of
ancient and Semitic languages, and had given lectures on the
conversion of the Jews. After the Disruption of 1843, when the Free
Church broke with the Church of Scotland, the first Free Church
General Assembly set up an Educational Committee that recommended the establishment of a college in Edinburgh to train
ministers for the Free Church. In the summer of 1843 the Free
Church appointed four professors: Thomas Chalmers became
Principal and Senior Professor of Theology, David Welsh Professor

of Church History, William Cunningham became junior Professor of Theology, and John Duncan Professor of Hebrew and Old Testament. It was said of Duncan that, with his mastery of languages, he could 'talk his way from Scotland to the Great Wall of China'.[19]

In 1861, aged 65, he was living at 3 Buccleuch Place with Mary Walker Sandeman, also 65, who was described as a friend. Mary Sandeman was born in Perth, and in 1841 she was living in Edinburgh, at 7 St Vincent Street, with three young sisters, and a servant. The sisters were Anna Maria Butter, aged 13; Charlotte Macnabb Butter, aged 12; and Isabella Macnabb Butter, aged six.

Mary Sandeman was living at No 10, when she died in May 1869. In June of that year *The Scotsman* ran an advertisement by a 'quiet family' in Esslingen, Germany offering places for 'YOUNG LADIES' who could study at a nearby seminary. Rev. Professor Smeaton of Mansionhouse Road, and Rev. John Duncan were given as referees.

The Scotsman, in March 1870 reported that the late Miss Sandeman of Dalrymple Crescent had left a legacy of £10-10s 'to provide better Housing for Working People'. This was part of the 12th list of contributions given by the Edinburgh Association for improving conditions of the poor. This was substantially greater than most contributions, which were between £1 and £2, an exception being the Earl of South Esk who donated £10.

John Duncan died in February 1870 and is buried in Grange Cemetery. *The Scotsman* reported on his funeral, which took place on 3 March. Professors and students of New College and a large number of Free Church ministers met at Grange Free Church, and proceeded to No 10. There were services at the church and at the house. The company then progressed to Grange Cemetery. Rev. Smeaton was chief mourner, and the names of the pall-bearers were also given.

Rev. Harry Anderson

Rev. Harry Anderson had been the minister at Juniper Green Free Church. He was born in Inverurie in 1810 to James Anderson and Susannah Watson. James Anderson was a baker, and had six children,

Harry being the youngest. His two eldest sisters, Helen and Susan did not marry, and lived with him at No 10. In 1841 Helen and Susan had been living at 7 Hamilton Place with their niece, Phoebe Cruikshank. She was the daughter of another sister, Mary Anne Anderson, who married a George Cruikshank.

Harry died in September 1870, having been ill for two or three years, and George Cruikshank reported his death. At the time George Cruikshank was living at the schoolhouse, Rayne, Aberdeenshire. Helen and Susan Anderson were still living at No 10 at the time of the 1871 census. They had one servant, Mary Anne Bayes, 26, from Currie near Edinburgh. They then moved to 9 South Mansionhouse Road, where Susan died in October 1877. In the 1881 census, Helen was living there with Phoebe, who was now widowed, and her son, Samuel Davidson, aged 14. Helen died in 1889, aged 92. In her death certificate she is described as a landowner, and her parents were James Anderson, a baker, and Susan Watson. She died of 'senile decay', and the death was reported by Samuel.

David Cowan Mudie

David Cowan Mudie bought number 10 and moved his family into it in 1872. In August 1874 two advertisements appear for a 'House and Laundry maid' and a 'house and table maid' wanted immediately 'for the Country'. Particulars could be got from a Mrs Rainey, 10 Dalrymple Crescent. As mentioned above, the history of the Mudie family is told in Chapter 6.

Harry Lawrence Usher

Harry Usher was Andrew Usher's youngest brother. He rented No 10 from 1896 to 1898. The story of the Usher family is also told in Chapter 6.

Robert S. Gracie

Robert Spenser Gracie was born on 15 March 1870. His father was

Robert Gracie and his mother was Mary Ann Theresa Mason Spencer. In the 1901 census his occupation was given as 'secretary of limited company'. His wife Margaret also came from Edinburgh, and had been born in November 1874. Her parents were Andrew Aitken and Joana Lawrie Anderson. Robert and Margaret had married in Edinburgh in 1900. At the time of the census they had one servant, Elizabeth Gentleman, 21, from Tillicoultry.

In November 1900 Robert Gracie was one of seven partners buying over the paint company of Craig and Rose. Craig and Rose was founded in 1829 by two Scots businessmen, James Craig and Hugh Rose, and is still in business today. It is the company who supplied the first paint for the Forth Rail Bridge. Three of the partners were from the Rose family; two were described as paint manufactures, and one as a chartered accountant apprentice. Robert Gracie is described as a cashier.

NO 11 DALRYMPLE CRESCENT

No 11 is also a detached house, similar in style to No 10, also built by Leadbetter and Smith. The Inland Revenue survey of 1912 describes its accommodation. Downstairs there was a dining room and sitting room, in good condition, with a marble fireplace in the sitting room. There was a kitchen and a servant's room, and a washhouse with tubs and a sink. Upstairs there were four bedrooms and a modern bathroom. Plate 8a shows a postcard of No 11 at the end of the 19th century.

George Tod Bathgate bought it in April 1863, but in March 1864 he advertised it in *The Scotsman* for sale by Public Roup*. It is described as an 'Excellent family house' with two public rooms, five bedrooms, a dressing room, bathroom, kitchen, and 2 WCs. There is a 'plot in front' and a garden behind. Additionally, 'If desired Grates, gas Lustres and Venetian Blinds can have a valuation'. The feu was £5-0-6d, and the upset price £950. It evidently did not sell, as the

* Roup is a Scots word for Auction

advertisement was repeated for a roup on 6 April, when the upset was reduced to £900. In May 1864, it was bought by Richard Lister.

On 2 March 1870 the house was advertised in *The Scotsman*, with very little detail, save that it was occupied by Richard Lister. The advertisement was repeated on 16 and 25 March, and is recorded as having been sold in May 1870 to Henry Haig Banks. In 1879 Henry Haig Banks sold no 11 to John Anderson. It was rented to John D. Gardiner in 1881 and 1882, and thereafter the Anderson family lived in it until 1901.

George Tod Bathgate

George Tod Bathgate was born in Peebles in March 1828. His parents were Alexander Bathgate and Janet Campbell. In 1862 he married Isabella Hay, who was born in Leith in 1830. A year later he bought No 11, and in the title deeds he is described as the secretary of the Scottish Trade Protection Society, based at 11 Bank Street. A year later, when he sold the house, he was described as manager of the Scottish Trade Protection Society.

In 1881 he was living at 16 Murdoch Terrace with Isabella and four children. At 53, he was described as a writer and accountant. His three daughters, Isabella, Catherine and Georgina had been born in Portobello, and his son, Alexander, in Musselburgh. The girls were 15, 14 and 13 years old and Alexander was eight.

In 1888 *The Scotsman* reported three rather unedifying stories about George Bathgate. In February he appeared as the complainer in a bill of suspension concerning a sentence passed on him the previous August. He had been ordered to pay a fine of 10 shillings or face five days in prison for assaulting a cabman. Bathgate claimed that he had a complaint against the cabman, which the Procurator Fiscal had refused to support, and he had also refused to postpone the trial or call witnesses forward. The Court of Session threw the case out, saying that they would not interfere with the original findings.

In July Bathgate sued John Ferguson & Son, confectioners, of the High Street for the sum of £1-1s 'less 6d paid to account' for the time and trouble with you relative to your business, and set of books which you wished me to commence for you; advising you as to your contract of copartnery.

Ferguson at first denied the charge, but then agreed that he had asked Bathgate to call. However Bathgate had been 'mirac'lous drunk', and that he did not pay the 6d on account, but gave him money to go away from his door. Bathgate threatened to bring an action for damages against Ferguson for saying that he was the worse for liquor.

Bathgate: If the man had been at all civil I wouldn't have charged him half so much
Ferguson: I'm quite prepared to prove assault against you when you were drunk. You are a man fit to give no man advice
Bathgate (laughing): That is only your opinion
Ferguson: You should take my advice and give up drink.

The magistrate tried to get the parties to come to an agreement, but Ferguson refused saying that Bathgate had even followed him to a public house where Ferguson was meeting a commercial traveller. Bathgate had offered to drop the case for 2 shillings. Bathgate claimed it was 'a gross falsehood'. Then Bathgate said he would take 15s, Ferguson offered 5, and the courts gave a decree for 10s and Court expenses. The Chairman remarked that it was 'not a very edifying case'.

In August he was described as living in Broughton Street, and was charged with stealing a waterproof coat from an office in Frederick Street. He pleaded not guilty, and the case was held over to the next day. Bathgate asked for bail, saying

'I am perfectly willing to appear tomorrow on my own recognisances. It is a matter of eighteen pence, and is capable of explanation'. Bail was set at £3, at which he exclaimed '£3; five shillings is more like it.'

George Bathgate died in Peebles in 1893, aged 65.

Richard Lister

Richard Lister bought No 10 in 1863 and sold it a year later. Subsequently he rented a house on the south side of the Crescent. His story is told in Chapter 6.

Henry Haig Banks

Henry Haig Banks was the second son of William Banks, who established his printing business in Edinburgh in 1852. William had previously been working for W. H. Lizars, and named his third son after him. The three sons were: William junior, born July 1833, Henry, born 1835 and Home Lizars, born 1840. Their mother was Margaret Robertson.

The name of the firm went from William Banks (1852 to 1857) to William Banks & Son (1858 to 1863) and to Banks & Co in 1864. Henry is described as an engraver and printer, with a business address of 1 North St David's Street.[20] At the time of the 1871 census he was married with four children. His wife, Mary Wilkie Banks was four years younger than him, and was born in Bonnington, Edinburgh. They also had a servant, Mary Stout, who was 31 and came from Lerwick. *The Scotsman* reported that another daughter was born on 23 February 1873, and a son on 18 August 1874. However, the daughter, Mary, died of bronchial pneumonia when she was only 11 weeks old.

In 1881 the family was living at 29 Mayfield Gardens. By that time he had seven children: William, born in 1862, working as a stationer; Margaret, born 1867, who was a scholar; Henry, born 1869, a scholar; Robert, born 1871, a scholar; Alexander, born 1874; Alfred, born 1877, and Alice, born 1879.

The firm continued to prosper. It moved from 26 Waterloo Place to 10 North St David's Street in 1868. In 1876 it opened a printing works at 92 Causewayside, and was renamed the Grange Printing Works. In 1884 the office moved from North St David's Street to 12 George Street, with the printing works still in Causewayside, and this arrangement lasted until well into the 20th century. Plate 9 is a copy

of an advertisement for the firm, taken from the 1895 Edinburgh and
Leith Post Office Directory.

An insight into the early work of the firm is obtained by some
letters written by Henry and his colleagues to the pioneering photographer William Fox Talbot.

On January 19th 1861:

Sir/

You will see from a Noto [*sic*] that I have enclosed in the
parcel with plates from Greigs the Engineers, that they
cannot case harden the steel from its thinness, this I was
doubtful of from the beginning as all the plates I can get
hardened were of a very thick description, fully ½ an inch
thick.

I am Sir yours respectfully

On July 30th 1861:

Sir/

With this you have proofs of three of the Blocks left with us –

We have bestowed every care upon them but have failed
to bring them up; you will see from the Impressions that they
are much too Shallow for Type printing as no care in the
world could prevent the Ink from going into the lines &
covering the surface at the same time – In cases where the
work is vignetted & does not come up to the outer edge of
the Block the surface beyond the work must be cut down
considerably below the level so as to bring the Vignette up
sharply & keep the edges clean –

We have a number of your steel plates carefully tied up –
shall we keep them until you return to Edinburgh, or send
them to your present address?

We are Sir

Yours respectfully

And

> The Glass with ruled lines you alude [*sic*] to in yours of the
> 24th has not been successful it is impossible to get a ground
> on such a large piece by means of heat. I have lost a large
> amount of time and material trying to get it done for you but
> to no purpose.
>
> However I will try some experiments with the ground in
> solution if you will give me authority to proceed, and can
> give time for it.[21]

John D. Gardiner

John Douglas Gardiner was a solicitor (SSC) whose workplace was at
58 Castle Street. He was born in Scone, Perthshire in April 1839. His
father was James Gardiner and his mother was Jess (or Janet)
Douglas.

He married Elizabeth Gladstone, who was born in Yetholm,
Roxburghshire in April 1841. They rented No 10 from the owner, John
Anderson, in 1881 and 1882. After living in Dalrymple Crescent they
moved to 16 Cumin Place, where he died in August 1890. His widow
was still in the house at the time of the 1891 census, with four
children: George, aged 19 was a law apprentice; Elizabeth junior was
17; William aged 11 and John aged eight were both described as
scholars. All the children were born in Edinburgh. Her widowed
mother, Christian Gladstone, was also living with them. She had
been born in Eckford, Roxburghshire in 1813.

Christian's maiden name was Scott, and she was the widow of
Archibald Gladstone who had been a baker at Yetholm. She died in
August 1897, when she was living at 1 Cameron Terrace. She was 84
years old.

John Anderson

John Anderson was a wholesale tea merchant whose premises were
at 140 Mitchell Street Leith. In 1881 John Anderson was unmarried

and living with his father, Duncan Anderson, who was Keeper of the Chapel Royal. His address is given as The Abbey, Holyrood Palace. John was born in Edinburgh in November 1849, and his father in Comrie, Perthshire in 1812. His mother, Susan (or Susannah) Andrews had died in 1880 at the age of 70. He also had an elder brother, Henry, who died at the age of 27.

By 1891, John Anderson, had married and was living at No 11. His wife's name was Charlotte Willmore, and she came from London. She was about ten years younger than John. They had four children: Susan aged five, Charlotte aged four, Elizabeth aged three and Henrietta aged two, who were all born in Edinburgh. Duncan, now aged 79, was also living with them. In addition there are three servants: a general servant, a sick nurse and a nursery nurse. The general servant was Jessie Hynd who was 26 and came from Perth. The sick nurse was Mary Morton, aged 40 from Cleish in Kinross, and the other nurse was Margaret Marshall who was also 26 and came from Stanley.

Also in 1891, John and others who jointly owned the steamship Newington of Leith, had an action against Macleod & Co, merchants, of Glasgow. Macleods had chartered the ship, and a contract had been drawn up between them and the owners that the ship should pick up a load of iron ore from Bilbao and carry it to Middlesborough-on-Tees. A rate for loading and discharging had been agreed, and also a cost if there was more than 10 days' delay. The ship sailed for Bilbao, and the owners informed the defendant of her departure. However she met stormy weather in the Channel and had to put into Dover for repairs. She was detained for 10 days, and arrived in Bilbao on 10 February 1890, but did not get her turn to load until 12 February, and completed loading on 23 February. Since the owners had informed the defendant of the departure from Dover, the Judge found in their favour, and awarded the sum of £142-6-6d plus expenses.

On a lighter note, the family owned a cottage in St Fillan's, by Loch Earn, and advertised it in *The Scotsman* for summer rent several times between 1888 and 1892.

Duncan died on 23 December 1894, and is buried in Grange

Cemetery. In *The Scotsman* of 21 February 1895 there was the announcement that Mary Morton, the sick nurse had died suddenly at the Royal Infirmary. She as described as 'Mary Morton of Blairadam, Fife, nurse at 11 Dalrymple Crescent for many years'.

John died in May 1898, but Charlotte, was still living at No 11 in 1901. Now aged 40, she was left with five children to bring up: Susan, now aged 15, Charlotte aged 14, Elizabeth aged 13, Henrietta aged 12 and Duncan aged five. To help her she had two young servant girls, a cook and a housemaid. The cook was Isabella M. Newton, aged 20, from Tranent, and the housemaid was Margaret A. Moffat, 19, from Lauder. Charlotte died in April 1906 at the age of 45.

The family headstone in Grange Cemetery (Plate 8b) commemorates the deaths of Henry, Susan, Duncan, John and Charlotte.

NO 12 DALRYMPLE CRESCENT

Throughout Victorian times the house on the north-east corner of the street was known as 25 Findhorn Place, but later became renumbered as 12 Dalrymple Crescent. It was owned by Robert Middlemass, and he and his family lived there throughout the period. The story of the Middlemass family is told in Chapter 6.

CHAPTER 4

The Southeast

~

The houses on the south side of Dalrymple Crescent fall into two groups: No 13 and Nos 24 to 27 are substantial detached houses, mostly lived in by their owners. Nos 14 to 23 are three-storey semi-detached villas, built by George Alexander specifically for renting. The landscape of the south side also affects the design of the houses. There is a substantial drop in the land running east to west through the grounds of the houses on the south side. Consequently most houses are two-storey at the front, facing the street, but three-storey at the back. Nos 24 to 26 were developed considerably later than the rest.

Obviously the inhabitants of George Alexander's villas were tenants, but No 13 was also rented for some part of its history. This chapter covers the houses from Nos 13 to 18, being the eastern half of the south side of the Crescent.

NO 13 DALRYMPLE CRESCENT

No 13 occupies the corner site on the south east of Dalrymple Crescent. The Inland Revenue record of 1912 describes it as a one and a half-storey detached house, with front wall of coursed rubble. It has two small gables with bargeboards projecting in front. There is a three-storey gable to the back, and a low two-storey part to this wing to the east. (The ground slopes to the rear, so the back has more storeys than the front). In the basement there was a kitchen with a concrete floor, and a 'jaw box' (a sink and drain) and a washhouse. There was also a WC with an old seat, a pulley, and cellarage. There were three steps up to the ground floor, where there was a bedroom, a dining room and a drawing room. In the wing there was a small bathroom with a zinc lined WC, and also a pantry. On the upper floor there were two good-sized bedrooms to the front, with camp ceilings, and another bedroom to the back. There was also a small store and two presses, with a small window to the back. Plate 10a is a picture of No 13 today.

Rev. Robert Gemmell bought the house from Alexander Henderson Chalmers, the transaction being dated 28 July 1865. From 1879 to 1881 the house was let out to William Jenkinson, but the Gemmells returned in 1882. Robert died there in November 1886, and the house was again let out. Benjamin Peach occupied it between 1887 and 1891. David Hugh Wilson lived there in 1893 and 1894, and Mrs Anne Kinmont rented it from 1895 to 1897, or possibly later.

In February 1899 the house was advertised for sale. It was described as having three public rooms, four bedrooms 'etc, etc'. The feu was £5-12-6d, and the upset price £1200. Elizabeth Gemmell sold the house to William Blues Scott, whose family lived there from 1899 to 1901.

Robert Gemmell

Rev. Robert Gemmell was a minister of the United Presbyterian Church, born in Irvine, Ayrshire in 1818. His father was Robert Gemmell, and his mother was Mary Dunlop. He married Elizabeth Boath, who came from Forfar and was ten years his younger.

He seems to have been a figure of contention. He is mentioned in *The Scotsman* in June 1867, when Rev. A. C. Rutherford had apparently previously published a letter in which he had made 'strong and offensive statements' about Robert Gemmell. The committee of the Presbytery had persuaded him to apologise, and Gemmell had accepted the apology and agreed to drop his complaint that Rutherford had misrepresented both him and his sermon.

In 1869, his mother, who was staying at the house, died in

February. In August of the same year he is quoted as a reference for Robertson Academy in East Preston Street, which advertised a 'Liberal education to boys in the Southern District.' Fees ranged from £1-1s in the 1st class to £2-10s in 7th class. Preparation was offered for 'University, Public Service exams or Mercantile Pursuits'. Rev. John Pulsford, living at No 15 Dalrymple Crescent was also quoted as a reference.

In the 1871 census Gemmell was recorded as the minister of Arthur Street Church and was living in No 13 with Elizabeth and three children: Robert aged 12, Elizabeth aged seven and Mary aged five. They had one servant, Janet Johnston, aged 21, from Musselburgh. In October of the same year, *The Scotsman* reported that young Robert had won a Sibbald bursary, which was worth £20 annually, and which was available to support four sessions at the High School, Edinburgh.

In 1875 *The Scotsman* reported the induction of Rev. T. B. Johnstone to the Arthur Street church. He is described as the colleague and successor to Rev. Robert Gemmell. After the service, members of the congregation 'dined together in Mr Darling's Hotel in Waterloo Place, where several sentiments appropriate to the occasion were proposed': These included 'Success to Mr Johnstone' proposed by Rev. Mr Gemmell, 'Prosperity to Arthur St Church' and 'The Presbytery of Kirkcaldy'.

Three years later, in May 1878 he was again writing to *The Scotsman* concerning his treatment by the Presbytery. It seems that that body had decided to reduce the stipends of ministers, but Robert Gemmell felt that the reduction of his retirement allowance from £80 to £20 (he was now 60) was excessive, particularly in view of the fact that another minister was receiving considerably more. There had been much friction between Mr Gemmell and his erstwhile congregation, and he effectively resigned from the Supreme Court of the United Presbyterian Church as a result.

The following year, he wrote another letter to *The Scotsman* from No 13, concerning the publication of a pamphlet by Rev. G. R. Badenoch LLD '(of what College I do not know or recollect)'. The pamphlet was entitled 'A Word of Warning against Mr Gladstone', and was directed at the electorate of Midlothian. Dr Badenoch had apparently been the treasurer of the Reformation Society of Scotland, and Gemmell wrote that 'Dr Badenoch knows right well what I and other directors know of him'. If supporters of Gladstone would contact him [Gemmell], 'I verily believe that I can give them some special information of which most likely they are still ignorant'. He further claimed that there were others like himself who 'had no sympathy whatever with the unfair and unwarrantable personal attacks made on Mr Gladstone'.

In the same year the family moved to 4 Morningside Park, and rented out No 13. By the time of the 1881 census young Robert had an MA from the University of Edinburgh, and was a theological student for the United Presbyterian Church. The two daughters were also still living at home.

Robert Gemmell's outspokenness continued to get him into trouble, and in May 1883 *The Scotsman* reported that the Synod of the United Presbyterian Church had taken most of the day on the case of Rev. Robert Gemmell. The conclusion was a 'deliverance interdicting Mr. Gemmell from appearing in any official capacity before the Edinburgh Presbytery, and instructing the Presbytery, in the event of Mr. Gemmell claiming to be heard as a member of any congregation within their bounds, to hear him only in committee and only so long as he submitted to the ruling of the chair'.

In 1885 he had become rather a laughing stock, as at the Synod held in May that year the Moderator stated that 'he had received letters, post-cards and newspapers to the number of over thirty from the Rev. Robert Gemmell (Laughter)'.

Undeterred, he was writing to *The Scotsman* again in February 1886, from No 13, and here we find the cause of the conflict. The letter is headed 'Disestablishment and United Presbyterian Principles'. It appears that the United Presbyterian Church in the main supported the idea of the disestablishment of the Church of Scotland, but Gemmell maintained that this was an opinion, and not a principle of the UPC. He was therefore publicly asking the 'Principal of our Church' to provide proof that disestablishment was indeed a principle.

May I respectfully request from you an answer to this communication within three days? And I reserve my right, after three days, to send this letter, either with, or without your reply, to the public papers. – I remain yours respectfully.

R. GEMMELL

In July 1886 *The Scotsman* reported that he was seriously ill. He was described as having been minister of Arthur Street United Presbyterian Church for many years. He was confined to his residence in Dalrymple Crescent, and was under medical treatment. He died on 5 November, aged 68. Elizabeth and his daughter Mary were living at No 13. Robert junior was a United Presbyterian Minister at Douglas in Lanarkshire, and young Elizabeth was living with him.

In 1890 and 1892 Elizabeth Gemmell was living at No 16 Mayfield Road, and renting out 13 Dalrymple Crescent, and in 1894 James Alexander was acting as her agent. In 1896 she borrowed £150 against the house, and from this record we know that young Elizabeth had married Rev. John Dundas and was living in Muirkirk, Ayrshire. Elizabeth senior and daughter Mary were living with them while Robert was still minister at Douglas.

In 1899, at the time the house was sold, Elizabeth Gemmell and Mary were living at Hillside, Burntisland.

William Jenkinson

William Jenkinson was a brewer, born in Leith in May 1847. His father, also William Jenkinson, was a spirit merchant, who came from Haddington in East Lothian. His mother, Marion Arklie, was also from East Lothian. He was one of six children, all born in South Leith. He married Margaret Wylie Wallace in September 1873. He was a partner in the firm of Jamieson and Jenkinson (brewers) whose premises were at 263 Cowgate. He rented the house from 1879 until 1882. Before 1879 his address was 1 Archibald Place, but in 1881 he was living at No 13 with his wife, Margaret, and four daughters: Helen aged five, Marion aged four, Margaret aged two and Edith aged one.

In October of that year *The Scotsman* reported that Mrs Jenkinson had given birth to a son. They had one servant, Johanna Smith, born in Falkirk in 1862.

Benjamin Peach

Benjamin Peach (Plate 11a) was a geologist with Her Majesty's Survey of Scotland. He was born in England in 1842, but his wife, Margaret, came from Kirkton in Sutherland. She was twelve years younger than him. In the 1891 census their children, Jeanie Peach aged 16, Elizabeth aged nine, Angus aged two and Benjamin aged seven days, were living with them. In addition they had three servants. Elizabeth Hardy was a nurse, aged 46, from Torryburn in Fife. Betty Cuthbert, 19, was the cook, from Crail, also in Fife. The housemaid was Isabella MacLean, 19, from Coigach in Ross and Cromarty. Peach rented the house between 1887 and 1891, and from there the family moved to 86 Findhorn Place.

The Geological Survey of Great Britain was established in 1835 to provide geological maps of the country. Work began on mapping Scotland in the 1850s, starting with the east central area (Berwickshire, Fife, Edinburgh and the Lothians). The Survey in Scotland was established with headquarters in Edinburgh in the 1870s. The terrain made the work difficult, and extra staff were drafted from England in the late 1880s.

Benjamin Neeve Peach was born in St Austell, Cornwall in September 1842. According to Angela Anderson in a booklet published by the Institute of Geological Sciences in 1970,[1]

> There can be few names in the history of Scottish geology
> better known than that of Ben Peach, whose classic work in
> the Geological Survey of Scotland from 1862 to 1905 laid the
> foundations for so much of our present understanding of
> the geological structure of this country.

Benjamin's father, Charles Peach, was an officer in the Coastguard service who was promoted first to Peterhead, and then to Wick in

1852. Charles Peach was a keen amateur geologist,[2] and was in contact with Sir Roderick Murchison, the director of the Geological Survey of Great Britain. Murchison undertook to send Benjamin to the Royal School of Mines in London. He graduated in 1862, and then joined the Geological Survey of Scotland, which had just been formed. He worked closely with John Horne, and published several joint works. He retired from the Geological Survey in 1905, but lived on until 1926, and published several papers on palaeontology in his retirement. He was also a good watercolour artist (Plate 11b is a sample of his work). He was awarded the Murchison Centenary Prize in 1892, and in the same year was elected Fellow of the Royal Society. He was also awarded the Neill Medal of the Royal Society of Edinburgh, an Honorary Doctor of Laws Degree (LLD), the Murchison Medal and the Wollaston Medal (in 1921).[3]

David Hugh Wilson

David Hugh Wilson was born in Dundonald, Ayrshire in July 1843. His parents were David Wilson and Jane Denniston. His father was a Free Church minister. He had two brothers and two sisters. He did not marry, and worked as Chief Clerk of the Board of Supervision for the Relief of the Poor. He lived in No 13 sometime between 1891 and 1894, and died at Craiglockart Hydropathic Hospital in November 1894. His death was reported by his brother John, a solicitor in Irvine, and the certificate was signed by Henry D. Littlejohn.

Sir Henry Duncan Littlejohn was no ordinary GP. Born in Edinburgh in 1826 he became the first Medical Officer of the city, following the collapse of a tenement building in 1862, with the loss of 35 lives. He was president of the Royal College of Surgeons, Edinburgh in 1875 and became Professor of Medical Jurisprudence at Edinburgh University in 1897.[4]

The Board of Supervision for the Relief of the Poor was set up in 1845 under the Poor Law (Scotland) Act. It consisted of the Lord Provosts of Edinburgh and Glasgow, the Solicitor General, the Sheriffs of Perth, Renfrew and Ross and Cromarty and three members appointed by the Crown, and its function was to oversee the operation of the Poor Law.[5]

As Chief Clerk of the Board of Supervision, David Hugh Wilson would have known Dr Littlejohn, who was their medical officer at that time, and this probably explains how he came to sign the death certificate.

Anne Kinmont

Anne Kinmont was born Anne McDonald Watson, in Brechin, Forfar in April 1837. Her father was David Watson, and her mother was Mary Hill. She married Thomas Rogers Kinmont in October 1864 in Dalkeith. He was a solicitor and bank agent, latterly working in Errol, Perthshire. He died in June 1894, aged 67. They had eight children: Mary Elizabeth, born in 1866, John in 1868, Anne Playfair in 1870, Charlotte Hill in 1871, Agnes Emily and David Watson (twins) in 1873, Margaret in 1875 and Patrick born in 1876. All the children were born in Errol.

David Hugh Wilson rented No 13 from 1893 to Whitsunday 1895, but in late 1894 he moved to the Hydropathic Hospital, where he died. Anne Kinmont sub-rented the property from his trustees, and then rented it in her own right.

Between 1894 and 1897 a number of advertisements appeared in *The Scotsman*, advertising tuition of English, arithmetic, French, drawing and music to young pupils. The advertisement was placed by 'M', and the address was 13 Dalrymple Crescent. 'M' described herself variously as a young lady (1894), a young governess (1896) and an experienced young lady (1897).

Also in 1897 the following advertisement appeared in *The Scotsman*:

> Mrs Kinmont, 13 Dalrymple Crescent, thoroughly recommends reliable, obliging, elderly nurse for invalid; would go abroad; free at term.

The family moved to Springfield, 1 South Oswald Road, in 1899. At the time of the 1901 census four of the children, all unmarried, were living at home. They were Charlotte, Agnes, Margaret and Patrick. Patrick was a registered medical practioner, although he was not working at the time of the census. Anne Kinmont's aunt, Anne Playfair was also living with them. She had been born in Alyth in April 1805. She died less than a month after the census was taken, and the record of her will describes her as 'sometime residing at Errol, Perthshire, afterwards at 13 Dalrymple Crescent, Edinburgh, latterly at Springfield, South Oswald Road'.

In 1905, Charlotte married James Gall Inglis, the son of Robert Inglis, who had bought the land on which No 4 was built, and who lived in Dick Place throughout the period.

William Blues Scott

William Blues Scott was born in Edinburgh in 1868. In 1891 he was living at No 4 South Gray Street, with his widowed mother, Janet Scott (née Blues). She was 66, and had been born in Kincardine. W. B. Scott was a student of art. His father was Rev. George Scott, Secretary to the City Mission in Glasgow, who had died in 1876. W. B. Scott and Janet had moved into No 13 by 1899, and Janet died there in December 1899. There was nobody in the house at the time of the 1901 census.

NO 14 DALRYMPLE CRESCENT

No 14 (Plate 10b) is an eight-roomed semi-detached villa, the first (from the east) of the houses built by George Alexander. In 1871, it was rented by Stephen Wellstood, and Robert Beattie was also listed as living there in that year. From 1873 to 1877 it was let to Miss Cleland, and William Brodie lived there from 1878 to 1881. The house was advertised to let in August 1881, the rent being £70 per annum. Donald MacKinnon occupied it from 1883 to 1886, and Jane and Isabella Paterson rented from 1888 to 1901.

Stephen Wellstood

Stephen Wellstood was an ironfounder and was born in Edinburgh in November 1812. His father, James Wellstood, was a shawl manufacturer from Paisley. His mother was Anne Geikie Wellstood. The family were Quakers, and one son, Robert, who died as an infant, is buried in the Quakers Burial Ground in the Pleasance, Edinburgh.[6] In 1830 the family moved to New York, where two of Stephen's brothers made a name for themselves.

John Geikie Wellstood was born in Edinburgh in January 1813, and became a bank-note engraver. The New York Times reported his death in an obituary dated 22 January 1893, in which it said that in the 1870s he designed and engraved most of the United States' banknotes, and praised the elaborate detail of his work.[7]

His other brother, William, was born in Edinburgh in December 1819 and became a book illustrator. His plates include portraits of Florence Nightingale, Ulysses S. Grant, and Henry W. Longfellow, as well as various landscapes.[8]

Meanwhile Stephen returned to Scotland and became a founding member of Smith and Wellstood who were manufacturers of American Stoves, based in Bonnybridge. Smith & Wellstood Ltd originated in a retail hardware business in Glasgow. Stephen Wellstood and James Smith became partners in 1858 and with the help of a third partner, George Ure, they opened the iron foundry at Bonnybridge, called 'The Columbian Stove Works'. They created the ESSE brand name as French-sounding names were in the fashion at the time. The company of Smith and Wellstood continued to produce the ESSE stoves, and the foundry was bought by the Ouzledale Foundry Company in 1984. The ESSE brand is still in existence, and the company celebrated its 150th anniversary in 2004.[9]

Stephen married Jessie Jack, a British subject, who had been born in 'Russia, Tartary' in 1825. In 1868 he was living in 14 Duncan Street, and moved to No 14, where he was living at the time of the 1871 census. At this time his widowed sister-in-law, Elizabeth, was living with them. She was born in Tayport, Fife in 1810. They also had two visitors: another Stephen Wellstood, aged 16, from New York, described as a student of chemistry, and Sophie Jack, aged 13, from England. They had two servants: Isabella Patton, 25, from Glasgow and Ann Milne, 20, from Rothes in Elginshire.

By 1873 they had moved back to Duncan Street, this time to No 15, but later, in 1886, the family was living at 29 Upper Gray Street. Stephen died there on 27 January 1886. Jessie subsequently moved to 20 Newington Road, where she died in April 1898. Stephen's sister-in-law, Elizabeth Wellstood (née Proudfoot) died in Newport, Fife, in 1896.

Stephen and Jessie are also buried in the Quaker Burial Ground in the Pleasance, Edinburgh.

Robert P. Beattie

Robert Purves Beattie was born in Edinburgh in February 1842. His father was William Beattie and his mother's name was Christina Purves. He was a plumber, gasfitter, brass founder and bath manufacturer, with business premises in 19 Castle Street. He lived at 8 Lauriston Park until 1871, when he moved into No 14. He had left the Crescent by 1873, and died in Kensington early in 1887, and in April 1888 the probate of his will described him as 'of 1 The Terrace, Kensington, and of 15 Holden Terrace, Pimlico, and of King Street, St James', all in Middlesex, and of 19 South Castle Street, Edinburgh, sanitary engineer'.

Miss Sophia Cleland

Sophia Cleland was born in the Gorbals, Lanarkshire in April 1841 to George Cleland and Sophia Smith Lang. In 1871 she was living at 4 Abercorn Terrace with her sister, Margaret, and two cousins. Margaret was two years younger than Sophia. The cousins were Grace and William Todd. Grace was born in 1845 in Dunbartonshire, and William was a student of arts at Edinburgh University. He was born in Edinburgh in 1853.

Miss Cleland lived in No 14 between 1873 and 1877. On 7 December 1874, an advertisement appeared in *The Scotsman*:

Dog (Liver and White Pointer) Strayed on Saturday night.
Answers to Grouse. Reward at 14 Dalrymple Crescent
Grange.

William Brodie

William Brodie, the tea merchant, was born in Dansie, Fife in
November 1828. His father, also William Brodie, was a carpenter, and
his mother was Barbara Ley.

His wife, Mary Doig,[10] was born in Edinburgh in December 1831,
and they were married on 4 July 1860, in the bride's home, 3 Seafield
Row, North Leith.

Brodie established Brodie's Coffee and Tea Merchants in 1867,
and the business is still in operation today.[11]

In 1881 William and Mary were living in No 14 with two servants,
Jane Thomson and Annie Hawkes, both aged 20. Jane came from
Annan, and Annie from London. The Brodies subsequently moved
to 8 James Street, Portobello, where William died on 17 December
1884. Mary lived on in the house until she died in 1898.

Donald MacKinnon

Donald MacKinnon (Plate 12a) was born on Colonsay in 1839.[12] He
had a remarkable career, from being the son of a crofter to the first
professor of Celtic at the University of Edinburgh. His biography is
given in 'Professor Donald MacKinnon and Doctor Roger McNeill:
Gaelic "lads o pairts" from Colonsay' by J. W. Sheets.[13]

The 1841 census shows him living at Killchatten on the west of
the island. His father, Duncan, was an agricultural labourer, and he
had two older brothers and four sisters. His mother, Mary Currie,
was also born on Colonsay.

At this time there were two schools on Colonsay. One, run by the
SSPCK (Scottish Society for the Propagation of Christian
Knowledge), had the attitude 'let there be no Gaelic'. The second,
nearer to his home, had a schoolmaster who had studied Gaelic
under Dr Norman McLeod of St Columba's church, Glasgow.[14] Here,

the approach was 'Gaelic first, then English', and this was the school that Donald attended.

In 1857 he went to Edinburgh, and attended the training college in Johnston Terrace, which was a popular avenue for students of 'rural origins and humble means' to go to University. After teaching in Sutherland for three years, he studied at Edinburgh University, and gained his degree in 1869.

In 1872 the Education (Scotland) Act made sweeping changes to the education system in Scotland. One result of this was the formation of the Edinburgh School Board, and Donald MacKinnon became its first Clerk and Treasurer, a post he held for ten years.

In November 1873 he married Catherine MacPhee (Plate 12b), also of Colonsay. Catherine was born in 1844, the daughter of Neil MacPhee and Kitty Bell. She was the youngest of six children, and lived in Killchatten.

The couple first lived at 14 Fettes Row, but by the time of the 1881 census they were living at 3 Greenhill Gardens. They had two children: Malcolm, aged six, was born on Colonsay, and Mary, aged one, was born in Edinburgh. Staying with them was Catherine's unmarried half-sister, Ann McCalder. She was a retired teacher, aged 47, and also came from Colonsay. There was also a servant, Flora McKehnie, 17, who came from Jura.

In 1882 Donald MacKinnon was the first person to be appointed to the Chair of Celtic Studies at Edinburgh University. The 1872 Education Act had made no mention of Gaelic, either as a teaching medium or as a specific area of study. This meant that people had to fight to get Gaelic recognised as a teaching medium. The Gaelic Society of London made efforts to found a Celtic Chair at Aberdeen University and a survey was held into the desirability of a University Celtic Chair. Professor John Stewart Blackie, Professor of Greek at Edinburgh University, was very keen to have a Celtic Chair established in Edinburgh and encouraged the Gaelic Society of Inverness to join him in fighting for its establishment. Professor MacKinnon held the post until his death in 1914.

In 1883 the Napier Commission, officially the Royal Commission of Inquiry into the Condition of Crofters and Cottars in the

Highlands and Islands was set up. Francis Napier, 10th Lord Napier, was its chairman, and it had five other members, including Professor MacKinnon.[15]

Donald MacKinnon and his family lived in Dalrymple Crescent from 1883 to 1887, when they moved to Merchiston Place. In July 1884 his young son, Neil, died at the age of 22 months. The following year, in August, Mrs MacKinnon gave birth to another son, Duncan.

Donald and Catherine were both buried on Colonsay. Their gravestone reads:

DONALD MACKINNON 1839 – 1914
PROFESSOR OF CELTIC IN EDINBURGH UNIVERSITY 1882 – 1914
CATHERINE MACPHEE HIS WIFE 1842 – 1917
HIS DAUGHTERS CATHERINE 1949 MARY 1960

Jane and Isabella Paterson

Jane and Isabella Paterson were both born in Edinburgh. Jane was born in 1827 and Isabella in 1835. Their father, Archibald Paterson was a silk mercer. In 1841 the family was living at 7 Annandale Street, Edinburgh. Their mother was Jean Scott, and six children were living at home. Jane was the eldest, aged 15, Isabella was the fourth child, and the youngest, Walter Scott Paterson, was two years old.

In 1881 the sisters were living with their elder brother, Thomas, at 12 Arniston Street. He was a grocer. Thomas died in 1884 at the age of 64, and the sisters moved to No 14 in 1888. At the time of the 1891 census Jane was 64 and Isabella 56. They had one servant, Ellen Innes, 29, from Portobello. Isabella died in 1900, and in 1901 Jane was living there alone, but now with two servants, Ellen and a Janet Innes, also from Portobello, who was two years younger.

NO 15 DALRYMPLE CRESCENT

No 15 seems to have been a much bigger house than No 14 as there were 13 rooms recorded in 1871. This is probably due to the slope of the ground, which means that there was more headroom in the basement of No 15, allowing for proper rooms and not just storage. It was rented by Rev. John Pulsford from 1869 to 1879. David K. B. Whyte occupied it from 1882 to 1885, and Mrs William Steel was living there between 1887 and 1890. Walter Strang had the house from 1891 to 1894. The Mackillop family lived there from 1895 to 1901, and the villa was again available for rent in October 1901.

John Pulsford

John Pulsford was the minister of Albany Street Congregational Chapel. He was born in Turnlow, Devon in 1816. He was brother to William Pulsford, also a minister, who had been the minister at the same church until 1864. William's successor, Rev. John Cranbrook did not seem to get on with his congregation, and in 1867 John Pulsford became their minister. Meanwhile, in 1871 William Pulsford, whose biography is given in 'Glimpses of old Glasgow',[16] became head of the Congregational Union of Scotland.

John Pulsford's wife, Alice Hourst Pulsford was born in Pontefract, Yorkshire in 1824. The couple had three daughters and two sons, all born in Hull. At the time of the 1871 census Ellie Elizabeth was 22, Annie Jane 21 and Clair 16. Francis, the elder son was 19 and an engineer apprentice, Alfred John, aged 12 was at school. They had one servant, Emma Bateman who was also born in Hull.

Alice died in October 1873, aged 49, and later, in 1878, John Pulsford was one of the victims of the City of Glasgow Bank fraud.

The Bank was established in 1839 to cater particularly for small investors, with branches opening in the evenings to receive deposits (unusual at the time). During 1857 financial difficulties meant that the directors had to stop payment for a few days, during which time panic spread through Glasgow and military assistance had to be sought from Edinburgh. The bank closed on 11 November 1857, but business resumed on 31 December 1857. In June 1878 the directors reported that there were now 133 branches and that business was booming with deposits at £8,000,000 and that a dividend of 12 per cent would be paid.

However on 2 October that same year the directors decided to close the bank. An audit showed that the estimated balance of loss, including the bank's capital, was £6,200,000. They had lent far more than they had collected in deposits and had been a major lender to the Racine & Mississippi Railroad which failed, owing the bank over one million pounds. It emerged that the balance sheets had been falsified over a number of years.

The directors, including Robert Stronach and C. S. Leresche were arrested, but Leresche later became a witness for the prosecution. The remaining defendants were tried at the High Court in Edinburgh in January 1879 and all were found guilty. Robert Stronach and Lewis Potter, a director since 1858, were found guilty of fraud and each sentenced to 18 months imprisonment and the others to 8 months each.

In the trial papers, the directors are accused of 'the crime of falsehood, fraud, and wilful imposition and fabrication, falsification, and uttering bank balance sheets and theft and breach of trust and embezzlement at Head Office of the City of Glasgow Bank, Virginia Street, Glasgow'.

The victims included: Robert Craig, Craig Esk House, Newbattle, Edinburgh; Renton and Kerr, stockbroker, Edinburgh; Thomson and Porteous, tobacco manufacturers, Edinburgh; Robert Christie, grocer, Edinburgh; Honeyman and Wilson, wholesale grocers, Edinburgh; James Ritchie, High Street, Edinburgh; Thomas Brownlie, Gresham Cottage, Uddingston, Lanarkshire; Hamilton and Inches, jewellers, Edinburgh; Mossman and Watches, provision merchants, Edinburgh; and John Pulsford, reverend, Dalrymple Crescent, Edinburgh.[17]

The failure of the bank was widely reported. On the 28 January 1879 it was reported in the *Grey River Argus*, a paper published in New Zealand,[18] with almost a full column devoted to the event. It emphasised that many of the shareholders were ruined. John and William Pulsford are specifically mentioned. One of the Edinburgh directors was a deacon at John Pulsford's church, but the paper emphasises that the Edinburgh directors 'were not aware of the doings of the Glasgow Board'.

In the same year (1879) his eldest daughter, Ellie Elizabeth married John L. Mitchell, who came from Edinburgh and was two years older than her. He was a cabinet-maker and upholsterer, and in 1881 they were living in Mansfield Place.

Having left Dalrymple Crescent, in 1881 John Pulsford was living at 14 Eildon Road. In 1885 he was awarded an honorary Doctorate of Divinity by Edinburgh University. *The Scotsman* reported the introductory speech by Professor Taylor:

> Mr Pulsford's record of pastoral service and literary work is long and honourable. The first series of his 'Quiet Hours' (was) issued in 1858 ... (and has) gone through many editions.

He then identified other religious writing by Mr Pulsford. Advertisements for these books appeared regularly in *The Scotsman*. John Pulsford died in 1903.

David K. B. Whyte

David Keith Bullow Whyte was born in Edinburgh in August 1840. His parents, William Whyte and Janet Bullow, were married in 1835. They had least three other children: William who was born in 1844, Jessie who was born in 1836 and Emilia who was born in 1839. David's father had died by the time of the 1851 census, and Janet was listed as a spirit dealer. At this time the family was living in Dunbar Close, Edinburgh. Janet married Peter McLeod in May 1851.

By the time of the 1871 census, Peter had died, and the family was living at 38 Findhorn Place. David, who was described as the head, was married to Elizabeth McIntosh, who had been born in Edinburgh in April 1843. They had a baby son, William, born in 1870. David worked as a clerk for HM Lighthouses.

As well as David and his family, Janet, and her other children were living in the house. Jessie, Emelia and William were all unmarried. Jessie was 35 and Emelia was 32. William styled himself W. Ritchie Whyte, and gave his occupation as an accountant.

By 1881 they had left Findhorn Place, and were living in 6 St Andrews Terrace. Janet was now described as the head of household. Jessie Emelia and W. Ritchie were still living with her, and W. Ritchie now gave his occupation as a teacher of music. David and Elizabeth now had six children: Keith, born in 1881, Jessie E. in 1874, David K. B. (Jr) in 1875, James in 1877, Elizabeth in 1872 and William R. (Jr) in 1870.

According to the Post Office Directories, David Whyte and W. Ritchie Whyte were both living at No 15 between 1882 and 1885. In 1890 David Whyte was living at 5 Gladstone Place, Leith, and in 1899 he was at 28 Broughton Place, when he was working in New Register House. In 1899 W. Ritchie Whyte, teacher of music, was living at 54 Marchmont Road.

William Steel

William Steel was a merchant from Greenock, who moved to 15 Dalrymple Crescent, some time after 1885, and died there in April 1887. His widow, Elizabeth Russell, continued to live there until 1890, when she moved to 45 Newington Road. She was there at the time of the 1891 census, living with her two daughters and a son. Elizabeth Steel was born in Blairgowrie in 1850. Her daughters, Wilhemina Jessie Carruthers and Adeline Euphemia were both born in Greenock, and christened at the Union Street United Presbyterian Church there. Wilhemina was christened in May 1877, and Adeline in January 1879. There was also a son, Rubens, born in Perth, but we have no more details.

Walter Strang

Walter Strang was a teacher of music, born in Edinburgh in 1826. He married Jane Logan in 1853 and they had three sons: David born in 1856, Robert born in 1858 and James born in 1860. All three were educated at the Edinburgh Academy. Jane had two sisters: Ellen and Mary. Ellen remained unmarried, but Mary married a merchant named William Black. Both William and Jane had died before 1881, and David died in February of that year. At the time of the census in

April, the rest of the family were living at 83 Great King Street. Mary was the head of the family, and was 66 years old. Ellen was 59. Robert was a Divinity student and James was an insurance clerk.

Mary died in 1891, and between then and 1894 both Walter Strang and Miss Logan gave their address as 15 Dalrymple Crescent. In 1895 Walter gave his address as 6 Tipperlinn Road. He died in 1898, at the age of 72, in James's house at 30 Cluny Gardens.

Archibald Mackillop

Archibald Mackillop was a Supervisor of Inland Revenue, born in Fortingall, Perthshire in 1814. In 1881 he was living at 25 Shillinghill, Alloa. He was widowed, and living with his two daughters, Isabella aged 31 and Mary aged 26, and his granddaughter, Helen Ann Thomson aged 14, who was born in Alloa. Isabella was born in Lochgilphead, and Mary in Ireland. The family moved to Dalrymple Crescent before 1895, and in March 1896 Helen married Samuel Ford Aitchison of Eagle Pass Texas. *The Scotsman* describes her as being the daughter of 'the late John Thomson of Alloa'.

Archibald, now retired, died at No 15 on 28 March 1897. The sisters put a notice in *The Scotsman* on 10 April 1897:

> The Misses Mackillop return sincere thanks for the many kind expressions of sympathy received by them in their recent bereavement. – 15 Dalrymple Crescent.

In 1901 they were living in the house with one servant, Maggie McMeillan, 17, from Bridge of Allan.

NO 16 DALRYMPLE CRESCENT

The Inland Revenue survey of 1912 describes No 16 as a semi-detached villa with a polished ashlar front wall. There is a two-storey bow window, with moulded quoins and a heavily moulded wall-head course. There is a three-storey bow window to the back. On the ground floor the accommodation consisted of a sitting room with a marble mantelpiece, a pantry, dining room and nursery room. On the first floor there was a small bedroom over the hall, another bedroom, a bathroom and a drawing room with a white marble mantelpiece. Downstairs there was a small bedroom, the kitchen, with a small room off it, and various storerooms and cellars. Nos 16 to 19 (Plate 12c) are slightly grander than the other houses built by George Alexander, as they all have bay windows on both floors. Nos 14, 15 and 20 to 23 have 'flat' frontages.

From 1869 to 1874 the house was occupied by John Sibbald. James Sime was living there in 1875 and 1876, and the Misses Cleland had the house between 1877 and 1879. In 1879 Hugh Andrew Brown died there. From 1881 to 1887 it was rented to Mrs Oliver Russell. From 1888 to 1897 it was the home of Alicia Sutherland. Miss Margaret Crawford died there in 1899, and from 1900 onwards it was rented to Agnes Gibson.

John Sibbald

John Sibbald was a renowned physician and surgeon who was living at 16 Dalrymple Crescent in 1871. He was born in Edinburgh on 24 June 1833 to William Sibbald and Jane Graham. His father was a banker. John attended Merchiston School in Edinburgh. He studied medicine in Paris and Edinburgh, obtaining his MD in 1854. He specialised in 'lunacy', being the medical superintendent of the Argyll District Asylum from 1862 to 1870.

In the mid-19th century there was official recognition of the fact that the organisation and provision of care for the mentally ill in Scotland was inadequate. The Royal Commission on Lunacy was set up in 1855 to investigate matters, and the Parliamentary report was presented in 1857. This proposed a number of radical recommendations, most of which were written into the Lunacy (Scotland) Act of 1857. The Act established the General Board of Commissioners in Lunacy for Scotland, and John Sibbald became Deputy Commissioner in 1870 and Commissioner in 1879, a post he held until he retired in 1899.[19]

In 1864 he married Sarah Jane Phelan,[20] born in Clonmel, Ireland
in 1841. They had six children: Emeline Sarah born in December
1864, Mary in August 1868, William in October 1866, all born in
Lochgilphead, Argyll; and Harriet in 1878, Mildred in June 1873 and
Bernard Jan in September 1871, all born in Edinburgh.

At the time of the 1871 census they were living at No 16, and had
a visitor, Mary Anne Phelan, Sarah Jane's unmarried sister, born in
Clonmel in 1846. She is described as the daughter of a wine
merchant. In addition there were two servants.

They moved to 3 St Margaret's Road in 1877. In 1881 Emeline was
not at home, and John Sibbald's unmarried sister, Christian Sibbald,
born in 1845 was living with them. In addition, there were two
servants and a governess.

Sir John Sibbald became a Fellow of the Royal Society of
Edinburgh in 1872,[21] and was knighted in 1899. He was also a Fellow
of the Royal College of Surgeons, Edinburgh and a Fellow of the
Royal College of Physicians, Edinburgh. In 1876 he was President of
the latter, and was also President of the Royal Medical Society in 1855-
56. He died at 18 Great King Street, Edinburgh on 20 April 1905. His
portrait, Plate 13, hangs in the main hall of the Royal Society of
Physicians, Edinburgh.

Sarah Jane was the grand-daughter of Bernard Phelan, who was
the founder of the Bordeaux wine producer, Chateau Phélan-Ségur.
Her father, Bernard Paul Phelan was a wine merchant in Clonmel.[22]

James Sime

James Sime established a boarding school for boys at Craigmount,
Dick Place in 1865. The house was designed by the famous architect
Frederick T. Pilkington, who also designed the Barclay Church in
Bruntsfield, Edinburgh, as well as many other buildings in
Edinburgh and elsewhere.[23] James Sime was born in Perth in 1829.
His parents were David Sime and Magdalene Findlay. He obtained
his MA at Edinburgh University, and from 1855 to 1864 he was rector
of the Free Church Normal School in Edinburgh, where he also
taught Religious Knowledge.[24] In 1871 James Sime was living at

Craigmount with his unmarried sisters Magdalene and Jessie, who
were 37 and 32. Also at the school were three teachers, 42 boarders
and ten servants. James Sime rented No 16 in 1875 and 1876, and in
the Valuation Roles he is described as 'MA, Craigmount, Dick Place',
but it is not clear why he moved out of Craigmount, as he continued
to run the school there until 1900 when it became a girls' school, run
by the Misses Gossip.

The Misses Cleland

The Misses Cleland were the daughters of William Cleland and Janet
Walker. There were ten children from the marriage: John, born (or
christened) in May 1814, Janet in July 1816, Margaret Guthrie in
September 1818, Robert in June 1820, William in November 1822,
Helen in September 1826, Elizabeth in December 1826, Mary Ann
Haig, in July 1828, Jane Briggs in March 1830 and Jemima in June 1832.
They were all born in Edinburgh.

William died in 1836, and in 1861 Janet (senior) was living at 7
Malta Terrace with Mary Ann and Jemima. She died in September
1862, aged 71. In 1871 Janet (junior) was living with Margaret at 50A
Fredrick Street. and in 1873 'the Misses Cleland' were living at 66N,
Frederick Street.

From 1877 to 1879 they lived at No 16 Dalrymple Crescent, but
they had moved by the time of the 1881 census, when Janet and Mary
Anne (or Marianne) were living at 13 North Mansionhouse Road,
with two boarders: Elizabeth and Catherine Scott. Catherine was a
widow, aged 62, born in Bengal, India, and Elizabeth was unmarried,
and born in Edinburgh in 1860.

Hugh Andrew Brown

Hugh Andrew Brown was born in 1820. His parents were Thomas
Brown, a Captain in the 79th Highlanders, and Isabel Miller. He
married Paulina Millicent Collins in Bengal in August 1848. He
became Personal Assistant to the Director General of the Post Office
in India. By 1879 he was a widower and had retired to Dalrymple

Crescent. He died of apoplexy in August of that year, and his son, H. Crawford Brown, reported his death.

Mrs Oliver Russell

Mrs Oliver Russell was born Jane Ann Smith, in Montrose, in 1825. Her sister, Agnes Smith was born in Farnell, Forfarshire some twenty years earlier. Jane married Oliver Russell, and they had two daughters: Helen Mary, born in Auchtermuchty in 1846, and Jane Sophia, born in Colinton in 1853. Oliver Russell died in 1860 while they were living in Gilmore Place. By 1871 Agnes, who never married, was living with her widowed sister at 4 Castle Terrace. No 16 Dalrymple Crescent was registered to Mrs Russell's name from 1881 to 1887. By 1900 they had moved to 30 Mayfield Road, where Agnes died on 1 January, at the age of 95.

Alicia Sutherland

Alicia Sutherland was born Alicia Tomkins MacDonald in Dores, Inverness-shire in 1816. She married Rev. David Sutherland of the Free East Church, Inverness. He was born in Fearn, Ross-shire in 1819. They had five children: Alicia Margaret, born 30 October 1851, Henry Craigie, 28 October 1852, Lydia in 1853, Caroline in 1855 and Anne in 1860; all were born in Inverness.

In 1871 they were living at 12 Ness Bank, Inverness. The four daughters were at home, but Henry was in the Navy.

David died in 1875, and in 1881 Alicia was living as a lodger at 4 Hope Street. With her were Annie and Caroline, and her seven-year-old grandson Edward Strathearn Mather. He was the eldest son of Lydia who had married Myles Edward Mather in 1873.

Alicia Margaret married William Miller, and in 1891 Alicia senior was living in No 16 with Annie and four of the Miller children. They were Hugh, aged 16, Alicia Harriet ('AH'), aged 12, Margaret, aged ten, and Beatrice, aged eight. All the children had been born in India. There was also a servant, Anne Gordon, aged 23, from West Calder. In October of that year *The Scotsman* reported that Miss Sutherland

(Annie) was a stallholder at a bazaar to raise funds for the Piershill Soldiers' Home.

William Miller was a Lieutenant Colonel of the 17th Regiment Madras Native Infantry, and he died at No 16 in December 1893. In January the following year Hugh was elected to a Queen's Honorary India Cadetship after his examination at Sandhurst.

The family subsequently moved to 7 Sciennes Road and Alicia died there in December 1900, at the age of 84.

Margaret Crawford

Margaret Crawford was the daughter of James Crawford, banker, of Cumnock and his wife Mary Wyllie. James was born in 1785 and Mary in 1786. They had at least eight children: James, born in November 1811, Hugh in April 1813, Janet in February 1815, Robert in June 1817, Jessie in 1822, Marion in April 1823 and Margaret in 1829.

There were also two sons called David, the first born in 1819 and the second in 1825. Naming a child after one who had died seems to have been a common practice.

In 1841 the family's address was Old Cumnock Village, Ayrshire. Robert, Janet, Margaret and Marion were living at home. In 1851 the address was The Square, Old Cumnock, and Margaret and Jessie were at home.

Mary died in Cumnock in 1873, and is described as the widow of James Crawford, banker.

Margaret never married, and in August 1899 *The Scotsman* reported her death at 16 Dalrymple Crescent. She is described as the daughter of the late James Crawford, banker, Cumnock. She was about 70 years old.

Agnes Gibson

Agnes Gibson moved into No 16 in 1900, and in the 1901 census she is described as a widow from Ettrick, Selkirkshire, aged 74. Living with her were her unmarried daughter, Christina, aged 31, and son Sharpe, aged 33, who was working as an insurance clerk. Both were born in Ettrick. They had one servant, Jane Robb, 49, from Auchinreath in Morayshire.

NO 17 DALRYMPLE CRESCENT

No 17 was built slightly later than some of George Alexander's houses. Margaret Rosie moved here from No 20 in 1872, and lived in it until 1874 when Archibald MacCalman was the tenant. He lived in the house until 1876. W. B. McLachlan rented it in 1877, and Rev. G. Fisher occupied it in 1878. From 1879 to 1886 it was the home of Margaret Lamb, and Leslie O. Paterson was the tenant from 1888 to 1893. John Bruce lived there in 1894, and George Stevenson and his family occupied it in 1895, and were still living there in 1901.

Margaret Rosie

Margaret Rosie ran a boarding school, first at No 20 and then at No 17. Her story is told in Chapter 6.

Archibald MacCalman

Archibald MacCalman was born in Muckairn, Argyllshire in October 1829. His father was Alexander MacCalman and his mother was Flora MacCallum. He married Jane MacDonald who was born in 1832, in Edinburgh, and they had at least eight children: Mary, born in 1858, Jane in 1860, Isabella in 1862, Alexander in 1866, Archibald in 1869, Annie in 1870, Elizabeth in 1872 and Hugh in 1873.

Archibald was a merchant, and the family lived in Tarbert, Argyllshire, where all the children were born. They moved to Edinburgh after 1871, and lived at No 17 from 1874 to 1876. By 1881 Archibald had died, and Jane and the children were living at 7 Gilmore Place. Mary and Isabella were governesses, and young Jane was described as an 'Artist, China Painter'. The younger children were still at school. Jane died in May 1882, at the age of about 50, when she was living at 6 Hailes Street, Edinburgh.

W. B. McLachlan

William Bremner McLachlan was a fish salesman, born in Edinburgh in 1830. His father was Robert MacLauchlan and his mother was Margaret McFarlane. (William appears to have dropped the 'u' in his name at some point). In September 1849 he married Margaret Harvey, also from Edinburgh, born around 1822.

In 1876 he was living at No 4 St Catherine's Place. He moved to Dalrymple Crescent in 1877 and on 5 December of that year his younger daughter, Margaret, married Patrick Laing from Kinross. *The Scotsman* announcement stated that the wedding took place at the house, officiated by Rev. Thomas Cochrane.

He did not stay long in the Crescent, and the 1881 census shows him living in Hastings, with his wife and daughter Margaret, and younger son, John. In addition he had a visitor, Robert Galacher from Greenock, who was also a fish salesman. Meanwhile Patrick, who was a provision merchant, was living with Margaret senior's brother, William Harvey, at No 7 Forth Street, Edinburgh. William was a fruit merchant, and was married with a son, and three unmarried daughters living at home. In addition, his married daughter, her husband and her son were living with them. In total there were ten people in the house, plus one servant.

William McLachlan moved back to Edinburgh and by 1882 he was living at Caruanan Villa, 57 Fountainhall Road. The house was designed for him by the architect John McLachlan, who does not seem to be a relation. In 1884, he moved into a new villa at 55 Fountainhall Road, also designed by John McLachlan.[25]

William's wife Margaret died in 1887, and by the time of the 1891 census he had married again. His new wife, Jane, came from Wales, and was some 20 years younger than him. A son was born in March 1891, and at the time of the census William's daughter, Margaret, was back in the family home. In the census she gave her name as Margaret McLachlan, and her status as unmarried. There was also a visitor, Elizabeth Edwards, who had been born in Edinburgh. She was unmarried, and the same age as Margaret. The address given in the census record was 60 Fountainhall Road.

William died in September 1897, by which time he was living in Portobello. The record of his will describes him as 'sometime merchant, Caruanan Villa, Fountainhall Road, Edinburgh, latterly at 24 Melville Street, Portobello'.

Rev. G. Fisher

The Edinburgh and Leith Post Office directories record a Rev. G. Fisher living in No 17 in 1878. However he also seems to have stayed at No 22, with Miss Eleanor Fowden, so his story is told with hers in Chapter 5.

Margaret Grieve Lamb

Margaret Grieve Lamb was a widow who was born in Yarrow, Selkirkshire in 1826, and was supported by the 'rent of lands'. Her maiden name was Ballantyne, her father's name was Robert, and her mother's was Catherine (maiden surname also Ballantyne). In 1841, aged 14, she was living on the family farm, named Tinnis. The farmer was her 21-year-old brother, David Ballantyne, and there were three other sisters and a governess. Ten years later, she was still at the farm, with her elder sister, Jessie, an aunt and a niece.

In 1859 she married John Lamb, a coffee planter who was living in Selkirk at that time. They had three children, Annie, Charles and Jessie, all of whom were born in Ceylon.

By 1881 John had died and Margaret and the children had returned to Scotland. They lived at No 17 from 1881 to 1886. At the time of the 1881 census Annie was 21, Jessie was 16, and Charles, who was 19, was a banker's clerk. They had one servant, Flora Mathieson, 26, from Lochaber.

Leslie O. Paterson

Leslie Ogilvie Paterson was a retired army surgeon, who lived at No 17 from 1888 to 1893. With him was his wife, Annie. Leslie was born in Edinburgh, to James Patterson and Mary Ogilvie. Annie came from Kent. At the time of the 1891 census Leslie was 60, and his wife ten years younger. They had two servants: Margaret Withers, 40, from Loanhead, was the cook, and Elizabeth Douglas, 33, from Dumfries was the parlour maid.

John Bruce

John Bruce lived in No 17 for a short period in 1894. This is probably the same John Bruce who was living at 10 Ventnor Terrace in 1891. He was a supervisor for the Inland Revenue, born in Kirkmichael, Perthshire in December 1836. His father, Robert Bruce was a farmer. He married Isabella Campbell in March 1872. He lived until May 1917, when he died in Pitlochry, aged 80.

George Stevenson

George Stevenson was a wholesale woollen merchant from Cullen in Banffshire, born in 1842. His parents were James and Margaret Stevenson. In 1891 he was living with his family at 3 Carlung Place. In 1901 they were living at No 17. Elizabeth, his wife, was born in Glasgow in 1857. They had five children and one servant, Christina Beattie, aged 23, from Dechmont in West Lothian. The children were: George who was aged 18, Elizabeth J. aged 15, Agnes aged 13, Mary aged 12 and James aged ten. All were born in Edinburgh, and George junior was a draper's apprentice.

NO 18 DALRYMPLE CRESCENT

No 18 is one of four semi-detached villas built slightly later than the rest, and with more architectural detail. It was not occupied at the time of the 1871 census, but Mrs Webster lived there later in the year, and Miss Webster was living there from 1872 to 1874. It was then rented by William Lawson from 1875 to 1881. Charlotte Dalziel lived there from 1882 to 1884. There was a change of tenancy in February 1885, when the 'household furniture and other effects' were auctioned at Dowell's auction house. The list advertised in *The Scotsman* is detailed:

> large mantelpiece mirror in gilt frame, rosewood chiffonniere with mirror back and fret panel doors, couch, three easy chairs and eight small chairs in damask; mahogany telescope dining table, couch, easy and twelve chairs in haircloth; mahogany and birch Elizabethan bedsteads with curtains and bedding, French and iron beds and bedding, mahogany and pine wardrobes, chest of drawers, washstands and ware, toilets and mirrors, arm-chair commodes; mahogany hat and umbrella stand, table and chairs; painted presses, carpet, rugs, waxcloth, window curtains, dinner service, crystal, outside meat larder, kitchen utensils – etcetera.

George Brook was resident in 1888. C. J. Shiells lived there in 1890 and 1891, and James H. Black in 1892 and 1893. Finally Alexander Mustard lived in the house from 1894 to 1901.

Jean Webster

Jean Webster was born Jean Don in Brechin, Angus in March 1798. On 12 February 1819 she married Joseph Webster, also from Brechin, and they had nine children, all born in Brechin: Joseph, born in October 1819, Thomas in November 1821, David in February 1824, George in March 1826, John in July 1828, Jane in September 1830, Ann in February 1833, William in February 1835 and Alexander in August 1837.

In 1841 they were living in Brechin High Street with seven of their children. Joseph senior was a mason journeyman, and Joseph junior was a teacher. George was a draper's apprentice. Thomas and David had left home.

The family may have emigrated to Australia, but by 1871 Jean was back in Edinburgh, with her daughter, Ann. They had moved into No 18 Dalrymple Crescent by May 1872, but Jean died in June, and

Ann continued to live there until 1875. In December 1873, her sister-in-law gave birth to a baby boy. The announcement in *The Scotsman* described her as the 'wife of Alexander Webster (of Melbourne)'. Her maiden name was Jane Margaret Brown, and the son was also called Alexander.

William Ramage Lawson

William Ramage Lawson was editor of the *Edinburgh Courant* from 1876–86.[26] He was the son of James Lawson, a draper, from Kirriemuir, and Margaret Webster. He was born in December 1840, and had six sisters: Emily, Jane, Elizabeth, Anne (Wilson), Mary and a Mary who died as an infant, and six brothers: George Webster, John Yeaman, David Wilkie, Alexander Webster, Robert and James, all born in Kirriemuir.

He married Ida Dora Eisenhuth in May 1864 in Kirriemuir. Ida was born in Germany in 1840. They sailed to Australia in September of that year, where Lawson became the editor of the *South Australian Register*.

They had five children: James Eisenhuth, born 18 July 1865 in Bowden, South Australia; Emil Alexander Webster, born 28 May 1867 in Digger, Adelaide, South Australia; Caroline, born 7 February 1869 in Digger, Adelaide, South Australia; William Eisenhuth, born 19 September 1871 in London, and Herbert Julius Eisenhuth born in 1879 in Edinburgh.

In the 1881 census they also had a visitor, Lerise Netz, from Germany. She was 26 and her occupation was ladies' help. They had two servants: a cook, Christine Kippen, 20, from Edinburgh, and a housemaid, Christine Miller, 17, from Wishaw. The family moved to Fountainhall Road in 1882.

The *Edinburgh Courant* was a broadsheet newspaper first published in February 1705. One of its earlier editors was Daniel Defoe, author of *Robinson Crusoe*. In 1879 (when Lawson was editor) it reported the Tay Bridge disaster. The paper seems to have ceased publishing in its existing form in 1886, and Lawson appears to have left Edinburgh about that time.

The family moved to London,where Lawson was instrumental in the founding of the *Financial Times*, and was its editor for some time. Ida died in May 1899, and William re-married, in Innerkip, Toronto.[27] His new wife was Eva Green, born in England, in 1861. They lived in, or had a home in, Glanymor, St David's, Pembrokeshire. Lawson died in 1922, and is buried in Worthing, Sussex.

Charlotte Dalziel

Charlotte Dalziel was born Charlotte Pearson, in Edinburgh in 1807. She married George Dalziel, a Writer to the Signet, in Edinburgh in October 1827. They had eight children, all born in Edinburgh: Charlotte, born in September 1828, Agnes in March 1830, Georgina in January 1832, Anne in August 1834, John in January 1837, Mary in July 1840, Eliza in May 1842 and George in January 1843.

At the time of the 1841 census they were living in Regent Terrace, and two of the eight children, young Charlotte and Georgina, were at home, although Charlotte herself was not. George died in 1869, when they were still living at 10 Regent Terrace. Two of the children, John and George followed their father into the law firm of Gibson-Craig, Dalziel & Brodie. In 1881 Charlotte, now aged 74, was living at 10 Lennox Street with her daughter Charlotte, who was unmarried and aged about 50. They moved into Dalrymple Crescent in the same year and Charlotte senior died in December 1884.

Mrs Margaret Anderson

The Valuation Rolls show a Mrs Margaret Anderson as the tenant at No 18 in 1885, but we know nothing more about her.

George Brook

George Brook was born in Huddersfield in March 1857. After his schooling he went into his father's business, but developed a keen interest in marine zoology. In 1879, he became a Fellow of the Linnean Society of London, a learned society whose remit is 'The cultivation of the Science of Natural History in all its branches'. He decided to make a career in the biological sciences, and in 1884 he was appointed lecturer in Comparative Embryology at the University of Edinburgh.

From 1884 to 1887 he held the post of scientific assistant to the Scottish Fishery Board, but the experience was not a happy one. He did not get on with the director, Professor Cossar Ewart, and was frustrated by the lack of communication with headquarters. He felt that money had been wasted, and that the work done had 'comparative little value'. He resigned in 1887 because he felt his position was 'an anomalous one', being nominally in charge of the scientific investigations, but in practice having no real control. He received written instructions to make certain investigations on the West Coast of Scotland, but at the same time 'received verbal instructions from Professor Ewart that no money could be spared'. He only managed to carry out his work because he was able to borrow his father's yacht.

The dispute spilled into the letter columns of *The Scotsman*, with Professor Ewart, and a former member of the Board, a Mr Grieve, exchanging insults. Professor Ewart claimed that Mr Grieve 'has remarkably strong prejudices against science' and that his 'views as to science are worthy of the Dark Ages'. Mr Grieve, in turn, claims that Professor Ewart was jealous of Mr Brook's appointment, and that he had deliberately sabotaged Mr Brook's position.

George Brook's personal life took a happier turn. In January 1888 he married Fanny Elizabeth Scott, the daughter of a contractor from Newcastle-on-Tyne. In November 1888 their daughter, Dorothy Cecil Brook was born at No 18 Dalrymple Crescent.

A further glimpse of the life of a junior academic can be gathered from *The Scotsman* archives. In 1889 George Brook is cited as an example of a lecturer working within the Faculty of Medicine at that time. It seems that a habit had grown up of having an 'extra-mural school' which gave lectures in competition to the Faculty, but which students were permitted to attend. One group argued that this was detrimental to the work of the Faculty, while the opposite view was that it acted as a type of training ground for future Professors. It mentioned a number of prominent men who were physicians and surgeons, original investigators, and were 'ornaments of the extra-mural school'. It goes on:

> Then take, on the other hand, the case of Mr George Brook.
> He is an inter-mural lecturer … His researches … have been
> of the highest value but he is so heavily handicapped by
> professorial competition that he has never been able to form
> a class. If any persons have the right to complain of lack of
> opportunity for original work, they are the assistants to the
> professors, who are so busily occupied in relieving their
> superiors that they have no time even for private study.

However George Brook survived these problems, and in 1889 he wrote a report on the Black Corals of the Challenger Expedition,* and this subsequently led to his engagement in 1890 to catalogue the collection of Stony Corals at the British Museum. He was also a Vice-President of the Royal Physical Society of Edinburgh, a Fellow of the Royal Society of Edinburgh and of the Zoological Society.

Unfortunately, his promising career was cut short by his sudden death in 1893. Edinburgh University's annual report refers to his 'lamented death in August last', saying that it had 'bereft the University of a very zealous and eminent man of science'.

The Linnean Society, in its obituary, throws further light on his death.

> He died suddenly on August 12th, 1893, from the effects of
> heat-apoplexy whilst out with a shooting-party on the
> moors near Newcastle-on-Tyne.

It concludes that

> His untimely death, at the early age of 36, robs British science
> of a promising naturalist, whose self-taught knowledge, clear

---

* The *Challenger* Expedition of 1872–76 was a scientific expedition that made many discoveries which laid the foundations of oceanography.

judgment, and bold independence, enlisted the admiration, as well as the affection of a large circle of friends.[28]

C. J. Shiells

Courtenay John Shiells was born in Edinburgh in December 1857. His father, John Lyall Shiells was a draper, and his mother was Mary Ann Kenward 'daughter of Henry Kenward'. John Lyall died in 1862, at which time the family was living at 16 St Vincent Street. Courtenay Shiells became a Chartered Accountant with an office in 16 South Charlotte Street. He was living in 18 Dalrymple Crescent in 1891, but there were only two servants staying at the house on census night. They were the cook, Margaret Ferguson, 25, from Borgue in Kirkcudbrightshire, and the housemaid, Margaret Little, 21, from Morebattle in Roxburghshire. By 1895 he had moved to 39 Queens Crescent. He had also moved offices, being the joint owners of 141 George Street, with his elder brother Henry Kenward Shiells. C. J. Shiells lived in Queens Crescent until 1900 or 1901, and then moved into 'Braidfoot' in Grange Road, but again he was not at home on census night.

James Henry Black

James Black was an assistant surveyor for the Post Office. He was born in Ireland in 1841. In 1891 he was living at 40 St Albans Road with his wife, Annie, who came from England. She was nine years younger than him. They had four children. The elder two, Louise and Lily were born in Ireland in 1873 and 1875. The younger two, Arthur and Gertrude were born in Edinburgh in 1878 and 1881. At the time of the 1891 census, James' sister, also Annie, was staying with them. She was unmarried, and born in 1848, also in Ireland. James Black rented No 18 in 1892 and 1893.

Alexander Mustard

Alexander Mustard was a Solicitor of the Supreme Court (SSC), with an office at 15 South Charlotte Street. He was born in Alves, Morayshire in September 1857 to James Mustard and Margaret Reid. He had four daughters, and on 23 January 1889 his wife, Annabella Low, died giving birth to their son, Alexander Low Mustard. He moved to No 18 in 1894 and was still living at there on census night 1901. He was still a widower, and was now living with his unmarried sister, Isabella, aged 36 and also from Alves, and Alexander, now aged 12. They had one servant, Ellen Marshall, 24, from Dalkeith.[29]

CHAPTER 5

The Southwest

~

This chapter continues the story of the houses on the south side of Dalrymple Crescent. Nos 19 to 23 were rented out by George Alexander. No 27 was the first of the detached houses to be built. It was first numbered 30, obviously in anticipation of more semi-detached villas being built. In the event the remaining three plots were taken up by substantial detached villas. No 26 was the first of these three, then No 25, and the building of the Crescent was not completed until 1886, when No 24 was finished.

NO 19 DALRYMPLE CRESCENT

We only have a description of the accommodation of No 19 from the Inland Revenue records of 1912. On the ground floor there was a drawing room, a dining room, one bedroom, a small press with a wash-hand basin, and another press in the hall. There was a small room used as a kitchen. In the basement there was another kitchen with a servant's room off it, a coal store and a washhouse. On the first floor there was a drawing room, a bedroom and a bathroom.

John Dick rented the house from 1872 to 1885, and during that time, in 1875, Charlotte Algeo died at the house. Archibald Oliver was the tenant from 1886 to 1894, and John G. Johnstone rented the house in 1897 and was still living there in 1901.

John Dick

John Dick was a medical doctor who was born in Whitburn, West Lothian in April 1813. His parents were George Dick and Jane Glasgow. He married twice: his first wife, Charlotte Calder died in July 1859 at Mid Calder, and he married his second wife, Bethia Hamilton Sommers in November of the same year.

He moved into No 19 in 1872, and we can presume that he was still practicing in 1875, when Charlotte Algeo died in his house. Michael Fry in his *History of Edinburgh* suggests that there is evidence that the medical facilities of Edinburgh encouraged people to move to the city, and that doctors would be able to supply 'lodgings for invalids with means to pay for private care'.[1] This could well have been the situation with Mrs Algeo.

By 1881 he had retired and the census shows him living with Bethia at No 19. They had no servants. Bethia was born in Mid Calder, Midlothian in February 1814. *The Scotsman* announced John Dick's death in January 1885 in a brief notice, describing him as 'late of Mid-Calder'. Bethia died in November 1887, when she was living at 35 Bruntsfield Place.

Charlotte Algeo

In November 1875, *The Scotsman* reported the death of Charlotte, 'widow of the late Captain Algeo', at No 19. According to the record of her will, her residence was 2 Morningside Place, and she had previously lived at 96 Charlotte Street, Fitzroy Square, London. They married in August 1843, and her maiden name was Wauch. Two years earlier in 1841 she had been living at 2 Athol Place with her mother (aged about 80), a woman of 25 named Anne Eleanor Alger (Algeo?) and a child of 3½ named Charlotte Newcomen. Captain Robert Newcomen Algeo had been a major in the Army. Charlotte's father, Robert Wauch, had been a captain in the army, and her mother had also been named Charlotte. Her death certificate said that 'Mrs Algeo had no particular disease, but died of natural decay at the age of 86'. The death was reported by her niece, also a Charlotte Algeo, who lived at 5 Upper Bayswater Street, London.

Archibald Oliver

Archibald Oliver was born in Cavers, Roxburgh in 1848 to James Oliver and Mary Hall. In 1881 he was a Law Clerk (Managing), living with his wife Marjory Norris Logan at 9 Warrender Park Terrace. They had two young sons James, three, and Jasper, eight months. By 1891 he had qualified as an SSC and was working with the firm of Davidson & Syme WS, whose premises were at 22 Castle Street.

In the 1891 census, Archibald was not at home, but they now had two more sons: Archibald aged nine and William aged five. All the family came from Edinburgh; Archibald was born in 1840, and Marjory in 1850. They had a cook, Sarah Allan, 19, from Edinburgh and a housemaid, Rachel Newton, also 19, from Manchester. Rachel may have joined the household in October 1890, when an advertisement was put in *The Scotsman* for a 'nurse-housemaid'.

Sarah may have left in March 1894 when an advertisement for a 'Cook (good plain)' appeared.

In June, Margaret Fraser, who was working as a domestic servant for the Oliver family, was married to Peter Riach, a mason, at No 19. The service was conducted by Rev. J. Bell Nichol and witnessed by Archibald Oliver. An announcement in *The Scotsman* described Margaret as the 'youngest daughter of John Fraser, Keith, Banffshire'.

In 1894 the family moved to 46 Lauder Road, where Archibald died in September 1901.

John G. Johnston

John George Johnston was a Chartered Accountant, born in Canada in 1862. In 1895 he was living at 48 India Street and had a practice at 1 George Street. By 1897, when he was living at No 19, his practice was at 46 Hanover Street. He was unmarried, and in 1901 was living with his mother, Margaret, a widow aged 71, who was born in London. They had one servant, Jessie Monteith, aged 38, who was born in Edinburgh.

NO 20 DALRYMPLE CRESCENT

The house was rented to Margaret Rosie from 1868 to 1871. Then Colonel W. Walker became the tenant from 1872 to 1874. Mrs Williamson lived there in 1876, and Thomas Ogilvy Cownie rented it in 1877 and 1878. Rev. Thomas Dymock lived there from 1881 until his death in 1888, and his widow continued to live in the house until she died in 1897. Her son, Thomas Dymock junior was living there in 1898, and in 1901 it was occupied by William F. Robertson.

Margaret Rosie

Margaret Rosie ran a boarding school at No 20 before moving to No 17. Her story is told in Chapter 6.

Col. William Walker

William Walker was a Colonel in the 1st Regiment of Grenadiers in the Bombay Native Infantry. He was born in August 1825 in Kinglassie, Fife to James Walker and Catherine Stark. He was married twice. His first wife, Margaret Hardy, bore him two children: Maud in 1861, and Helen Bell in November 1862; both born in Bhooj, Maharashtra, India.

Margaret died before 1866, when he married Eliza Murray Dalziel, whose mother later rented No 18. Eliza was born in Edinburgh in May 1842. They were married in Edinburgh and returned to India, where two more children were born: Hugh Dalziel in 1868, and Pearson in 1869, both born in Belgauns.

By 1871 they had returned to Scotland, and were living in Forfarshire at the time of the census. Another son, William, was born that year, and they then returned to India where two more children were born: Agnes in 1873 and Charlotte in 1874, both born in Poona.

However they rented the house at No 20 between 1872 and 1874 through Eliza's brother, John, who was a solicitor. We can only presume that some of the children were at school in Edinburgh.

By 1881 they were all back in Scotland, living in Arthurseat

House, Old Machar, Aberdeen. William died in February 1889, aged 74. At that time he was living at 42 Albany Street. His will describes him as 'Major-General, retired, Bombay Army, formerly Col., 1st Regiment of Grenadiers, Bombay Native Infantry, sometime residing at Ruthrieston House, Ruthrieston, Aberdeen, thereafter at 42 Albany Street, Edinburgh'.

Mary Williamson

Mary Williamson was born in Anstruther in August 1788. Her father was James Rodger and her mother was Mary Bertram. She married Captain Charles Robb, RN in 1811, and their daughter, Ann, was born in Leith in 1813. Captain Robb died soon after, and Mary married Stephen Williamson in 1820.

In 1841 the family was living in Castle Street, Anstruther. Stephen is described as a Navy Surgeon. They had three children: James, born around 1823, an apprentice surgeon, Mary, born around 1826, and Thomas, born around 1823. Ann Robb, now about 28, was also living with them.

By 1868 Stephen had retired, and they were living at Gladstone Terrace, Burntisland when he died in July of that year. Mary was staying at No 20 when she died in August 1876.

Thomas Ogilvy Cownie

Thomas Ogilvy Cownie was a member of the Cownie family, whose story is told in Chapter 6.

Rev. Thomas Dymock

In April 1881, a Free Church minister, Thomas Dymock was living at No 20, with his wife and family. He was 76, and had been born in Kelso in October 1804. He attended Glasgow Grammar School, where his father was rector, and was ordained in Arbroath in 1834. At the Disruption he joined the Free Church, and served as senior minister at the Free Middle Church in Perth from 1846 to 1881, when he retired through ill health. His wife, Ruth (née Bentley), aged 64, came from Aberdeen. They had three sons and two daughters. Three of their children were living with them in 1881: Mary (or Margaret) was 34, Thomas 32 and Ruth 27. They were all born in Perth, and all unmarried at that time. The eldest son, John, and the second son were both ministers, and the youngest, Thomas junior, was a chartered accountant. They had one servant. Elizabeth Clicterdale, 22, also from Perth.

Thomas died in February 1888, when *The Scotsman* published his obituary. The heading was 'Death of a pre-Disruption Minister'. The article stated that he was buried at Wellshill cemetery in Perth. For over forty years he was 'ever striving to do good and faithfully fulfilling the injunctions of his high calling'. He had a kind nature and 'an open heart' and was 'trusted and revered wherever he went'.

His widow, Ruth, continued to live in the house and was still there at the time of the 1891 census. Mary and Ruth junior were still living at home, but Thomas junior was not in the house. They also had a retired servant, Elspeth Grant, who was 86 and came from Grantown in Morayshire. There was also a cook, Margaret McGregor, 26, from Thornton in Fife, and a housemaid, Ellen Lamb, 18, from Pentcaitland.

Ruth died in 1897, and in 1898, Thomas gave his work address as 8 Castle Street, and his home address as 20 Dalrymple Crescent. However, he had moved by the time of the 1901 census.

William Ford Robertson

William Robertson was a registered medical practitioner and pathologist to the Association of Scottish Asylums. He was born in Sprouston, Roxburghshire in 1868. His wife, Marion, was five years younger and came from Preston in Lancashire. In 1899 they were living in Charterhall Road, but had moved to Dalrymple Crescent by the time of the 1901 census. At this time they had twin sons one year old, Alexander and William, and another son called Francis who had been born at home on 19 March 1901. Living with them was a 'private sick nurse (own account)', Mary McFarlane, a widow aged 40 from

Heriot in Midlothian. There was also a domestic nurse, Agnes Blyth, 20, from Edinburgh and a servant, Georgina Anderson, 25, from Aberdeen.

NO 21 DALRYMPLE CRESCENT

The house was first occupied by John Simpson, from 1868 to 1873. Mrs Mary Amelia Downie and her daughter Mrs Jean Campbell Firmstone were both living there in 1875. The Misses Plummer were living there some time in 1876, and James Gibb Cownie rented it from 1877 to 1878. The house was advertised to let in *The Scotsman* in May 1878. It was described as having seven rooms, bathroom, kitchen, servants' room, and garden. Grates, gas-fittings and window blinds were included. On 31 May the advertisement stated that the rent had been reduced to £75.

In 1879 the tenant was Alexander Kemp, and then it was rented by David Crouch from 1881 to 1891. Mrs Louisa Nicoll lived there in 1895 and 1896, and Robert Pennefather was the tenant from 1897 to 1900. Subsequently Frank J. Pearson was renting the house in 1901.

John Simpson

John Simpson was born in Bathgate in February 1837. He was the nephew of Professor James Young Simpson, the renowned physician who first used chloroform as an anaesthetic. James Young Simpson was also born in Bathgate, the youngest of the eight children of David Simpson, the village baker. James showed his great ability at the village school, and his father and brothers together paid for him to go to University. John Simpson's father, Alexander, was the third son of David Simpson, being some fourteen years older than James (who adopted the middle name 'Young' later in life).[2]

In 1841 John's family was living in Main Street, Bathgate, and Alexander was also a baker. John became a chemist and druggist and worked for Duncan Flockhart and Co., the firm who supplied the chloroform for the experiments James Young Simpson carried out in 1847.

John Simpson was one of the witnesses for the prosecution at the trial of Dr Edward Pritchard, who was hanged in 1865 for poisoning his wife and her mother. The mother, Mrs Jane Taylor lived at 1 Lauder Road.[3]

Dr and Mrs Pritchard lived in Glasgow, but in October 1864 Mrs Pritchard was ill, and went through to Edinburgh to recuperate, staying with her parents at 1 Lauder Road. She recovered, and went back to Glasgow for Christmas, but was ill again, so Mrs Taylor went through to look after her. Mrs Taylor also became ill, and died in February 1865. Mary Pritchard herself died about three weeks later. Dr Pritchard himself signed both death certificates, and mother and daughter were buried in Grange Cemetery. However, the Procurator Fiscal received an anonymous letter, and on the basis of this, Dr Pritchard was arrested, and the bodies of both women were exhumed. They were shown to contain antimony, a poison with effects similar to arsenic.

At the trial, John Simpson described how his company often sold Battley's Sedative Solution to Dr Pritchard, and confirmed that there was no antimony in the medicine. In the description of the trial, John Simpson is described as a partner in the firm of Duncan Flockhart and Co.

In August 1866 he married Christina Petrie, who was five years younger than him, and came from the Isle of Man. In October 1868, *The Scotsman* announced the birth of his son, Peter, who was two years old at the time of the 1871 census. As well as Peter, they had an older son, Alexander, aged three, and a younger daughter, Elizabeth who was seven months old at the time of the census. All the children were born in Edinburgh. They had a general servant, Isabelle Murray, 24 and a nursemaid, Jane Sutherland, 22, both from Olrig in Caithness.

The family moved to No 29 Lauder Road, where John died in 1876, at the age of 39. His widow continued to live there, and in the 1891 census, aged 50, she was living with her three children. Alexander, now 23, was a law student, and Peter was a medical student.

Mary Amelia Downie

Mary Amelia Downie was born Mary Emilia Lockhart in Cambusnethan, Lanarkshire in 1805, and was christened on 25 August of that year. Her father, Robert Lockhart, was a minister, and her mother was born Elizabeth Ann Newman. In April 1834 she married Alexander Downie, a merchant who was 12 years older than her. In 1841 they were living at Crossbasket in East Kilbride, with five children. The eldest, Sara, who was aged 14, must have been a daughter of a previous marriage. The other children were Eliza Anne aged six, John aged four, Alexander aged three and Jane Campbell aged five months.

Jane (or Jean) Campbell married Joseph Firmstone in Kensington in 1868, when she was 27 and he was 52. They had one son, Joseph A. L. Firmstone, born the following year, but Joseph senior died in February of that year at Abberley House, Worcester Park, Surrey.

In 1875 Mary and Jean were living at No 21, but Mary died there in October. In her will she is described as the widow of Alexander Downie, a merchant from Glasgow.

Jean died on 2 January 1876. *The Scotsman* announcement of her death described her as the daughter of the late Alexander Downie of Glasgow. She had lived at 9 Grange Road, prior to living in Dalrymple Crescent, and in February 1876 her executors placed an advertisement in *The Scotsman* looking for anyone who had a claim against her estate.

In 1881 her son, Joseph A. L. Firmstone, aged 11 was living with Mary's sister Louisa in Hamilton, Lanarkshire. Louisa was 23 years younger that Mary, and in 1881 she was the widow of Lieutenant Colonel McGrigor.

The Misses Plummer

The Misses Plummer were two sisters, Margaret and Sarah, who came from Dalkeith. Margaret was born in June 1817 and Sarah in April 1825. Their father, William Plummer, was a master flesher, and their mother was Sarah King. In 1841 the family was living in New Road, Dalkeith. Their mother had died, so the family consisted of

William, the two sisters, and their brother, George. In the census he is described as a farmer of 61 acres, who employed three labourers.

William died in 1870, and in 1876 the sisters were staying No 21. From there they moved to 32 Queens Crescent, where they were living at the time of the 1881 census. Margaret Plummer died at the same address in November 1889, when she was 72.

James Gibb Cownie

James Cownie was a member of the Cownie family, whose story is told in Chapter 6.

Alexander Kemp

Alexander Kemp was a builder, born in Crieff in 1830. His wife was Margaret McGregor, but by 1871 he was widowed, and living at 8 Montague Street with his two daughters, Jane and Elizabeth, aged eight and six. Both were born in Edinburgh. They moved into Dalrymple Crescent sometime between 1878 and 1879, but in October of that year, Alexander died, aged 49. In 1881 the two girls, now aged 18 and 16, were living at 10 Gilmore Road with their unmarried aunt, Jane McGregor, born in Auchterarder, Perthshire in 1837.

Alexander Kemp was mentioned in *The Scotsman* in December 1870, when a tenement in the High Street collapsed, and he was the builder contracted to demolish it.

David Crouch

David Crouch was a member of the Crouch family, whose story is told in Chapter 6.

Louisa Nicholls

Louisa Nicholls lived at No 21 in 1895 and 1896. She was born Louisa Heron Brien in Glasserton, Wigtownshire on 27 February 1840. Her baptism record says that 'William Brien and Stewart* McBurnie had a Legitimate daughter born this day and baptised 3d March'. In the 1841 census, at the age of one, she was staying in Monreith Village with John Heron, an agricultural labourer aged 34, and Louisa Heron, aged 19. In the 1851 census, William and Stewart now had two more children, Marion and William junior. William (senior) is described as a tailor, and Stewart as the wife of William.

Louisa married Gordon Nichol (Nicholls) in Glasserton, in November 1866. In 1871 they were living in Monreith, and Gordon's occupation was given as 'mariner'. Ten years later they were living in Mochrum, Wigtownshire. Gordon was not at home at the time of the census, but Louisa and the children were recorded. There were four daughters and two sons: Catherine, born in 1869 in Glasserton, John in 1871 in Whithorn, Marion Louisa in 1873 in Glasserton, Agnes in 1875 in Whithorn, Georgina in 1877 in Port William, and William in 1878 in Port William.

Louisa Heron, now 66 and described as her aunt, was also staying with them.

Louisa Nicholls died in Glasgow in 1933, at the age of 92.

Robert Pennefather

Robert Percival Pennefather was born in May 1841 in Karnal, Bengal.[4] His father was also Robert Percival, then a Captain in the Bengal Army. His mother was Elizabeth Jane Denson. She had travelled to India in 1819 and they were married in November 1823. Robert junior followed his father into the army, being admitted to Addiscombe Military Seminary in 1857. He rose to the rank of Lieutenant Colonel in the Royal Engineers.

In April 1890 he married Margaret MacDonald Lowe, a widow with a son aged 17 and moved into the house where she was living, 10 Albert Terrace, Edinburgh. Margaret was born Margaret MacDonald Graham in Paisley in March 1851. Her parents were Margaret Frier and George Graham, who was a Major in the Royal Scots Fusiliers.

---

* Stewart was definitely the Christian name of a girl.

Her previous husband, Thomas Lowe, had also been in the army, and her son, George, was born in India.

At the time of the 1891 census, they were in Albert Terrace, and George was studying medicine. Soon after they moved to 28 Hartington Place, where Margaret died in November 1894.

Robert moved to No 21 in 1897, and he died there in March 1900. In April his furniture was advertised for auction in *The Scotsman*. This included

> a 'cottage pianoforte', a carved oak sideboard with mirror back, an oak 'telescope' dining table, a dining room suite in 'figured marone Utrecht velvet', book cases, cabinets, a drawing room suite, in 'blue Utrecht velvet', bamboo whatnots, and bedroom furniture.

Frank Pearson

Frank Robert T. Pearson was a maths master who was born in Ulverston, just south of the Lake District in the last quarter of 1870. In 1901 he was living in No 21 with his wife, Eliza. Frank was 30 years old and his wife was some nine years older and came from Traquair, near Peebles. They had a 13-year-old boarder, Alexander Patrick, from Hawick, and one servant, Christina Forsyth, 30, from Peebles.

NO 22 DALRYMPLE CRESCENT

No 22 had a large number of tenants over the period. Mrs J. Forster Pratt was living here in 1869 and 1870. At the time of the 1871 census, it was occupied by Charlotte Brand. Then Richard Lister rented it from 1872 to 1876, and he was followed by Rev. James T. Stuart in 1877 and 1878. Eleanor Fowden rented the property from 1878 to 1880, and Mrs Jas Hay Ower was living there from 1881 to 1884. In 1887 it was occupied by R. L. Lundin Brown, and from 1889 to 1893 Jane McJerrow rented it. During this time, in 1892, Mrs H. M. Parry gave her address as 23 Dalrymple Crescent. From 1895 to 1900 it was occupied by George A. Young. Finally, James Robertson was renting it in 1901.

Mrs J. Forster Pratt

Mrs Forster Pratt was born Frances Ligonier Balfour in Orkney about 1826.[5] Her father was William Balfour 4th, of Trenabie, who had been in the Navy. She married John Forster Pratt who was a solicitor in Berwick-on Tweed. His father was John Pratt, of Addlestone Mains, Northumberland. They married in Edinburgh, and the marriage was reported in *The Gentleman's Magazine* in July 1853. John Forster Pratt died in Berwick in 1858, and his widow was living in Dalrymple Crescent in 1869 and 1870. She died in June 1889, aged 63, when her home was at 58 Queen Street, although she actually died at Riva in the Tyrol, Austria.

Charlotte Brand

Charlotte Brand's maiden name was Inglis, and she was born in Locklee near Forfar in 1811. She married Robert Brand in Montrose in 1834 and they had three children: Alexander, Charlotte and Robert. Robert senior was a shipmaster and he died in Montrose in 1854. In 1871, aged 60, Charlotte was living in Dalrymple Crescent. At the time of the census she had two visitors: Jane Inglis, 45, from Locklee, and Isabella Campbell, 30, from Montrose. Both were unmarried. She also had four boarders: Amelia Burns, 33, born in South Leith, Flora Burns, 29, from Glasgow, Charlotte Graves, 13, born in Besaphore, India, and her sister Amy, 10 born in Chinore, India. There was one servant, Isabella Newton, 19, from Inverkeithing. Charlotte had moved to 55 Grange Road by 1873, and died there in 1882, aged 71.

Rev. James T. Stuart

James Thomson Stuart (Plate 14) was the first minister at Mayfield

Free Church. He was born in Dundee in July 1837, and his parents were Alexander Stuart and Sarah Brown. In May 1878, *The Scotsman* reported the death of Hannah Isabella aged 12½, his eldest child.

Mayfield Church (Plate 15) was designed by Hippolyte Blanc,[6] a well-known Edinburgh architect, who also designed the manse at No 18 West Mayfield. This was where Mr Stuart was living, with his family, in 1881, although he was not at home on census day. His wife, Hannah Elizabeth Thompson, also came from Dundee, and was born in 1843. They had four surviving children: Alexander aged 13, Georgina aged eight, Katie aged five and Sara aged two. All were born in Kelso. They also had two boarders, Alfred Duke, aged 14 from Brechin, and Miss Jane McQueen, aged 62, from Fortrose. In addition they had a visitor, Duncan McDonald, a professor of Biology, born in Edinburgh in 1847.

James Stuart died in Crieff in April 1885, at the age of 47. His gravestone in Grange Cemetery reads:

IN LOVING REMEMBRANCE OF

JAMES THOMSON STUART M.A.

FIRST MINISTER OF MAYFIELD FREE CHURCH EDINBURGH

WHO DIED AT CRIEFF ON 12TH APRIL 1885 AGED 47 YEARS.

ALSO HIS CHILDREN

SARAH BROWN AND JOHN W. THOMSON

WHO DIED IN INFANCY AND ARE INTERRED AT KELSO.

HANNAH ISABELLA WHO DIED 14TH MAY 1878 AGED 12 YEARS

SARAH CHRISTIAN WHO DIED 30TH NOVEMBER 1881 AGED 3 YEARS

AND ARE INTERRED HERE

ALSO OF HIS WIDOW HANNAH E. THOMSON

WHO DIED AT EDINBURGH 11TH DECEMBER 1892 AGED 50 YEARS

'THEM ALSO WHO SLEEP IN JESUS WILL GOD BRING WITH HIM'

I THESS IV 14[7]

Eleanor Fowden

Eleanor Fowden was born in Chorlton Upon Medlock, Manchester, in February 1836. Her father was William Fowden, and her mother's name was Mary Ann (her surname is not given). The family were still living there in 1851, but William died before 1861. At this time Mary Ann and Eleanor were living with three servants in Chorley in Cheshire. Mary Ann was 69 and Eleanor was 25. Ten years later they had moved to Weston-super-Mare in Somerset, and had two boarders, George Fisher, aged 46 and Elizabeth Fisher, aged 42. Both were apparently born in Nottinghamshire. Eleanor then appeared in the valuation records for No 22, renting it from 1878 to 1880. In 1878 a Rev. George Fisher was listed in the Post Office directories as living at 17 Dalrymple Crescent, and in 1879 and 1880 his address was 22 Dalrymple Crescent. Eleanor had moved south again by 1881, to Clifton, near Bristol. According to the census, the head of house was a Baptist minister, George Fisher, aged 56, but born in Northamptonshire. His wife, Elizabeth Fisher, was also born in Northamptonshire, and was a year older. Their border was Eleanor Fowden, now 45, whose income came from owning land and nine houses. Eleanor died in Devon in 1920.

Mrs James Hay Ower

Mrs Hay Ower was born Caroline Legendre in Invergowrie, Angus about 1822. Her father was Jules Legendre, a French teacher, born in Chartre, France. Her mother's name was Jean Inches. In 1840 Jules died of heart disease, in Dundee, at the age of 55. Caroline married James Hay Ower in 1849, and they had at least two children: Elizabeth born in 1857, and Jane born in 1864. James died in Dundee, in 1876, and Caroline rented No 22 between 1882 and 1884.

In 1882 she advertised in *The Scotsman* for a Cook (Good Plain) and a House-Table maid. 'Wages £16 and £14. Good references indispensable.' Two years later another advertisement appeared in *The Scotsman*: 'Cat (Large, Black-and-grey Pet) Found. Apply 22 Dalrymple Crescent, Grange'.

She moved to 121 Mayfield Road, and in the 1891 census she was living there with Jane and Elizabeth, both of whom were unmarried.

R. L. Lundin Brown

Richard Lundin Brown was the son of Robert Brown, a Free Church minister, and Elizabeth Lundin, daughter of Christopher Lundin of Auchtermairnie in Fife. When Elizabeth inherited the estate (which was subsequently sold), the children adopted the name Lundin Brown. Robert and Elizabeth had seven children, all born in Largo, Fife where their father had his church. Richard, the second oldest, was born in December 1829. According to Professor T. A. Lee,[8] 'he married into the landowning families of Maitland Christie of Durie and Lindsay of Balcarres'. 'Maitland Christie' was Charles Maitland Christie of Durie and 'Lindsay of Balcarres' was the Hon. Robert Lindsay, son of the fifth Earl of Balcarres. Richard Lundin Brown's wife was Margaret Christie, the fourth daughter of Charles Maitland, and Mary Butler, who was the eldest daughter of the Hon. Robert Lindsay. Richard and Margaret had one daughter, whose name is not recorded.[9]

Richard became known as R. L. Lundin Brown, to distinguish him from R. C. Lundin Brown (Robert Christopher). The latter was his younger brother who was a missionary in British Columbia.[10] Richard Lundin Brown rented the house from 1895 to 1900. He died in St Andrews in 1905 at the age of 76, and Margaret died in 1924 in Aberlour, Banff at the age of 95.

Jane McJerrow

Jane McJerrow (neé Little) was born in Annan in 1838. She married David McJerrow, also from Annan, in 1860, and they had seven sons and two daughters: David was born in 1862, John in 1864, Sarah in 1866, James in 1868, William in 1869, Thomas in 1870, Jessie in 1873, Christopher in 1875 and Gordon in 1876.

David senior was the son of a master baker, and Jane was the daughter of a draper. David died in 1877 at the age of 50, and in 1881

Jane was living in the Brewery House in Annan with her nine
children. David junior was a lawyer's apprentice clerk, and John was
a medical student at Edinburgh.

The family rented No 22 from 1889 to 1893. By 1891, three sons
had left the family home: David, James and Thomas. At the time of
the census John was still a medical student (aged 27), William was a
captain in the mercantile marines, and Christopher and Gordon
were 'scholars'. The girls were unmarried and still at home. In
addition, a nephew, W. Lother Nicholson, from England was staying
with them. He was 19 and studying engineering. There was one
servant, Jane Palmer, aged 24, from Wishaw.

Mrs Hannah M. Parry

Hannah Parry was the wife of William Parry of the Indian Civil
Service. In 1891 she was living at 16 Greenhill Place with her daughter
and three of her sons. She had been born in India in 1841. All the
children were born in India. The eldest, Edgar, was born in 1868, and
was a medical student in 1891. The other children were Eleanor, aged
20, Frank, aged 14 and Trevor, aged 10. Edgar joined the Indian
Medical Service in 1892, and in the same year Hannah was listed as
living at No 22. By 1901 William had retired, and was living at 57 Nile
Grove with Hannah, Eleanor, Trevor, and another son, Will, who was
an apprentice gardener. Trevor was now studying medicine.[11]

George A. Young

George Adam Young was a bookseller and publisher who had a shop
in South Bridge. He was born in India in 1857, but was a British
subject. He had two older sisters, Margaret and Jane who were also
born in India about 1859. In addition he had a brother, John, born in
Edinburgh in 1862, and two sisters, Annie and Kate, also born in
Edinburgh. Annie was born in 1864, and Kate in 1867. Their father
was Robert Young and their mother was Margaret Turnbull. In 1891
George, Margaret, John, Annie, and Kate were living at 14 Grange
Terrace, although George was not at home on census night. In

addition they had a visitor, Barbara Reeve, a spinster aged 60 from Burntisland.

The family lived at No 22 between 1895 and 1900, but by 1901 John, Jane and Annie were living at 82 Thirlestane Road. At the time of the census Jane was a piano teacher and Annie a violin teacher. There was also a visitor, Margaret Woods, aged 22, a clerkess who had been born in India.

James Robertson

At the time of the 1901 census James Robertson, a retired ironmonger, was living in No 22 with his wife Euphemia. James was born in Minto, Roxburghshire in 1841, and Euphemia in Jedburgh in 1845. Their son, Alexander was a lawyers' clerk. He had been born in Jedburgh in 1878. They had one servant, Margaret Levock, 19, from Edinburgh.

NO 23 DALRYMPLE CRESCENT

No 23 was also rented by a large number of people. Henry Brougham Crouch was the tenant from 1869 to 1971, and he was followed by Robert Dick in 1873 and 1874. John H. Banks was living there in 1876, and from 1877 to 1884 the tenant was James J. Fulton. George Mackie lived there in 1887 and 1888, and Mary S. Edgar was the tenant at the time of the 1891 census. Mrs G. C. Rosebank Hay was living there in 1894, and Mrs Anne S. Paterson in 1896. Rev. Alex Paterson was there in 1897 and 1898, and John Stewart of Ensay died there in 1899. Mrs J. A. Bryden was in residence at the time of the 1901 census.

Henry Brougham Crouch

The story of Henry Crouch and his family is told in the Chapter 6.

Robert Dick

Robert Dick was a chemist and druggist working for the firm of

Duncan Flockhart and Co. He was born in Mid Calder in November 1843. His father, William Dick was a 'local agent' and his mother was Jane Spiers Brash. He married Jane Dickson, who was born in Peebles in November 1841. Her father was Alexander Dickson, and her mother was Joan Wilson.

On 18 April 1874 *The Scotsman* reported that a son had been born to Mrs Robert Dick, and then on 7 May, that Johanna Russell Wilson Dick, 'beloved daughter' of Robert Dick had died aged one year and eleven months. She died of scarletina after four days of illness. On 9 May, her mother Jane died of kidney failure after 'many months' of illness. Two days later the baby, christened William Andrew, also died of scarletina. In November 1874 an advertisement appeared in *The Scotsman* for an experienced servant to 'Cook, wash and dress'.

We know that Robert Dick was still in Dalrymple Crescent in March 1876, when he was listed as one of the members of the General Committee to elect members of the Edinburgh School Board. On 13 April 1876 he remarried, while he was still living in Dalrymple Crescent. His new wife was Margaret B. Aitken, living at 13 Chalmers Crescent, where the marriage took place. It was conducted by Rev. John Young, the minister at Newington United Presbyterian Church. Margaret was born in 1855 in Bladnock, Wigtownshire. Her father was Alexander Aitken, the tea salesman who had lived at No 2 Dalrymple Crescent in 1864 and 1865, when Margaret was about ten.

By 1881 Robert and Margaret had moved to 4 St Andrews Terrace. They now had two daughters: Agnes born in 1879, and Jeannie born in 1880. In addition a nephew, William Walter Brownlee, and Margaret's brother, Charles Aitken, were staying with them. Charles was 8, born in Edinburgh in 1873. William was the son of Robert's younger sister Jane Spiers Brash Dick, who married Robert Dick Brownlee. He was born in Kirkcaldy in April 1872.

John Henry Banks

John Banks was born in Edinburgh in January 1819. His father was Henry Banks and his mother was Jean Paterson. He became a surveyor for the Inland Revenue, and the position took him round the country. In 1851 he was living in Old Machar in Aberdeenshire. He was married to Janet Wilson, born in Edinburgh in 1825, and they had two children: a son, Henry Charles, born in 1846, and a daughter, Margaret, in 1849.

In 1876 he was living at No 23, and was based at 14 Waterloo Place. His post was described as 'surveyor, HM stamps & taxes'. He was living in No 23 in 1876, and in March 1877 an advertisement in *The Scotsman* stated

> Servant (Good General) Wanted at Term for Glasgow. Small Family; liberal wages will be given to a suitable person. Apply 23 Dalrymple Crescent, Grange.

By 1881 the family had moved to Apsley House, Dumbarton Road, Govan. At the time of the 1881 census they had two sons living with them. Henry C. Banks was now a master mariner. Abernethy Banks was considerably younger, being born in Glasgow in 1863, and was a commercial clerk.

John Banks died in Apsley House in January 1883 the day after his 64th birthday, and Janet died three years later.

James Fulton

James John Fulton was a master brewer and maltster, born in Kilmarnock in Ayrshire in 1849. His wife was Isabella Stewart Irvine, born around 1846. In 1877 they were living at 23 Buccleuch Place, where their daughter Isabel was born. They moved to 23 Dalrymple Crescent that same year, but his wife, Isabella, died in November, of congestion of the kidneys. At the time of the 1881 census he was still living in Dalrymple Crescent with his daughter, a nurse and a general servant. The nurse was Elizabeth McNeil, 30, from Tranent, and the general servant was Elizabeth Law, 24, from Strathmiglo in Fife.

He remarried in 1883, to Eleanor Rendle Deas, and they had a daughter, Madge (Margaret Crooks), but *The Scotsman* reported her death in February 1886, at the age of 22 months. They moved from Dalrymple Crescent soon after.

George Mackie

George Mackie lived in No 23 in 1887 and 1888. He was an accountant, with his office first situated in York Buildings, and later at 116 George Street. *The Scotsman* announced the birth of a daughter on 26 November 1887. A year later, in November 1888 an advertisement appeared in *The Scotsman* for a servant, and then in December, this urgent message: 'Girl (about 14) wanted at once to look after baby; go home at night'. By 1890 the family had moved to 119 Dalkeith Road.

Mary S. Edgar

Mary Edgar was born Mary Sybilla Cowan in Kelton, Kircudbrightshire in 1845. Her parents were Samuel Cowan and Mary Campbell. She married Andrew Edgar, the Minister of Mauchline Parish, Ayrshire. He came from Catrine in Ayrshire, and was born in 1831. In 1881 they were living at the manse in Mauchline with eight children: Andrew, born in 1867, Mary in 1869, Campbell in 1871, John in 1873 and Charles in 1875, born in Tongland; and Jane in 1876, Sybil in 1878 and Madeleine in 1880, born in Mauchline.

Another daughter, Audrey, was born in 1884, in Mauchline. Andrew died in March 1890, and at the time of the 1891 census Mary was living in Dalrymple Crescent with her three of her daughters, Mary, Madeleine and Audrey. Also staying with them was her 82-year-old mother, Mary. They had a cook, Isabella Johnston, 23, from Mauchline, and a housemaid, Eliza Armstrong, 44, from Kelton.

Mary Cowan, now aged 90, died in May 1899, when she was living at 36 Fountainhall Road.

Mrs G. C. Hay

Mrs G. C. Hay (of Rosebank) was born Marianne Binny, the daughter of Graham Binny and Marianne Kyd. She was christened in the parish of St Cuthbert's, Edinburgh in August 1832. Graham Binny was a Writer to the Signet, and Marianne was one of six children. She married George Charles Hay, MD, and a daughter, Isobel, was born in the parish of Inveresk and Musselburgh in 1854.

The family moved to the Cape Colony, where three more children were born: Mary in 1863, Fanny Ellen in 1869 and John in 1870. By 1881, she was widowed, and living back in Edinburgh at 12 Scotland Street. John was a pupil at the Edinburgh Academy between 1879 and 1886. He became a GP, and subsequently moved to Australia, where he married Edith Mary Puckle, the daughter of Walter Puckle, a prominent banker. In fact, the address given for them in the Edinburgh Academy Register was 'Lyndhurst, Puckle Street, Moonnee Ponds, Victoria'.[12]

Marianne Hay lived at No 23 in 1894, and died in 1896 in Echuca, Victoria, Australia. She is described as the widow of George Hay, 'sometime residing in Dalkeith, afterwards in Dalrymple Crescent, Edinburgh, latterly at Echuca, Victoria'.

Mrs Anne S. Paterson

Anne Paterson was born Anne Salmon in Inverarity, Angus, in August 1832. Her parents were John Paterson, a land agent, and Margaret Mitchell. She married John Paterson of Milton and Moat of Urr in December 1858. In the 1841 census, John is shown as a farmer, living at Craigdarroch in Sanquhar, Dumfriesshire. In 1881 they were still living at Craigdarroch, with three of their children: John Salmon Paterson, aged 19, Margaret Mitchell Paterson, aged 11 and William Edgar Paterson, aged 21. Young John attended the Edinburgh Academy, whose register gives his occupation as 'farmer'. He married Agnes Brown, the daughter of Jas. R. Wilson of Sanquhar.

John senior died at Craigdarroch in May 1886, at the age of 77. Anne lived at No 23 in 1896 and she died there in January 1897. Her death was reported by another son, James O. Paterson, who was living in Fingal Place in Edinburgh.

Rev. Alex Paterson

Rev. Alex Paterson was a United Presbyterian Minister, who lived at No 23 in 1897 and 1898. He was born in Glasgow in 1847. His wife

Anna was four years younger than him, and was also born in Glasgow. He was the minister of the United Presbyterian Church in Lilliesleaf, Roxburghshire in 1881. His three children were all born there: George in 1877, Mary in 1882 and Alison in 1886. By 1896 they had moved to 153 Dalkeith Road, and then spent two years at No 23. By 1901 they were living at 6 Sea View Terrace, Duddingston. Alex Paterson was now retired, at the age of 54.

John Stewart of Ensay

In March 1899, *The Scotsman* announced the death of John Stewart of Ensay, aged 74. He died at 23 Dalrymple Crescent, and the funeral was to be at Luskentyre.

John Stewart was the son of Donald Stewart, factor to Lord Dunmore, and Isabella MacRae, daughter of Donald MacRae of Cluanie, Heights of Kintail. He married Jessy MacRae of Auchteryre, and they had two sons and five daughters: Jane MacRae; William, a Captain in the 91st Highlanders; Isabella Christian who married Gordon Fraser of Nairn in 1882; Mary who died in 1891; Donald Alexander who married Isabella Mary Anderson in 1894; Jessy Chisholm who married Thomas Scott in 1888; and Hannah who married Captain Ronald Macdonald (Aberarder family) of the 92nd Highlanders.

Jessy died in 1860. In January 1899 *The Scotsman* reported that their grandson, Mr John Stewart Gordon Fraser, who was the son of Isabella and Gordon Fraser, and had been given a grant of £40 by the Argyll Naval Fund, a fund set up under the auspices of the Highland and Agricultural Society.

In his will, John Stewart is described as 'of Ensay, Pabbay, &c., and Joint Tenant, Farm of Scorrybreck, Isle of Skye'. He was famous for his herd of Highland cattle. James Cameron,[13] writing in 1919 about Highland cattle says:

> Practically nothing is known regarding the origin of the breed. (It) owed a great deal in many respects to the brothers Donald and Archibald Stewart, who shifted with the best of

their stock to the Hebrides in the early part of last century –
Donald taking a Lewis farm in 1802, and Luskentyre, in
Harris seven years later.

He goes on to say that John Stewart was one of the outstanding
breeders of the century:

Following his father's example, (he) blended the best of the
island and mainland strains of cattle, and having large
numbers to deal with on extensive feeding ranges he was able
to practice line breeding most effectively.

The herd was sold at auction in 1901. It was described as the property
of representatives of the late John Stewart Esq., of Ensay, and was
sold on account of the termination of the lease of Scorrybreck.

Others took a less benevolent view of Donald and Archibald
Stewart. This was the time of the Highland Clearances, and there are
several reports on their behaviour at that time.

Stewarts of Ensay were previously the Stewarts of
Luskentyre, Cadets of the Stewarts of Garth. Before they
settled in Ensay they had settled in Harris and made
themselves so unpopular that it is feared they are still
remembered with oaths and curses.[14]

In 1800 there were a large number of settlements round
the coastline from Lemreway to Seaforth Head. Some of
these were clachans with one, two or three crofters, while
others were townships with nearly a score of crofters. They
lived in comfortable circumstances but this life was doomed
to a cruel end through the machinations of one Donald
Stewart, a 'hireling shepherd' from Perthshire who became
manager for the partners who had obtained the lease of
Bhalamus. Clearances of the crofters soon began and by the
time the Stewarts left Bhalamus for Aline and Eilean Ensay in
1842 practically all the crofters had been evicted from the
area. This Donald Stewart later became factor in Harris,

settled in Luskentyre and cleared it as well as most of North
and South Harris. He became a drover and later a breeder of
Highland cattle.[15]

Perhaps the most damning comments come from the evidence given
to the Crofters Commission[16] in June 1883 by one M. Macleod, cotter
and fisherman, Ardhesie. There were 11 families living in the area,
which was overcrowded. Their troubles began in the time of Donald
Stewart who was factor for Macleod of Harris. He 'cleared seven
townships at one stroke' and

> His next move was to turn his attention to Macleod [of
> Harris] himself, and devise to make a fool of him, and he
> succeeded, because before the end came they used to call
> Macleod a beggar. Macleod latterly was, through his factor's
> instrumentality, reduced to such a poor condition that he
> obtained his support in Donald Stewart's own house.

The hearing also heard that 'Stewart came originally to the farm of
Pairc as a shepherd and from the Pairc he came here [Harris]'. John
Stewart rebuffed these claims in a letter to *The Scotsman* sent in July
1883. According to him, the claims of Macleod of Ardhesie were 'so
utterly false that I cannot let them pass without contradiction'. He
could prove the 'untruthfulness of his evidence' from the records he
had of the time and by the testimony of 'many Harris men of much
greater respectability than M. Macleod'. Furthermore the clearances
to which Macleod of Ardhesie referred did not take place during
Donald Stewart's factorship. Macleod of Harris was not a fool, and
stayed at John's father's house as a guest.

He refuted the remark that his father first went to Harris as a
shepherd, rather he was of the 'old and respected family of Stewart of
Garth'. He finishes

> That any man whose only claim to being heard before the
> Royal Commission consisted of an inventive and vicious
> imagination and a voluble tongue, should give evidence

regarding a period entirely beyond his recollection, and vilify the memory of men who were esteemed and respected before he was born, is, to say the least, unfortunate.

In April 1899 another advertisement appeared in *The Scotsman*:

House (furnished) wanted about nine rooms within walking distance of George Watson's schools. 23 Dalrymple Crescent.

Eliza Bryden

Eliza or Lizza Bryden was the widow of John Adam Bryden, of the firm of John Bryden & Sons, bell-hangers and window-blind makers. Lizza was born in Edinburgh in 1857 and she married John Bryden in 1880. Her maiden surname was Cotton. John died in March 1898, when they were living at 3 Salisbury Road. In 1901 Lizza was living in Dalrymple Crescent with three children, Molly aged 19, Eva aged 15, and John who was 11, They were all born in Edinburgh. They had a cook, Eliza McPherson, 55, from Wick in Caithness, and a general servant, Jessie McDonald, from Croy in Inverness-shire.

NO 24 DALRYMPLE CRESCENT

No 24 (Plate 16a) is built on one of three plots of land owned by John Paterson. The site passed through various hands (See Chapter 2) and there is no record of a house on the site until December 1886, when John Robb Matthew bought the property. This makes it the last house to be built in the Crescent. It is a detached house of 13 rooms. John Matthew died shortly after buying the house, but his widow continued to live there until the end of the century.

John Robb Matthew

John Robb Matthew was a draper and warehouseman, based in the Lawnmarket. In 1881 he was living at 11 Tantallon Place with his wife,

Jessie, and 11 children: Elizabeth, born in 1852, Jane in 1854, Robert in 1859, Jessie junior in 1860, George in 1862, Duncan in 1864, Joan in 1866, Mary in 1867, Bert in 1869, Christian in 1870 and Stewart in 1872.

John was born in Forfar in 1825, and Jessie was two years younger than him, and came from Callander. They were married in Edinburgh in 1849, and Jessie's official name was Janet McLaren. All the children were born in Edinburgh. Robert was a draper superintendent, George a draper's apprentice, and Duncan a joiner's apprentice. In addition Jessie's unmarried sister Margaret McLaren was visiting them at the time of the 1881 census.

Jessie junior married a William Hunter in 1885, and early in 1887 the rest of the family moved into No 24. John died on 7 November of that year, aged 57, and is buried in Grange Cemetery, along with other members of his family. In the notice of his death in *The Scotsman* he was described as being 'of James Matthew and Son, 473 Lawnmarket'.

In 1889 Duncan married Frances Hogg, in Edinburgh, and at the time of the 1891 census, Jessie was living at No 24 with Elizabeth, Bert and Stewart. Bert was now a draper's superintendent, and Stewart a draper's apprentice. They had a housemaid, Christine McNab, 29, from Couch Fern, Argyllshire and Marie Blackie, 17, a general servant from Davidson's Mains, just outside Edinburgh.

In December 1899, Robert died of acute pneumonia at 67 Newington Road, aged 40. On 15 September 1900, Christian died at No 24. She was aged 30.

In 1901 Jessie, now 74, was living with Elizabeth (48 and unmarried), and another of her sisters, Elizabeth McLaren, who was 56. She also had a grand-niece, Jean Robertson, 20, born in Callander staying with her, and one servant: Jane Brown, 20, from Musselburgh.

The family headstone in Grange Cemetery has the following inscription:

IN MEMORY OF
JOHN MATTHEW
SECOND SON OF

JOHN ROBB MATHEW

WHO DIED 17TH AUGUST 1868

AGED 14 YEARS
JOHN ROBB MATTHEW
WHO DIED 7TH NOVEMBER 1887

AGED 57 YEARS
CHRISTIAN McLAREN
HIS YOUNGEST DAUGHTER

WHO DIED 15TH SEPTEMBER 1900

AGED 30 YEARS
JOAN ROBB STEWART
FOURTH DAUGHTER

WHO DIED 30TH JULY

AGED 37 YEARS
JESSIE McLAREN
WIFE OF THE ABOVE

JOHN ROBB MATTHEW

WHO DIED 29TH MARCH 1904

AGED 77 YEARS

THEIR DAUGHTERS
JEAN
DIED 22ND APRIL 1915
ELIZABETH
DIED 7TH NOVEMBER 1927

NO 25 DALRYMPLE CRESCENT

No 25 (Plate 16b) is also a detached house, built in a classic style. It is
the middle plot of the three bought by John Paterson. His estate sold
it to George Stratton, who built the house, which he then rented out.
The first tenant was Rev. James Gregory, who lived there from 1880
to 1887. It was then let to James Hay between 1888 and 1898. George

Stratton died in 1897, and his trustees sold the house to James Hall, who lived there from 1899 onwards.

The Inland Revenue survey gives a full description of the house. The sale to James Hall was completed at Whitsun 1900, the sale price being £1500. He was still living in the house in 1912, and the description shows that he was a man who kept up with the times, and kept his house in good condition.

The house was described as a two-storey detached house with a ribbed ashlar front wall, moulded architrave, splayed quoins and a moulded wallhead. There were no bow windows to the front. The side and back walls were coursed rubble. On the west wall was a motor garage of brick and wood with a zinc flat roof.

In the basement there was a coal cellar, and a large store over the whole front area of the house. It also had a larder, a pantry, a servant's room and a bedroom with a bow window to the back, as well as a WC. The surveyor reported that there was gas lighting here. In the garden was a hot-house in good condition, with a boiler for heating. The garden walls had been well pointed.

On the ground floor there was electric lighting, and the paper and paint were in very good condition. Accommodation consisted of a dining room, a breakfast room a bedroom, a kitchen and a scullery. On the first floor there was also electric lighting, and the paper and paint were 'good'. There was a small bedroom, a bathroom and WC with a towel heater, as well as the drawing room and another bedroom.

James Gregory

Rev. James Gregory was born in Bradford in 1844. He was the son of Ellen and James Gregory. James Gregory senior was also a minister. In 1871 he married Martha Wickwar, in Bradford. On 14 November 1879 *The Scotsman* reported that the Augustine Congregational Church, George IV Bridge, would have Rev. James Gregory of Leeds as its new pastor, succeeding Rev. Dr Lindsay Alexander, who had become the Principal of the Congregational Theological Hall. James Gregory came from Belgrave Chapel, Leeds, and preached his first sermon, on 17 January 1880.

At the time of the 1881 census, James and Martha were living at No 25, and had five children, all but the youngest being born in England. At that time John was six, Ellen was four, James junior was two and Arnold was one. Ralph was six months old and was born in Edinburgh. They had one servant, Anne Brown, 26, also from England. James' mother, Ellen was staying with them, when she died in January 1882.

Two more children were born to them. In May 1884, *The Scotsman* announced the birth of a son, and in May 1885 another son, Joseph Alexander (Aleck) died of diphtheria in the City Hospital. He was aged three years and eight months, meaning that he was born in late 1881.

The family left Dalrymple Crescent in 1887.

James Hay

James Craig Hay was one of seven children born to Andrew Hay and Sarah Ann Craig. He was born in Edinburgh in November 1839, and became a leather merchant.

In 1863 he married Hannah Wilson Pringle, who was two years younger than him, and was born in Earlston, Berwickshire. They had four children: Andrew, born in 1864, Thomas Craig in 1868, James in 1870, and William in 1872. Hannah died in December 1874, at the age of 33.

James married again. His new wife was Grace Fairley, also from Edinburgh, and ten years younger than him. In 1881 they were living at 2 Carlung Place and with six children. Andrew was 17 and a shipbroker's apprentice; Thomas was 12, James was ten, and William was eight. James senior had two children by his new wife: Grace, aged two, and Sarah who was born in March 1881.

They moved to No 25 in 1888, and at the time of the 1891 census, Andrew and William were no longer at home. Thomas was a cashier, and James junior a warehouseman. Two more children had been born: Harriet and John, both aged six. There were also two students staying with them, daughters of Grace's sister, Isabella. They were Margaret and Harriet Ferguson, 20 and 18, from Newport, Fife. They had two servants. The housemaid was Maria Hogg, aged 18, from Musselburgh, and the cook was Mary Sketheway, aged 24, from Shappinsey in Orkney.

James Hay died at 7 Warrender Park Terrace, Edinburgh, in May 1914, at the age of 75, and Grace died a year later. The two Ferguson sisters never married, and lived well into the 20th century: Margaret died in 1944 at the age of 74, and Harriet in 1958 at the age of 86. Both were living at 'Fairlea', Youngsdale Place, Newport in Fife.

James Hall

James Hall was a house agent and valuator from Rosskeen in Ross-shire. His wife, Mary, came from London. He bought the house in 1899, and in 1901, at the time of the census, he was 52 and she was 50. They had four children, all born in Edinburgh. They were James, aged 15, Mary, aged 14, Dorothy, aged 13, and Ethel, aged 11. They had one servant, Rose O'Donnell, 22, from Ireland.

NO 26 DALRYMPLE CRESCENT

No 26 (Plates 17a and b) is the most westerly of the three plots owned by John Paterson, and was sold to Thomas Ogilvie Cownie in 1878. He lived there with his family until he died in 1898. The house was put up for auction soon after he died. It was described as:

> Convenient and Commodious DETACHED VILLA of 3 Public Rooms, 6 Bed-Rooms, Dressing-Room, Bath-Room and Lavatories, Kitchen, Laundry, Servants' Accommodation, Housemaid's Pantry with Lift, and other Pantries, Closets and Presses. Ground Quarter Acre.

The upset price was 'moderate' and the Feu duty £6-5s. However it was not sold, and his widow, Margaret Cownie, continued to live in it until 1901.

In the Inland Revenue survey of 1912 the house is described as a one and three-quarter-storey detached house with coursed rubble walls, gables and back wall. The gable to the front was fitted with bargeboards and half-timber work, and projecting eaves. There was one small attic, and the front canopy over the door was supported by wooden trusses. The boundary walls were rubble, and there was a parapet wall and railings to the front. There was a small tool house on the south boundary.

Accommodation consisted of a basement kitchen with a good range. There was also a scullery with sink and a small service hoist. There was a washhouse with a brick floor, two wooden tubs, and a boiler. On this floor there was also a bedroom, a coal cellar, a WC, and a wine cellar with stone shelves. There was a larder under the stair. In addition there was a nursery with a window giving on to the garden, and a press containing a washbasin.

On the ground floor, there was a dining room, another small room, a small bedroom, and a pantry. Wooden stairs led to the first floor, where there were four bedrooms, a small dressing room, a bathroom and WC.

Margaret Cownie was still the occupier, with the property registered to the trustees of the late Thomas Cownie.

The story of the Cownie family is told in Chapter 6.

NO 27 DALRYMPLE CRESCENT

The last house on the southwest side of the Crescent is another large detached house, built in 1874. The land had been sold to James Hogg, a builder and joiner, and during 1874 three advertisements appeared in *The Scotsman*:

The first, on 10 January, read:

Grange – Dalrymple Crescent – For sale, detached Villa, 8 Apartments, In course of finishing. Apply to Mr Hogg, at Building; or to J. Douglas Gardiner, S.S.C., 35 George IV Bridge.

The second appeared on the 12 May, and read:

> Grange – 30 Dalrymple Crescent – detached Villa for sale.
> Three Public, Four Bedrooms. Stable and Coach-House can
> be had if required. Apply to the Joiner at the Villa.

The final advertisement was on the 10 October and read:

> Grange (Dalrymple Crescent) – Detached Villa for Sale –
> Dining, Drawing Room, parlour, 4 Bed-Rooms, Dressing
> Room, bath, and other conveniences. Ground, Quarter of an
> Acre. Feu £6-6s.

By 1875 the house had been bought by Camilla More and her family.
They were still there in 1912 when the Inland Revenue survey took
place. It described the building as a two-storey detached house with
rubble walls and two-storey bow windows. There was a hot-house in
the back garden, with a parapet wall and railings to the front.

On the ground floor there was a dining room, a bedroom, a
small room with an old grate and open fire. The kitchen and pantry
both had jaw-boxes (sinks and drain). In addition there was a
servant's room, a press and a WC. Outside there was a washhouse
with two tubs, and a stone floor. The coal cellar was in the basement
under the kitchen.

There was a stone stair to the upper floor, where there were three
bedrooms, a dressing room, the bathroom and the drawing room. A
small stair led to a large room in the attic, which was 'not finished'.

Camilla More

The More family came from Perth, and were part of the family of
Alexander More and Euphemia Lockhart. Alexander was the
Collector of Her Majesty's Customs at Dartmouth, and died in the
1850s, with Euphemia dying shortly afterwards.

There were six children. The eldest, John, was born in October
1834. Camilla was born in October 1835, Elizabeth in February 1837,

James in February 1839, Catherine in November 1840, and Charles in January 1843. Four of the family, Camilla, Elizabeth, Catherine and Charles moved into Dalrymple Crescent, having previously lived in the family home at 5 Danube Street. Elizabeth died in 1878.

In the 1881 census the house was numbered 27 and Camilla, Catherine and Charles were living there, with one servant, Jessie Clerk, 22, from Ayr. All three of them gave their means of support as 'interest'. They were still there in 1891, and in July of that year contributed to the Russian Refugees Relief Fund. By August 1899 Charles was no longer living there, since an advertisement in August of that year looks for a servant for 'two ladies, quiet place; no washing'.

Catherine died on 27 January 1901, and in the March census Camilla, now 65, was living alone with one servant, Isabella Bannerman, a 54-year-old widow from Haddington. Charles appears to have been out of the country at this time, and he died in Lasswade, Midlothian in 1924, at the age of 82.

CHAPTER 6

The families

~

In quite a number of cases, families were linked to Dalrymple Crescent in a less simple way. Some families lived in more than one house in the street, and in other cases, more than one member of the family lived in the street.

Thomas Ogilvy Cownie rented No 20 in 1877 and 1878, and then bought No 26, where he and his family lived until the end of the century. His brother James Gibb Cownie rented No 21 in 1877. David Crouch rented No 21 from 1881 to 1893 and his brother Henry Brougham Crouch rented No 23 from 1869 to 1873. Richard Lister bought No 11 in 1864 and sold it in 1869. He later rented No 22 from 1872 to 1876. Robert Middlemass bought No 12 (then known as 25 Findhorn Place) in 1862 and lived there until the end of the century. His son, John Middlemass bought No 6 in 1886 and lived there until 1897, when he sold it. He and his father also owned the land on which No 24 was built, although they never lived there. David Cowan Mudie bought No 9 in 1865 and lived there until 1871. He then bought No 10, and moved into it, renting out No 9. After his death in 1893, his family continued to rent out both houses. Margaret Rosie rented No 20 from 1868 to 1871 and then rented No 17 in 1872 and 1873. Andrew Usher rented No 9 from 1878 to 1888, and his brother Harry Lawrence Usher rented No 10 from 1895 to 1898.

THE COWNIE FAMILY

William Cownie was a clothier, who had a shop at 63 South Bridge.

He was born in Alyth, Perthshire in 1798. He married Helen Gibb, who was about five years younger. In 1841 they were living at 5 South College Street, with five children:[1] William, born in Alyth in 1826, David, born in Alyth in 1828, Jane (or Jean), born in 1832, James Gibb, born in May 1836 and Thomas Ogilvie, born in Edinburgh in January 1840.

Young William's occupation is given as apprentice clothier, and David's as apprentice pawnbroker. An advertisement from *The Scotsman* in 1862 gives us an idea of the family business.

w. COWNIE & SONS, Clothiers, 63 South Bridge, invite attention to the large and Varied Stock of SCOTCH TWEEDS and other GOODS, suitable for the present Season, embracing the *Newest Styles and Best Qualities Manufactured*, at the most Moderate Prices.

GENTLEMEN'S CLOTHING made to Order on the Premises
by First-Class Workmen
DRESS SUITS, from 65s. to 110s.
SCOTCH TWEED DO. from 40s. to 90s.
HATS, SHIRTS, GLOVES, TIES, HOSIERY, &C.

By this time two more children had been born, Alexander Brodie Cownie in 1842, and Helen Alison Hutton Cownie in 1846. The younger William was now 36, David was 34, James was 26 and Thomas was 22. All were working for the firm.

William senior died on 24 May 1864, when he was living in Hope Terrace, off Whitehouse Loan. Almost immediately, on 4 June 1864, the younger William put an advertisement in *The Scotsman*:

MONDAY THE 6TH
WILLIAM COWNIE, having withdrawn from the Firm of w.
COWNIE & SONS, SOUTH BRIDGE, begs to inform his Friends and the Public that he will OPEN these Extensive and Commodious PREMISES, No 5 NICOLSON STREET on MONDAY THE 6TH INSTANT, with a Large and Varied Stock

of Goods for LADIES' and GENTLEMEN'S WEAR, all in the most FASHIONABLE STYLES and FABRICS, at UNUSUALLY LOW PRICES.

To the various Branches carried out by the old Firm, W.C. has added that of DRESSMAKING, under the superintendance of a most experienced hand.

WILLIAM COWNIE,
TAILOR, CLOTHIER AND GENERAL DRAPER,
5 NICOLSON STREET.

The other brothers continued to run the original firm.

Ten years later, in 1877, both Thomas and James moved into Dalrymple Crescent. Thomas rented No 20 and James No 21. Both were married by this time, and both had baby daughters, born four months apart.

Thomas had married Margaret Howie Smith at Alyth in March 1865, and James had married Helen Heron in Edinburgh in 1864. By this time, in 1877, Thomas and Margaret already had seven children: Margaret Howie, born on 13 February 1866, Helen Gibb, 9 September 1867, Jane, 14 October 1869, William Brodie, 9 March 1871, David Smith, 23 January 1873, Isabella Hogg, 4 Dec 1874 and Annie, born in 1876.

The new arrival was Ruth, born on 26 December 1877, and announced in *The Scotsman* two days later.

James and Helen also had a large family: Mary Brown, born 1 July 1865, Edward William, 19 May 1867, Henry, 26 Nov 1868, Charles James, 19 March 1873, Ethel Helen Gibb, 19 October 1874 and Colin Brown, born in 1876.

In January 1878 they advertised in *The Scotsman* for a servant '(good, general), able to Wash', and announced the birth of their new baby on 24 April 1878. She was Elspeth Brown H. Cownie, born the previous day. They also had another son, Allan, who was born in 1871 but died four years later.

They must have moved almost immediately, as the house was

advertised to let on 2 May. The 1881 census shows them living at 7 Brunstane Road. Another son, Douglas had been born by then, and they were to have two more children: Ernest, born in 1883, and Daisy Jane, born in 1885.

According to the Register of Sasines, Thomas bought 'lot 235 on the Feuing plan' part of the estate of the late John Paterson. This would imply that he had the house (No 26) built, and he certainly borrowed money at that time. By 1881 the family had moved in, and a son, Thomas, had been born in 1879. Three more children were to be born: John Smith Cownie in October 1882, Mary in 1884, and Walter in 1887. At the time of the 1881 census they had two servants, Jessie Kean, 18, from Peebles-shire and Elizabeth Lindsay, 16, from Kirriemuir.

The family were still at No 26 in 1891. Thomas was now 50 and Margaret was 47. Eleven children were living at home, Margaret junior having married Frederick Sly in 1889. In addition, Margaret's sister, Mrs Jean Galloway was staying with them at the time of the census. She was ten years older than Margaret, living in Alyth, and married to a mechanic, William Galloway. Their two servants were now a housemaid, Jessie McInnes, 16 and a cook, Mary Mathieson, 18, both from Edinburgh.

Between 1881 and 1891, the family had seen three deaths. In July 1884, James and Thomas's mother, Helen Gibb Cownie, died at Windsor Villa, Wardie Road, aged about 80. In April of the same year, their brother David Cownie had died aged 56. He had also worked in the family business, and left a wife and nine children. In March 1890, their sister, Jane, who had not married, and had been living with their mother in Windsor Villa, died at the age of 58.

In the 1890s two of Thomas' daughters were married: Helen to John Edward Philpott in 1893 and Jane to Walter Midgely Robertshaw in 1895.

Then, on 3 January 1898 Thomas died. The story related by his great-grandson was that he was coming home from work on a tramcar, riding on the top floor. As he started down the stair, he tripped, fell down the stairs, and hit his head.[2]

The house was advertised to be sold by auction on 2 February of the same year, but plans must have changed, because Margaret still owned it and was living in it in 1901. By this time, Annie had married John Henry Morgan in 1898 and Isabella married George Montague Philpott, the brother of John Philpott, in 1899. However Isabella was living at No 26 at the time of the census, and the three unmarried sons, David, Thomas and Walter, were also living at home. David was a clothier, Thomas an insurance clerk, and Walter a tailor's apprentice. Ruth, aged 23, and Mary, 18, were also living at home. With them was Margaret's unmarried niece, Margaret Galloway, the daughter of Jean, who had been staying with them in 1891. Margaret was 46, and was born in Alyth. There was one servant, Mary Byrne, 23, from Newcraighall near Edinburgh.

WILLIAM CROUCH AND SONS

The advertisements in *The Scotsman* give a vivid picture of the fortunes of a merchant family in Victorian Edinburgh.

William Crouch was a watchmaker and jeweller who was born in Edinburgh in 1797 or 1798. In June 1829 he married Jane Pratt, who also came from Edinburgh, and was born in October 1804. They had eight children altogether. At the time of the 1841 census they were living at 37 North Bridge, with five children: Morgan, born in May 1831, Jane, born in April 1834, Henry, born in June 1836, David, born in January 1838 and William Albert, born in June 1840.

Three more children were to be born in the ensuing years: Joseph in June 1842, Anne in November 1849 and Isabella in March 1851. Then in February 1858, *The Scotsman* reported the death of his eldest daughter Jane. At this time the family was living at 11 Lutton Place, and the shop was at 40 North Bridge.

In February 1866 the shop premises at 32 North Bridge were put up for auction.

SHOP NO 32 NORTH BRIDGE with Extensive PREMISES below, occupied by Messrs Wm Crouch & Son, Jewellers. Rent £150.

1a. Dalrymple Crescent in 2008. Photograph by T. Lamb

1b. Edinburgh in 1816, from James Knox, Map of the Shires of Edinburgh. Reproduced by permission of the Trustees of the National Library of Scotland

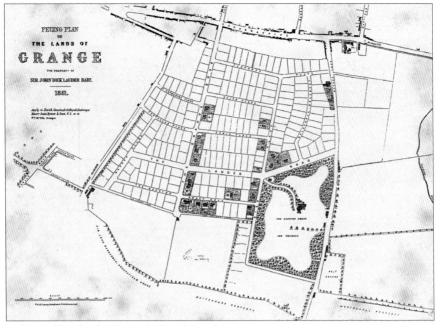

2a. Feuing Plan for the Grange by David Cousins, 1851
Reproduced by permission of the Grange Association

2b. The lot numbers of the 'pieces of land' in Dalrymple Crescent, auctioned in 1862 and 1864

It is Contracted and agreed between the parties following viz, Sir John Dick Lauder of Grange and Fountainhall, Baronet, Heir of Entail in possession of the estate of Grange, and others with consent of Robert Hunter, Sculptor South Clerk Street Edinburgh, on the one part, and Samuel Hunter, Sculptor, Bellevue Broughton, Edinburgh, on the other part, in manner following. That is to say the said Sir John Dick Lauder, considering, that under the authority, and by virtue of an Act of Parliament dated the twenty second day of June Eighteen hundred and twenty five, entituled " An act to enable Sir Thomas "Dick Lauder, Baronet, and the heirs of entail succeeding to him in the estate "of Grange, to grant feus thereof upon certain terms and conditions;" as also under the authority of the Lord Benholme, Ordinary on the Bills in the Court of Session in Scotland, obtained upon the petition and application of the said Sir John Dick Lauder, and service thereof, and the previous advertisements, all as required by the said Act, the said Sir John Dick Lauder, upon the thirty first day of March eighteen hundred and sixty two, exposed by public auction certain portions or pieces of land, being parts of the entailed lands and estate of Grange, to be let, granted, or dis-posed in feu farm in sixty six different lots, the piece of ground here-inafter disposed being lot number one hundred and eighty two thereof and numbered one hundred and eighty two on a Feuing Plan prepared by Robert Reid Raeburn, architect in Edinburgh, dated first April Eigh-teen hundred and fifty eight, referred to in the Articles of Roup after men-tioned, and signed by the said Sir John Dick Lauder, as relative to the foresaid petition; and that conform to, and in terms of, Articles and Conditions of Auction or Roup, subscribed by the said Sir John Dick Lauder upon the twelfth day of March Eighteen hundred and sixty two, and to which the authority of the said Lord Ordinary was duly interponed, as required by the said Act; By which Articles it is inter alia declared, that the pieces of ground or feus therein described are to be measured and staked off by the said Robert Reid Raeburn, or by any other architect or surveyor to be appointed by the said Sir John Dick Lauder, or the heirs of entail succeeding to him in the said estate of Grange and whose measurements should be final and binding on the feuars, and not sub-ject to challenge or objection on any ground whatever; and further, that the feuars were to have the privilege or use of the roads or streets called Mansion house Road, Dick Place, Findhorn Place, The Lauder Road, Cumin Place, The Grange Road, Tantallon Place, Seton Place, Saint Catherine Place, and Dalrymple Crescent, so soon as the said several roads or streets should have been formed and completed all as therein described; and the said several roads or streets, including the footpaths there mentioned, being of the respective breadths specified in the said Articles and Conditions of Roup; and it is by the said articles also declared, that the pieces of ground or feus situated in the said road or street of Dalrymple Crescent, in which road or street the lot or piece of ground herein after disposed is situated, were to be feued only for the purpose of building villas or dwelling houses, and offices, or other-wise as therein mentioned, the said villas or dwelling houses to be of two storeys and attics, with the exception of those on the pieces of ground

Jn. Dick Lauder

Wm. Fraser

Robert Hunter

Samuel Hunter

3. The last page of a Feu Contract for a house in Dalrymple Crescent

Right. 4a. Article reporting the murder of Marion and Elizabeth Hunter, October 1865. *The Scotsman* archive

Below. 4b. Advertisement for Samuel Hunter, Builder and Sculptor, Edinburgh and Leith Post Office Directory 1877. Reproduced by permission of Edinburgh City Library

DREADFUL TRAGEDY AT THE GRANGE

MURDER BY A MANIAC OF HIS MOTHER AND SISTER.

A DREADFUL tragedy was enacted in Dalrymple Crescent, Grange, yesterday morning, in the deliberate murder by a maniac of his mother and sister. The names of the unhappy victims of the murder were Mrs Hunter, aged 68, wife of Robert Hunter, sculptor, and her eldest daughter, Elizabeth Hunter, aged 42. The murderer is John Hunter, aged about 30. The young man has been weakly in body, and erratic in his disposition, from his boyhood. Within the last six years, however, it has been found necessary by his friends to keep him in close confinement within his father's house, though not under restraint—his fatuity being apparently of so mild and inoffensive a type that no danger was apprehended from the measure of freedom that was allowed him. The theory of the murder is, that the young man, who has been exhibiting some symptoms of restlessness within the last few days, was attempting to leave the house, when he was interrupted by his mother and sister, and that, irritated by their interference, he committed the deed. At the same time, it is apparent from his having armed himself with an iron rod with which he committed the murder that he was prepared to resist any attempt to detain him. Shortly after ten o'clock, he was seen from the window of a neighbouring house in the flower-plot in front of his father's house, making his way to the street; the two ladies following, and attempting to stay him from leaving. Outside the gate, his mother laid her hand on his shoulder, and appeared to be remonstrating with him, when he turned round upon her, and knocked down first his mother and afterwards his sister with a piece of iron bar, and afterwards hit them repeatedly while they were lying on the pavement on which they had fallen. The deaths of both ladies must have been instantaneous.

I Dalrymple Crescent, Edinboro

Above. 5a. No 1 Dalrymple Crescent around 1900. Malcolm Cant Collection

Left. 5b. Jessie Ann Willison (née Bett). Reproduced by kind permission of Anne Stewart

6a. The Willison family circa 1888. *Left to right;* Douglas, Jessie Ann Bett, Toosie (Ida), Campbell, Ella, John, Jenny, John Willison and James. Reproduced by kind permission of Anne Stewart

6b. Advertisement for Brechin Brothers, Edinburgh and Leith Post Office Directory 1894. Reproduced by permission of Edinburgh City Library

7a. No 9 Dalrymple Crescent in 2007. Photograph by T. Lamb

7b. Sketch of No 10 Dalrymple Crescent in 1991. Reproduced by kind permission of the present owners

8a. No 11 Dalrymple Crescent at the end of the 19th century. Malcolm Cant Collection

8b. Headstone of the family of Duncan Anderson, Grange Cemetery.
Photograph by Joanne Lamb

9. Advertisement for Banks Printing Company, Edinburgh and Leith Post Office Directory 1895. Reproduced by permission of Edinburgh City Library

10a. No 13 Dalrymple Crescent in 2010. Photograph by Joanne Lamb

10b. No 14 Dalrymple Crescent in 2010. Photograph by Joanne Lamb

Left. 11a. Portrait of Benjamin Peach. IPR/128-15CT British Geological Survey ©NERC. All rights Reserved

Below. 11b. Brankholm House: a water-colour by Benjamin Peach. IPR/128-15CT British Geological Survey ©NERC. All rights reserved

12a. Professor Donald MacKinnon.
Reproduced by kind permission of
Professor John W. Sheets

12b. Catherine MacKinnon (née MacPhee).
Reproduced by kind permission of
Professor John W. Sheets

12c. Nos 18 and 19 Dalrymple Crescent in 2010. Photograph by Joanne Lamb

13. Sir John Sibbald, MD, FRCPE, FRCSE, FRSE. Reproduced by kind permission of the Royal College of Physicians of Edinburgh

14. Rev. James T. Stuart, first Minister of Mayfield Free Church. Reproduced by kind permission of William Mearns

MAYFIELD · FREE · CHURCH · N·B · HIPPOLYTE · J · BLANC · A·R·S·A · ARCH[T]

15. Mayfield Free Church, 1894. Reproduced by kind permission of William Mearns

16a. No 24 Dalrymple Crescent in 2010. Photograph by Joanne Lamb

16b. No 25 Dalrymple Crescent in 2010. Photograph by Joanne Lamb

Left. 17a. No 26 Dalrymple Crescent (Greenbank) around 1890. Reproduced by kind permission of Andrew Carnon

Below. 17b. No 26 Dalrymple Crescent in 2010. Photograph by Joanne Lamb

Right. 18a. Headstone of the family of William Crouch, Grange Cemetery. Photograph by Joanne Lamb

Below. 18b. The fashions of the century: 1860. From 'Edinburgh in the Nineteenth Century', W. M. Gilbert

1860.

19. Victorian wallpaper in Dalrymple Crescent. Photograph by Joanne Lamb

20a. John Middlemass and two sisters, 1866. Photograph by David Doull, reproduced by permission of Edinburgh City Library

20b. Fashion plate of 1875. From 'A Hundred Years in Princes Street' illustrated by C. Walter Hodges

Left. 21a. The fashions of the century: 1890 and 1900. From 'Edinburgh in the Nineteenth Century', W. M. Gilbert

Below. 21b. No 3 Dalrymple Crescent in 2010. Photograph by Joanne Lamb

1890.   1900.

22a. Thomas and Margaret Cownie, and their children. circa 1886. *Left to right;* Maggie, Nellie, Walter, Margaret, Tom, Jack, Willie, May, Thomas, Annie, Janie, Bella, David and Ruth. Reproduced by kind permission of Andrew Carnon

22b. Wedding group at the marriage of Margaret Cownie and Frederick Sly, 1889. Reproduced by kind permission of Andrew Carnon

Left. 23a. Fashion plate of 1895. From 'A Hundred Years in Princes Street' illustrated by C. Walter Hodges

Below. 23b. Dalrymple Crescent street party, 2008. Photograph by Joanne Lamb

1895

24a. Edinburgh and Leith, extracted from: Plate 63 of J. G. Bartholomew's Survey Atlas of Scotland, 1912. Reproduced by permission of the Trustees of the National Library of Scotland

24b. South Edinburgh, extracted from: Plate 63 of J. G. Bartholomew's Survey Atlas of Scotland, 1912. Reproduced by permission of the Trustees of the National Library of Scotland

Although the property changed hands, the firm continued to operate from 32 North Bridge. In March 1867, *The Scotsman* printed an article that stated that the Queen Mary Casket, which had been designed and manufactured for the Paris Exhibition by 'Messrs W. Crouch and Sons', was on view at their showrooms in North Bridge. It seems that the shop also acted as a repository for lost and found jewellery, as illustrated by these advertisements from 1865 and 1869:

> LOST, on Wednesday evening, between Queen Street Hall and Bank Street, an EARDROP, Pink Topaz Set in Gold. Finder Rewarded. Apply at William Crouch & Son's, 32 North Bridge.

and

> BROOCH, Oval Gold, Blue Enamelled and Pearls, between Morningside and Portobello, last Monday. Apply Messrs W. Crouch & Son, 32 North Bridge.

Meanwhile, Henry Brougham Crouch married Maria Jane Hunter in 1869, and they moved into No 23 Dalrymple Crescent in the same year. Maria was born in Edinburgh in 1851, making her 13 years younger than Henry. He had not gone into the family business, but set up on his own as a goldsmith. In the 1871 census Henry and Maria had a boarder, Maria Louisa Laing, aged 22, and a servant, Anne Howie, 21, both of whom came from Edinburgh.

Henry had established a business at 27 Hanover Street, and in November 1875 a special announcement offered for sale the astronomical instruments in solid silver that had been in the possession of Sir John Herschel, the celebrated astronomer. In March 1877 he attended the tenth annual soirée of the goldsmiths of Edinburgh. In 1876 his home address was 7 Mansionhouse Road, and by 1881 he and Maria had moved to 1 Cobden Road. At the time of the census they had two children, Henry aged six, and Maria aged four.

Meantime the family business had expanded, and in May 1872 it was described as 'Manufacturing Jewellers, Silversmiths, Watch and

Clock Makers, based at 32 North Bridge Edinburgh and 221 and 264 Regent Street London'. However, the advertisement in *The Scotsman* announced that stock was being sold off at 20% below usual prices, due to the 'dissolution of the partnership' of 'William Crouch and Sons'.

A similar advertisement appeared in November 1874. The only address given now was 32 North Bridge, but owing to 'a change in their Firm' they were offering their stock at 20% to 50% below normal. In 1875 much of the stock was auctioned off.

Then, in February 1877, David, 'having succeeded to the old established business carried on by Wm Crouch & Son, 32 North Bridge' announced that he was selling 'a large and well-assorted stock of first class jewellery and plate' at a 20% reduction. From this time, the firm was referred to as 'W. Crouch and Son'.

In June 1879 the firm was tangentially involved in a bankruptcy case, and *The Scotsman* reported the details of the Court hearing quite fully. They were minor creditors, but the case is interesting for the light it throws on the financial difficulties of Victorian women.

Two sisters, Helen and Elizabeth Mackay were the subjects of the bankruptcy case. They had lived with their father, who had died in 1868. Their brother, Robert who was the heir, had made an annuity to each of them of £250 a year, and this was their only income. He had married in 1869, but had no family, and when he died he left the bulk of the estate to his widow. The elder sister spoke for them, trying to explain why they had got into financial difficulties. She had paid some of her father's debts, and had received an advance of £200 from the annuity to furnish the house where they were living.

> Her liabilities exceeded her income because of the expense of her fathers & sisters illnesses & she had given away more than she should have done to the needy poor.

She had no idea that her liabilities were so extensive. She was willing to restrict her expenditure so that her creditors could receive a portion of the annuity.

With regard to a claim made by Messrs Crouch, jewellers,
Edinburgh, for jewellery ... she said that the articles ... were
returned to Messrs Crouch, and she therefore did not
consider that the account was due.

She had tried to retrench before, but failed because her sister needed
medical attendance. She had never represented to her creditors that
she had been left annuities and ready cash, nor that she was not in
debt, nor that she kept a carriage, neither did she represent herself as
a close relation to Sir William Forbes with an account at the Union
Bank. She might have said that her aunt was a granddaughter of Sir
William, which was a fact! The case was held at the Edinburgh
Bankruptcy Court, and the Sheriff administered 'the oath' – the
sisters' liabilities were held to be £1095 between them. Their assets
were the interest from the annuities. It seems that the Sheriff was
satisfied that the debt could be paid off.

In 1881 David married Margaret Bertram, the daughter of
George Bertram, the founder of Bertram of Sciennes, who were
manufacturers of paper-making machinery. She was the sister of
David Noble Bertram, who lived at No 3 between 1886 and 1889.
David and Margaret Crouch lived at 21 Dalrymple Crescent from
1881 until 1893. Margaret was four years younger than David. At the
time of the 1881 census they had one servant, Mary McGaugh, 29,
from Ireland.

His father and mother, William and Jane were now living at St
Anne's Villa, Craigmillar Road with Isabella, who was the only one of
the children still at home. William was now 83, and he died in
September 1881.

In the early 1880s, W. Crouch and Son, under David, continued
to advertise in *The Scotsman*, with grand clearance sales, and
Christmas specials at 32 North Bridge (only address). At the
International Forestry Exhibition held in Donaldson's Hospital in
July 1884, several jewellers were exhibitors, including W. Crouch &
Son:

Several of Messrs Crouch's exhibits are made of oak from St

Giles Cathedral. This firm also show new brooches made of natural Scottish hazel nuts and English filberts.

In February 1885, a removal sale was advertised, as the business was moving to 'large and Central premises in 56 New Buildings North Bridge (Opposite the general Post Office)'.

In 1886, a very different type of story was reported in *The Scotsman:*

> William Crouch, jeweller, 21 Dalrymple Crescent, and George McIntosh, cattle-drover, Grassmarket, were remitted to the Sheriff for an alleged contravention of the Criminal Law Amendment Act

This was David's brother William Albert, who had at one time lived in London, but was now back in Edinburgh. The Criminal Law Amendment Act of 1885 was aimed at protecting girls from under-age sex and prostitution, but also had a section which criminalized male homosexuality.

The family was in the news again in July 1887. At court, a John Davidson was charged with stealing a 'large number of articles' from several jewellers, including William Crouch and Son, and Henry Brougham Crouch (whose shop was now in Princes Street). Davidson had been employed by these jewellers at the time of the thefts, and had an accomplice, Annie Hamilton. The judge said that Davidson had betrayed a position of trust, and sentenced him to 5 years penal servitude, but Hamilton was regarded as being under his influence, and was sentenced relatively lightly, being given 3 months imprisonment.

In 1887 Henry was living at 13 Morningside Drive, and his business address was 67 Princes Street. However in October of that year, 'Henry Brougham Crouch, Goldsmith and Jeweller, 67 Princes Street, Edinburgh' was offered for sale. A liquidation sale offered 25% off stock, but in addition, 'Offers for the entire stock and business' would be received by his solicitor.

1888 was an eventful year for the Crouch family. In January there was an 'Extraordinary Sequel to a Criminal Prosecution' (*The Scotsman*). John Davidson, who had been the defendant in the 1887 jewellery thefts, had pleaded guilty to the theft of 248 articles, about half of the 477 quoted in the indictment. Most of the stolen goods were still in the hands of the Procurator Fiscal. Davidson claimed that the other 229 goods were his, and that he had bought them at auction sales. It transpired that all the articles except 'a silver bouquet holder and a gold ring' were claimed by other people, and the judge accepted these claims. It appears that when the police had searched the house before the original trial, the jewellery had been found hidden in different parts of the house, in a hole behind the skirting in the bathroom, for example. Davidson was ordered to pay expenses. So the Crouch family were able to retrieve all the property stolen from them.

Also in January, Henry and David's mother, Jane, died at the age of 85, and a month later their brother William Albert died at David's house in 21 Dalrymple Crescent, at the age of 48.

In March, 'owing to the winding up of the trust Estate of the late Wm Crouch', the shop on North Bridge was having another sale.

Henry's wife Maria Jane Crouch died in 1891 at the age of 49. David and Margaret were still living at 21 Dalrymple Crescent, where, at the time of the census, they had two servants. The cook, Isabella Mackenzie, aged 30, was from Fort Augustus, and the waiting maid, Elizabeth McNabola, aged 19, was from Ireland. David moved to 34 Mayfield Terrace in 1893.

W. Crouch & Son continued to advertise and give discounts until the end of the century. In March 1895 there was a Compulsory Sale due to the rebuilding of North Bridge. The foundation stone for the new bridge was laid by the Lord Provost in May 1896, and the bridge was opened in September 1897. Finally in May 1897, another sale was advertised. The address was given as 32 North Bridge, and the firm had to vacate the premises, due to the demolition of the property. Again discounts of 30% to 50% were advertised.

Henry Brougham Crouch died in Dumfries, in 1902 at the age of 65. Isabella died in 1929, and is buried in Grange Cemetery along with her parents and brother William Albert. (Plate 18a)

RICHARD LISTER

Richard Lister was a commercial traveller who bought No 11
Dalrymple Crescent in May 1864. At the time he was living at 41
South Clerk Street, with his wife Mary Anne and son, also Richard.
Richard senior was born in 1828, and his wife a year earlier. Young
Richard was 12 at the time of the 1861 census. All three were born in
England. A daughter, Gertrude was born in July 1861, and a second
daughter, Rose was born at No 11 in March 1865.

On 15 March 1869 *The Scotsman* reported on Warrender Golf
Club's spring meeting, where they competed for the Silver Claret Jug.
A Richard Lister came sixth, and won a dozen golf balls. The name is
sufficiently unusual for us to be reasonably certain that it was the
same Richard Lister.

He advertised the house for sale in *The Scotsman* of 2 March
1870, and repeated the advertisement on 16 and 25 March. The sale to
Henry Haig Banks was completed in May 1870. The family do not
appear to have been in Scotland in 1871, but in 1872 they rented
No 22 Dalrymple Crescent.

In February 1873 *The Scotsman* described a small debt case
against 'Mr Lister, Dalrymple Crescent'. Elizabeth Easton sued him
for £1-16s-8d, being wages for one month and 25 days. The defence
claimed that she had 'packed up her boxes and left without a
moment's notice'. She replied that she had been 'dismissed by her
mistress, and was not allowed to serve until the end of the month'.
The bench advised the defender to pay the claim, 'as the money had
been worked for', and he agreed.

Richard Lister died on 26 May 1876 'in his 49th year', and *The
Scotsman* reported his death. In 1881 Mary Anne Lister was an
annuitant living at 14 Cairds Row in the parish of Inveresk, with
Gertrude and Rose, both of whom are described as school teachers.

ROBERT AND JOHN MIDDLEMASS

Throughout Victorian times the house built on lot 184 was known as

25 Findhorn Place, but later it was renumbered as 12 Dalrymple Crescent. It was feued by Robert Middlemass, and he and his family lived there throughout the period.

Middlemass' Biscuit Factory was started in 1835 by Robert Middlemass on a site on the northeast corner of West Preston Street. The factory later moved to Causewayside. Prior to Middlemass' enterprise, biscuit making in the area had originated in Leith where substantial 'ship's biscuits' were produced. By 1897, the distinctive building extended to Upper Gray Street and fronted on to Salisbury Place. At first, Middlemass' biscuits were made and packaged by hand, but by 1896, machinery had been introduced.

The factory produced their famous 'Albert Biscuit' during Queen Victoria's reign, but their proudest achievement was the 'invention' of the 'Digestive' biscuit, destined to become a household name. However in 1869, Robert was engaged in an exchange of letters to *The Scotsman* with 'Mackenzie and Mackenzie, purveyors of biscuits to Her Majesty'. The issue concerned whether Robert had copied the label that Mackenzie and Mackenzie used for their Albert biscuits. Robert refuted the claim in some detail. In a column in *The Scotsman* he says:

> I may add that any one who cares to examine the two labels will see that they are dissimilar in all essential particulars; while the *'Trade Marks'* which stamp publicly the manufacture of each party, are as unlike each other as any two Trade marks can possibly be. No one, having the use of his eyes, can mistake my 'Spread Eagle' for my assailants' 'Star of Denmark',
>
> In proof of the dissimilarity of the Labels and of the unfounded statement that I sought to imitate Messrs Mackenzie's, I refer to the following letter from the eminent firm by which my London label was designed and executed:

Atlas Paper Works Borough Road
London 24th May 1869
Having recently furnished Mr Middlemass of

Edinburgh with a very large quantity of labels for his 'Albert Biscuit' Tins, and seeing the same referred to in an unpleasant manner in 'Mackenzie & Mackenzie's' Advertisement, we beg to state we were not instructed to follow or imitate any label; and on our attention being again called to the label, we find that in every detail it is totally distinct, and could not possibly be mistaken for that of the opposing firm. – We are &c.

(Signed) CRESCENS ROBINSON & CO

Their views are fully corroborated by Messrs Banks & Co. of Edinburgh, who state the result of their examination of the labels in these terms:

10 North St David Street
Edinburgh, May 26 1869
We have examined the labels used by Mr Middlemass and Messrs Mackenzie & Mackenzie for Albert Biscuit Canisters and find, although there may be some trifling resemblance in a few unimportant details, that the Trade Mark is so *distinct* in character, and the name of the maker so boldly printed on each, that no one could possibly mistake the one for the other.

(Signed) BANKS & Co
Engravers & Steam Printers

ROBERT MIDDLEMASS
PRESTON STREET 26 MAY 1869

Robert Middlemass was born in Peebles in February 1819. He married Helen Mathieson from Ettrick in June 1851. She was about ten years younger than him. They had nine children, all of whom were born in Edinburgh: John born in March 1852, Agnes in October 1853, Christiana in November 1855, Helen in October 1857, Mary in

October 1859, Jane in October 1861, George in March 1864, Robert in June 1866 and Annie in June 1868.

In 1866 the photographer David Doull took a photograph of John and two of his sisters, probably Jane and Mary. David Doull also took photographs of the children of Robert's brother, James Middlemass who lived at 8 Dick Place. James Middlemass and his brother Andrew, owned J. & A. Middlemass, wholesale and retail clothiers, robemakers, shirtmakers and outfitters of 16, 18, 20 South Bridge.

In 1871 Robert was living in the house, which had twelve rooms, with Helen and the nine children. They had two servants, Janet Hodge, 31, from Kilconquhar, Fife, and Isabella Cunningham, 18, from Falkirk.

In 1876 the architect Charles Leadbetter extended or modified the house, which was now known as Rathan, and by the 1881 census it had 16 rooms. The Journal of Decorative Art of 1877[3] described it as a 'luxurious decorative scheme by Joseph Shaw & Co'.

At the time of the 1881 census, Robert was visiting a friend, Robert Stewart, a farmer who lived near Peebles. Helen was staying in the house with four children: Christiana, Mary, Robert and Anne. They had three servants: Jane Campbell, 27, from Elgin, Isabella Wilson, 24, from Linlithgow, and Elsie Irving, 18, from Forres.

Robert was away again at the census of 1891, when Helen was living with four unmarried children: Christiana, now 35, Jane, 29, Robert Lee, 24, also a biscuit manufacturer, and Annie, 22. Also at the house was Agnes, whose married name was Johnston, and her son, Henry, aged 4. There were two servants, a housemaid, Joan Puddock, 17, from Grange in Banffshire, and a laundry maid, Jane Lawrie, 21, from Kirknewton.

In 1901, Robert, now 82, was at home at the time of the census, but Helen was not. With Robert was his son, Robert Lee. Young Helen was a widow aged 42, and was staying at the house with her two children: Robert M. Donald, 18, who was a laboratory apprentice, and Helen E. Donald, aged 16 and at school. There were two servants. Elizabeth Milne, 20, from Ruthven, Banffshire, and the cook, Jane McCall, 27, from Ireland.

Robert died in 1904. The West Blacket Association's newsletter[4] reports that he and his family did much for the social welfare of the factory's neighbourhood. The factory closed in 1974 and when plans were drawn up for the extension of the National Library of Scotland in 1983, the biscuit factory was demolished.

John Middlemass, the eldest son, also had connections with Dalrymple Crescent. He was born in 1852, and in 1877 he married Annie Grant, a year younger than him, who came from Cupar in Fife. In 1881 they were living at 80 South Clerk Street, and John's occupation was given as baker. A year later, in 1882, John bought the land on which No 24 Dalrymple Crescent later stood, but he did not develop it, and sold it to his father in 1886. He then bought No 6 Dalrymple Crescent, and lived there from 1886 until 1897, but at the time of the 1891 census, there was nobody at home. They moved to 137 Warrender Park Road, where John died in December 1898. Ann was living there in 1901, with her niece, Louise Grant, who was 17, and a draper's shopkeeper.

DAVID COWAN MUDIE

David Mudie was born in St Andrews in April 1816, the son of William Mudie, a bookseller, and Elizabeth Cowan.[5] He spent seven years of his boyhood in Shetland with his grandmother, Elizabeth Tod or Cowan and Aunt Margaret Cowan who kept house for his uncle, Rev. Charles Cowan, at the manse of Fetlar. He graduated from St Andrews University in 1832 with a degree in mathematics. He trained as an engineer and went into partnership with Mr. Gershom Gourlay, forming the firm of Gourlay, Mudie and Co.[6]

Dundee in the 19th century had three locomotive factories. James and Charles Carmichael produced the first locomotives in Scotland in 1833 for the Dundee and Newtyle Railway. Kinmond Hutton & Steel started to build locomotives in 1838. Six were supplied to Glasgow, Paisley, Kilmarnock & Ayr Railway. These were sent dismantled by sea to Ayr and re-erected there. Three were sent to Canada and nine were supplied to Glasgow, Dumfries and Carlisle Railway. The third company, Stirling, James & Co, developed interests in steam engines and ships' machinery. In 1834 a locomotive named 'Trotter' was constructed for the Dundee & Newtyle Railway. Three locomotives were supplied to the Arbroath & Forfar Railway in 1838/9: Then about 1843 the company was taken over by Gourlay Mudie & Co., who built two locomotives for the Dundee, Perth and Aberdeen Railway in 1847/8, and a further two followed for the Dundee & Arbroath Railway.[7]

In 1846 they took ownership of the Dundee Foundry, which had been established about 1790 and was a pioneer in heavy engineering and machine-making in Dundee. The Foundry had made a conspicuous contribution to the building of locomotives for the Dundee and Newtyle and the Arbroath and Forfar Railways, and according to Professor Lythe:[8] 'In the engineering world of the 1830's and 1840's, "Dundee Foundry" was a name to conjure with.'

The firm was dissolved in 1853 and Mudie moved to Edinburgh where he took over the Panmure Foundry on the north side of the Canongate, which he managed until he retired. The Panmure foundry is mentioned in Cassell's *Old and New Edinburgh* by James Grant. Panmure Close leads off the Royal Mile, leading to Panmure House, former town residence of the Earls of Panmure, and home of Adam Smith from 1778 until his death in 1790,[9] but 'it became greatly altered after being brought into juxtaposition with the prosaic details of the Panmure Iron Foundry'.[10]

David Cowan Mudie married twice. His first wife was Isabella Petrie, whom he married in Edinburgh in July 1855, two years after he came to Edinburgh. They had a daughter, Isabella Elizabeth, who was born in March 1857. Isabella was the daughter of Alexander Petrie and Isabella Sim, and was born at Arbilot, now on the outskirts of Arbroath. Isabella senior died of tuberculosis in Panmure House in January 1862. Mudie moved into Dalrymple Crescent with his young daughter in 1865, and married Joanna Low Anderson in 1868. Joanna was born in Dundee in 1826.

At the time of the 1871 census they were living at No 9, and had a visitor, Jessie Bell, who was 17, a farmer's daughter, born in Anstruther. They had one servant, Mary Skinner, 28, from Pathhead in Fife.

They moved to No 10 in 1872, and Mudie retired in February 1875. In September 1877, 'D. C. Mudie, 10 Dalrymple Crescent' is reported to have donated £2 for famine relief in India. In 1880 Isabella junior married John Yeaman, a solicitor and banker from Alyth, Perthshire, and in 1881 they were living at the Royal Bank, Meigle, Perthshire. David Mudie and Joanna were not at home on census night, but were staying at 112 South Street, St Andrews, with one servant, Annie Taylor, aged 17. No 10 was only occupied by their servant, Christina Donald, 24, from Kincardineshire.

In November 1882, David Cowan Mudie was elected Fellow of the Society of Antiquaries of Scotland,[11] which was founded in 1780 and was incorporated by Royal Charter in 1783. It is the second oldest antiquarian society in Britain. The purpose of the Society is 'the Study of the Antiquities and History of Scotland, more especially by means of archaeological research'; the Society is still active today, concerned with every aspect of the human past in Scotland.

Joanna died in December 1887, and the 1891 census reports D. C. Mudie living alone with two servants: Elizabeth Home, a widow aged 49 from Balbigggin, Perthshire and Catherine Henderson, 14, from Branston Mains, Haddington. Mudie died at No 10 in April 1893.

MARGARET ROSIE

Margaret Rosie was a widowed teacher, born in Edinburgh in September 1820. Her parents were John Leitch and Catherine Calder. She ran a boarding school, and was based first in No 20, and then in No 17. She was living at No 20 at the time of the 1871 census. With her was her unmarried sister, Johanna Leitch, also a teacher, some seven years younger. Their niece, Catherine Walker Leitch, aged 20, was visiting at the time of the census. She was the daughter of their sister, Catherine, who married Alexander Leitch. In addition, they had four boarders, all scholars. Three were from Paisley: Helen Symington, 17, Jeanie Abercrombie, 19, Fanny Begg, 14. Jeanie Smith, 13, was from London. In addition they had three servants, sisters from the Isle of

Mull. They were Grace McDiarmid, 21, Flora, 19, and Marion, 17.

They moved to No 17 in 1872 and were there until 1874. By 1881 they had moved into new premises at 16 Merchiston Avenue. There were still only three boarders, Eliza Fairweather, 16, from Brechin, Annie Hewat, 17, born in Edinburgh, and Ronald Mackenzie, 15, from Beauly in Inverness. As well as Joanna (or Johanna) there was a governess, Elise Klerigenberg from Detmold and a visitor from Stow, Maggie Gibson, aged 18. There were two servants.

Margaret died in February 1897, aged 75. At the time she was living at 13 Hartington Gardens. Her niece Catherine also lived at 13 Hartington Gardens, and she died in January 1900, aged 49.

THE USHER FAMILY

The Usher family is an illustrious one, and a full history can be found in a book written in 1956, and freely available on the Internet.[12]

For our purposes, the story begins with James Usher who lived in West Nicholson Street in the 'old mansion house, the front of which is covered by a luxuriant pear tree'. This is now a pub called, appropriately enough, the Pear Tree. James started the brewery, and was later joined by his younger brother, Thomas. The firm of James and Thomas Usher was established, but James died comparatively young, and Thomas bought out his brother's interest. The company was registered as a limited company in 1895, as Thomas Usher & Son Limited, with Thomas as the first Chairman.

Thomas Usher was the father of Andrew William Usher and Harry Lawrence Usher, both of whom lived in Dalrymple Crescent. He was born in Edinburgh in 1821. Their mother was Eliza Caroline Henderson, born in May 1830. They had 12 children. Andrew was the eldest, and Harry the second youngest.[13]

Andrew William Usher was born in Edinburgh in July 1852, and married Isabella Purdie in July 1874. Isabella was also born in Edinburgh, in June 1852. They lived at 9 Dalrymple Crescent from 1878 to 1888, when they moved to 4 Bruntsfield Terrace. They had three children: George, born in June 1875, Edward, born in January

1880, and Dora, born in November 1887. In the 1881 census, they had one servant, Mary Wilson, 20, who came from Haddington.

When Thomas Usher died in 1896, Andrew William took on the running of the business. However he died shortly afterwards in June 1902, and is buried in the family vault in the Grange Cemetery. Edward died in the same year, in June, but George then became a director of the firm, although Andrew's brother, Thomas Leslie, was initially responsible for its running. George retired from the firm in 1948, and he died in January 1961, aged 85. Isabella died in January 1939, aged 87, and is also buried in Grange Cemetery with her husband. Dora lived until 1972, but she never married.

Harry Lawrence Usher was born in Edinburgh in November 1866 at the family home at 22 Minto Street, and was a pupil at the Edinburgh Academy. He married Alice Showell in July 1893 in Oldbury in Worcestershire. She was a brewer's daughter. They lived in 10 Dalrymple Crescent between 1896 and 1898. They had three children: Alice Margaret born in August 1894, Jean Elspeth born in March 1897, and Hester Showell Usher born in April 1899. By 1901 they were living at 51 Braid Avenue.

Harry was an accountant, and also one of the original directors of the Company when it was registered in 1895. Andrew William, Harry Lawrence, and Thomas Leslie are all mentioned as having taken shares when the company formed in 1895.

Harry Usher died on 26 Oct 1947 in Dunbar, East Lothian, at the age of 81.

CHAPTER 7

A servant's lot

~

In Victorian times, as in the present day, the houses of the Grange were much sought-after residential property. However, life in these houses was very different. There was no central heating, no vacuum cleaners, washing machines, or electric cookers. Instead there were servants. From the census returns for Dalrymple Crescent we can get some idea of who these servants were, and the people they worked for. Of course these were only the 'living in' servants, and we know from advertisements in *The Scotsman* ('Girl wanted, go home at night') that not all servants lived on the premises. However, we can build up a picture of the servants whose presence was recorded in the census. In the four census returns of the period there were 89 households. Ten of these had no servants, 46 had one servant, 29 had two servants, and four had three servants. The size of household varied considerably, from three servants looking after one householder, to one servant for a family of eight.

The following is a brief summary of the servants in Dalrymple Crescent and the families they worked for.

In 1871:

No 1 had five adults and one servant, aged 33.
No 2 had a married couple with a young son and one servant, aged 21.
No 3 had a bachelor with two servants: a widow and her daughter.
No 4 had a married couple in their 60s and one servant, aged 16.

No 5 had a married couple in their 50s and one servant, aged 21.

No 6 had five adults and one servant, aged 16.

No 7 had a married couple in their 60s and one servant, aged 23.

No 8 had five adults and no servants.

No 9 had a couple with a teenage daughter and one servant, aged 28.

No 10 had two elderly sisters and one servant, aged 26.

No 11 had a couple with three children and a baby, and one servant, aged 31.

No 13 had a couple with three children and one servant, aged 21.

No 14 had a married couple, three children, two visitors and two servants, in their 20s.

No 15 had four adults, three teenagers and one servant, aged 30.

No 16 had a married couple, a visitor, three young children and two servants, aged 34 and 19.

No 20 was a school, with three adults, three teenage boarders and three servants, who were sisters.

No 21 had a married couple, with two young children and a baby, with a general servant and a nursemaid.

No 22 had a widow, two visitors, four boarders and one servant, aged 19.

No 23 had a married couple, with a boarder and one servant, aged 21.

In 1881:

No 1 had two adults and one servant, aged 17.

No 2 had a married couple with a teenage son and one servant, aged 25.

No 3 had a married couple and one servant, aged 53.

No 4 had a married couple in their 70s and one servant, aged 18.

No 5 had a married couple in their 60s and one servant, aged 21.

No 6 had three adults, three lodgers and no servants.

No 7 had a married couple in their 70s and one servant, aged 46.

No 8 had a married couple with three teenage children, a lodger and no servants.

No 9 had a couple with two children and one servant, aged 20.

No 13 had a couple with four young children, and one servant, aged 19.

No 14 had a married couple in their 40s with two servants: a cook and a general servant.

No 17 had a widow with three older children, and one servant, aged 26.

No 18 had a married couple, a visitor, five children and two servants: a cook and a housemaid.

No 19 had a retired couple with no servants.

No 20 had five adults and one servant, aged 22.

No 21 had a married couple and one servant, aged 29.

No 23 had a widower with a young daughter, a nurse and a general servant.

No 25 had a married couple, with four young children, a baby and one servant, aged 26.

No 26 had a couple with ten children and two servants, aged 18 and 19.

No 27 had three adults and one servant, aged 22.

In 1891:

No 1 had two adults, and one servant, aged 49.

No 2 had one adult (72), a visitor and two servants: a cook and an attendant.

No 4 had a married couple, four daughters and one servant, aged 24.

No 5 had a married couple in their 70s and two servants.

No 7 had a widow in her 80s, a visitor and one servant, aged 21.

No 8 had four adults and no servants.

No 9 had three adults and one servant, aged 28.

No 10 had a widower with two servants, aged 49 and 14.

No 11 had a couple with four young children, an elderly father and three servants: a sick nurse, a nurse, and a general servant.

No 13 had a couple with three children and three servants: a cook, a nurse and a general servant.

No 14 had two unmarried sisters and one servant, aged 29.

No 16 had two adults, four children and one servant, aged 23.

No 17 had a couple in their 50s and two servants: a cook and a parlour maid.

No 19 had a married couple, with four children and two servants: a cook and a housemaid.

No 20 had three adults and two servants: a cook and a housemaid.

No 21 had a married couple and two servants: a cook, and a waiting maid.

No 22 had six adults, two teenagers and one servant, aged 24.

No 23 had three adults, two children and two servants: a cook and a housemaid.

No 24 had four adults and two servants: a housemaid and a general servant.

No 25 had six adults, four children and two servants: a cook and a housemaid.

No 26 had seven adults, seven children and two servants: a cook and a housemaid.

No 27 had three adults and no servants.

In 1901:

No 1 had two adults and one servant, aged 32.

No 2 had three adults, a child and no servants.

No 3 had a couple with two children, an elderly mother, visitor and two servants: a nurse and a cook.

No 4 had two adults, four children and two servants: a cook and a housemaid.

No 5 had a married couple and one servant, aged 25.

No 7 had four adults and no servants.

No 8 had three adults and no servants.

No 9 had a couple with five children and two servants: a nurse and a general servant.

No 10 had a married couple with one servant, aged 21.

No 11 had a widow with five children and two servants: a cook and a housemaid.

No 12 had five adults and two servants: a cook and a general
    servant.

No 14 had an elderly spinster with two general servants.

No 15 had two unmarried sisters and one servant, aged 17.

No 16 had three adults and one servant, aged 49.

No 17 had a couple with five older children and one servant,
    aged 23.

No 18 had two adults, a child and one servant, aged 24.

No 19 had two adults and one servant, aged 38.

No 20 had three adults, three children and two servants: a nurse
    and a general servant.

No 21 had a married couple, a boarder and one servant, aged 30.

No 22 had three adults and one servant, aged 19.

No 23 had three adults, a child and two servants: a cook and a
    general servant.

No 24 had four adults and one servant, aged 20.

No 25 had a married couple, four teenagers and one servant,
    aged 22.

No 26 had eight adults and one servant, aged 23.

No 27 had two adults and one servant, aged 54.

Summing up, we can see that most households in Dalrymple
Crescent had one servant who lived in. Towards the end of the
century, some households also had a cook. Where there was another
servant, it was generally a nurse to look after young children, or the
elderly.

THE LIFE OF A SERVANT

Unless the members of the household helped her, the lot of a single
servant looking after up to eight people was hard. Judith Flanders[1] in
The Victorian House describes in detail the daily tasks of such a
'maid-of-all-work'. The following is a brief summary.

    She would rise at six; open all the blinds, shutters and curtains;
light the fire, polish the range and put on the kettle. Then she would

clean the household's boots and the knives, clean the fire in the breakfast room and light it; clean the furniture, wash the mantel-piece, and dust the ornaments in the breakfast room. Next she would sweep the carpet, shake out the mats and rugs; clean the front hall and empty the downstairs fireplaces of cinders.

Having done all this, she would change into a clean dress in order to lay the table, and then cook and serve breakfast. While the family was having breakfast, she would air the bedrooms and strip the beds for airing. Then she had to turn the mattresses, empty the slops and wash the chamber pots. Three times a week she would wash the floors. Then she would make the beds. One room each day would be thoroughly cleaned, and the others would be dusted. She then had to collect the lamps and candlesticks for cleaning downstairs. Once downstairs, she would clear away the breakfast things, sweep the carpet and wash the breakfast things.

Dinner might be any time from after midday to early evening. For this she would prepare the dinner, tidy the dining room, and set the table. After serving the first course, she would check the drawing room fire and close the curtains, then dish up the second course. When the family had finished, she would clear up the dining room, clean the kitchen and wash the pots and pans. Then she had to draw the blinds and prepare the bedrooms. Before going to bed, her last tasks were to put out all the fires and lamps; lock the front door; turn off the gas and rake the kitchen fire and lay it ready for morning.

Flanders goes on to say that 'All this was regarded as normal, and not too much for one person', although 'even Mrs Beeton' said that the general servant was 'perhaps the only one of her class deserving of commiseration'.[2]

WHO WERE THEY AND WHERE DID THEY COME FROM?

The census can tell us quite a bit about the servants of Dalrymple Crescent living in the street at the time of the four census returns. Without exception they were female; most were young girls between the age of 16 and 25; the rest were older women, either spinsters or widows. Not surprisingly, given their age group, they did not stay long at one position. The census shows only one instance of a servant being at the same house for two consecutive returns, and *The Scotsman* papers of the day are full of advertisements for servants. However, when a family came from outwith Edinburgh, quite often the servant was born in the same area.

For the four census returns, 112 servants were recorded as living in Dalrymple Crescent. Fourteen of them came from Edinburgh, and a further 18 came from the counties closest to Edinburgh (Midlothian and East Lothian). Four came from England, and four from Ireland. The rest (approximately 65%) came from all over Scotland, from Shetland to Berwickshire.

We can get more of an insight into the lives of the servants and their employers by looking at some particular cases. I have selected some unusual cases (which are therefore easier to track down). The first concerns three sisters from Mull; the second describes a servant who continued to live with her employers after she retired. The third looks at the only case where a servant stayed in the same place over two census years. We also have a case where a servant was married from her employer's house, and an example of a mother and daughter being employed in the same house.

The McDiarmid sisters

In 1871, the three servants working for Margaret Rosie at No 20 were sisters from the Isle of Mull, and it is interesting to look at their background, which was very rural, and quite unlike Edinburgh.

Grace, Flora and Marion McDiarmid were aged 21, 19 and 17. Their father, Duncan McDiarmid, was born in Perth, and their mother, Jessie McKinnon, in the parish of Kilfinichen, Mull.[3] Jessie's father, Archibald McKinnon, owned a farm called Torrans, which was 2000 acres in size, and Jessie and Duncan were staying there when the 1851 census was taken. At that time Jessie was 19, Duncan was 50 and Grace was one year old, Archibald McKinnon was 65 and his wife, Flora, was 49. Also living with them was Jessie's brother, Donald, 17, two visitors and a lodger, Donald MacDonald. The visitors were a Gaelic teacher, James Matheson, 73, and a Free Church student of divinity, Angus MacDonald, 25. There were two servants, also surnamed McKinnon: Catherine, 25, a housemaid, and Archie, 24, a labourer. In addition, the other servants and farm workers were: Christy MacGilvray, 35, dairymaid, Mary MacGilvray, 19, housemaid, John MacGilvray, 24, joiner, Charles MacGilvray, 18, herd, Mary McNeil, 46, cook, Duncan MacLean, 28, ploughman, Donald Paterson, 22, shepherd and Archie Campbell, 16, herd.

Archibald and Flora had been living in the same farm in 1841, when the household consisted of Murdock McKinnon (aged 102!), Flora McKinnon, (aged between 75 and 80) – presumably Archibald's parents. Jessie was ten, Donald was five, and there were four other relations: Hana (between 15 to 20), John (between 15 and 20), Hector, five and Lachlan (between 35 and 40). They had five servants and farm workers: three male and two female.

By 1861, Duncan and Jessie and their family had left Torrans. Flora was now head of the household, and Donald and Hector were working the farm. A granddaughter, Catherine Elliot, aged 16, was acting as housekeeper. They had five servants: a cook, a dairymaid, a ploughman, a cowherd and an agricultural labourer. In addition they had a boarder, Archibald McKinnon, 30, whose occupation was listed as 'pauper', and a visitor, William Mackintosh, who was a pedlar.

This was the rural environment into which the three McDiarmid sisters had been born. Duncan may have died in Edinburgh in 1855. Jessie was living at Kinlochspelvie, Argyll in 1861, with Grace and the other children. It has been difficult to trace their movements after 1871, but in 1876 Marion appears to have married Roderick Campbell, a master grocer, and in 1881 they were living in Edinburgh at 1 Elizabeth Villa, St Leonards Hill. They had two daughters, Anne Rachel and Jessie Marion.

Elspeth Grant

Elspeth Grant was born in the parish of Cromdale, Inverallan and Advie, Morayshire, in February 1803. According to her death certificate, her father was John Grant, a tailor, and her mother's first name was Penuel, but there is no record of her parents' marriage.

By 1861 she was working as a servant in Rev. Thomas Dymock's house at 3 Atholl Crescent, Perth, with two other servants. At this time, she was 57, and the other two servants were aged 36 and 19. She may well have been working for the Dymock family in 1841, when they were living in Carnoustie. They certainly had a servant named Elspeth Grant, of the right age. Her place of birth was given as Angus, but since the rest of the household came from Angus, this may have been a mistake on the recorder's part.

The Dymock family moved to Dalrymple Crescent in 1881, but there is no record of Elspeth's whereabouts for that year. However in the 1891 census she was living with the family at No 20. Her age was given as 86, and she was described as a retired domestic servant. She died of influenza in June of that year, having been with the Dymock family for at least 50 years.

Ellen Innes

In the four census returns for Dalrymple Crescent, there is only one instance of a servant being with the same family on two census days. Ellen Innes worked at No 14 in both 1891 and 1901. Helen, or Ellen Innes was born in April 1861 to William Innes and his wife Anna, whose maiden name was Garden. They were living at 174 High Street, Portobello, and had been married at Duddingston Church in July 1846. William Innes was a railway labourer.

In 1881, aged 19, she was working as a servant in 7 Lee Crescent, just off Portobello High Street. Her employer was a widowed pharmaceutical chemist, living with his unmarried daughter. In 1901 she was joined by Jane, or Janet, Innes, who may have been a relative. Her father was also a William Innes, but his wife was Agnes, née Lyon. Moreover, although Ellen's father could write, this William Innes only put his mark on the birth certificate. He was a road stone-breaker, living at 14 Maryfield, Portobello. Janet was born in June 1860, so was just a year older than Ellen. In 1881 she was working as a housemaid for Mr Henry Doig, a carver and guilder, at 90A George Street Edinburgh.

Margaret Fraser

Margaret Fraser was born in Keith, Banffshire in August 1869. Her father, John Fraser was a quarry labourer, and her mother's maiden name was Jane Mann. In 1881, when Margaret was 11, they were living at 82 Mid Street, Banff. At that time she had four brothers living at home. The eldest, Duncan, was 22 and an engine cleaner. The second, Robert, was 20 years old and worked as a flesher. The next one, John, was eight, and the youngest, William, was only three years old.

Between 1891 and 1894 she became a servant in Archibald Oliver's household at No 19 Dalrymple Crescent. In June 1894 she married Peter Riach, a mason, who also came from Keith. He was about three years older than she was, having been born in November 1867. His parents were James Riach and Helen Milne. In 1881 he was living at 6 Duff Street with his parents, a brother and two younger sisters. His father was an agricultural labourer, and his elder brother, Alexander, was a carpenter's apprentice.

Peter and Margaret were married at 19 Dalrymple Crescent by Rev. J. Bell Nichol, and all four parents were alive at the time. Mr Oliver was one of the witnesses, and a notice of the marriage was put in *The Scotsman*. In 1901 the couple were still living in Edinburgh.

Margaret and Anne Sommerville

Margaret Sommerville and her daughter Anne were servants working for Edward Lothian in April 1871. At the time of the census, Edward and his two servants were the only occupiers of No 3. Margaret was born Margaret Kerr in Kirkliston in 1813. She was one of five children born to Robert Kerr and Margaret Livingstone. In 1838 she married William Sommerville, a farm steward, and they had three daughters. In 1841 she and William were living at 1 Lyle House, Cramond, Midlothian. William was described as an agricultural labourer, and their eldest daughter, also Margaret, was one year old. Janet, the second daughter was also born at Cramond, but Anne, born in 1846, was born in Cockpen, Midlothian. By 1851, Margaret was a widow, and was living at 'Butterfield', Cockpen with her three children. Living with them was her brother, William Kerr, who was described as a farm labourer.

No record has been found of her whereabouts in 1861, but we have seen that she and Anne (or Annie) were working at No 3 in 1871. A year later Annie married John R. Liddle, a coach painter, living at 40 Sciennes. He was a year younger than Annie. His father, Thomas Liddle had been a coachman, and his mother's maiden name was Agnes Ramsay. Interestingly one of the witnesses was David Noble Bertram, who later (in 1886) rented No 3. D. N. Bertram was the son of George Bertram, who owned Bertrams, the manufacturer of paper-making machinery. The factory was also in Sciennes, and George Bertram lived in Sciennes Hill House*. David was about 18 at the time of the Liddles' marriage, four years younger than John. It is possible that John and his father worked for Bertram's factory.

Margaret Sommerville died at No 3 in November 1877, of 'chronic vascular disease of the heart'. She was 67, and Annie was with her at the end. In the same year Edward Lothian sold No 3 to Duncan Francis Stewart, and moved to Corstorphine Road on the west side of Edinburgh.

Mary Morton

Mary Morton was the sick nurse to Duncan Anderson, the father of John Anderson, who owned No 11. She was born in Cleish, Kinross in December 1838. Her father, George Morton was a saw miller, who came from England. Her mother was Jane Farney (or Farnie or Fernie). At the time of the 1841 census they were living in the village of Kelty, in the parish of Cleish. Mary was two years old, and her younger sister, Elizabeth, was one. A son, Thomas was born in April 1842, but Jane died in the same year. George married again. His new wife was Isabella Mackay, and they had four more children. By 1881 Mary, now about 45 years old, was a teacher of dressmaking, and was

---

* Sciennes Hill House was once the home of Adam Ferguson, who hosted a dinner there where Robert Burns and the young Walter Scott met for the one and only time in the winter of 1786–87.

living with two elderly aunts, Jane and Mary MacDonald. They were living at 87 Montrose Street, Glasgow. It is probable that she developed her sick-nursing skills while looking after her aunts.

John Anderson moved into No 11 Dalrymple Crescent in 1883, with his father who was now 71. By 1891 Mary had joined the household as a sick nurse. Duncan died in December 1894, and Mary did not live much longer. An announcement in *The Scotsman* said that she died suddenly at the Royal Infirmary on 20 February 1895. She was described as 'of Blairadam, Fife, nurse at 11 Dalrymple Crescent for many years.' Blairadam House lies just outside Kelty. It was built by Sir William Adam in 1733, and has extensive forest, built to create an attractive landscape, but also to produce commercial timber. Mary's father probably worked on the estate. The record of her death says that she died of a hernia, and her death was recorded by her mother's sister Jane Susan Farney, who was living at 46 Comely Bank Avenue, Edinburgh.

IN CONCLUSION

In most of the cases we have looked at, employers and servants may have had closer ties than was usual, and this has helped to tease out the story of these servants. Judging by the number of advertisements in *The Scotsman*, there was quite a large turnover of servants. No doubt this was often because they got married, or found better positions. In some cases there would have been disputes and bad feeling, and we know that Richard Little's servant went to court to obtain her wages from him. So we have at least one example where a servant was not afraid to stand up for her rights. However, there is reason to believe that servants and their employers were normally on good terms. A servant's life may have been hard work, but it was not necessarily miserable.

PART 3

*Life in
Victorian Times*

CHAPTER 8

Life in the 1860s

~

There were many changes in Victorian life in the forty years we have been looking at. In order to get a better feel for the changes over this period of time, the next four chapters will look at life in each of the four decades: 1862 to 1871, 1872 to 1881, 1882 to 1891, and 1892 to 1901. Each chapter has three sections. The first looks at some of the main changes that took place in the decade. The second looks life in the Crescent during that decade, chronologically, and in the third section we will home in on one particular day, and look at *The Scotsman* for the day after the census that ends each decade. The articles and letters in the paper are very illuminating, as they reflect the attitudes of the times. They cover home and foreign affairs, and give us an insight into the Victorian view of the world.

THE 1860s

By 1862, when Dalrymple Crescent was first feued, Queen Victoria had been on the throne for 25 years, and the transition to what we think of as Victorian times was complete. Nevertheless the 1860s are something of a watershed between early Victorian times and later. Two events overshadowed the rest of the century. Darwin published *The Origin of Species* in 1859, and Prince Albert died in December 1861. Further afield the American Civil War had started in 1861, and the South surrendered in April 1865.

At home, the emphasis was on Law and Order, and on health. In

1862 the General Police and Improvement (Scotland) Act was passed, and Dr. Henry Littlejohn became the first Medical Officer of Health in Edinburgh. In 1864 the Compulsory Vaccination Act (Scotland) was passed, and in 1865 there was a Report on the Sanitary Condition of Edinburgh.

The Church was well represented in Dalrymple Crescent, and in the latter half of the 19th century, it was at the heart of religious and political controversy. The Disruption had occurred almost twenty years previously, but the issues that caused it were still very much live.

One of the major bones of contention between Church and State was patronage – the right of land-owners to appoint ministers to a Parish. The law enforced it, but it went against the Church's beliefs. In the Age of Enlightenment, a rational, tolerant and rather laissez-faire attitude had grown up within the Church, but later there came a division between the Moderates, who followed this approach, and Reformers, who were more evangelical and were concerned for the autonomy of the Church. This conflict came to a head in 1843 with the Disruption, in which 474 ministers broke away to form the Free Church of Scotland. This entailed giving up their livelihood, and all the property that the established Church of Scotland owned. Money poured in to support the cause: the new Free Church built 500 churches, established its own colleges and collected money at the astonishing rate of £1000 a day. This event gave a boost to the religious and social conscience of Victorian Scotland, and these effects were felt to the end of the century.

The Victorian era is seen as a period of invention and innovation, with its advances in technology, transport and manufacturing. Compared with the previous century the world was more complex and stressful. Work, for many levels of society, moved from being located in or near home to taking place in a separate environment. The Victorian home was seen as a sanctuary from this turbulent world. At this time it was generally assumed that the only career path open to middle-class women was marriage; only poor women worked for a living. With servants to do the housework, Victorian ladies had a life of constant leisure. They read, sewed, played music and entertained. Life was a constant round of social calls. This domesticity was an important component in defining middle-class Victorian life. A man's wife and home showed his standing to his contemporaries.

In Victorian times there were no pension schemes and no form of social security. Therefore, as soon as a man earned any surplus money, it was invested to keep him in his old age, and to provide for his family when he had gone. Capital money had to be invested to give his heirs a steady income, ideally in the form of an annuity. This key element of Victorian life is illustrated in the Crescent in three ways.

First, almost all the building in Dalrymple, and around Edinburgh at that time was speculative. Builders borrowed money, built their houses, sold them, repaid the debt, and moved on to the next project. We have seen that James Hunter had difficulties in keeping all his projects afloat, and bankruptcy was quite common at that time. From the other point of view, those with capital could easily lend it out and expect to live on the interest. Once houses had been built, they were often rented out, and we have seen examples of this, both by businessmen such as George Alexander and individuals such as Elizabeth Johnston or Elizabeth and Janet Sinclair. Finally, there was the possibility of taking in boarders and lodgers. The Thompson sisters at No 6 had three lodgers in 1881, and there are examples of boarders at No 20 and No 22 in 1871.

The 1860s was also a dividing point in fashion (See Plate 18b). By this time the crinoline had reached its ultimate width, and soon it would transform to the bustle. W. M. Gilbert writing in *Edinburgh in the Nineteenth Century* is most scathing of the style:

> It was a period of ugliness and want of taste, and was especially fatal to youth and beauty, which looked matronly in such attire. In the fifties, it has been said, there were no young people. Even children looked triple their years. ... It is generally admitted that in no period in the nineteenth century were ladies' dresses so devoid of any redeeming quality in style as in the fifties and sixties. From 1868 skirts grew gradually narrower.[1]

The ladies of Dalrymple Crescent would have been very relieved, since although the street was built in a comparatively short time, we have to imagine ladies in these crinolines picking their way through the dust and the mud of what was effectively a building site. Richard Rodger[2] evokes the same feeling of discomfort describing the building of an earlier part of Edinburgh:

> Relatively rapidly the main New Town thoroughfares and residences were constructed ... [It] took many years to complete the remainder of the New Town. ... [The] street [was] an ongoing building site [with] mud and dust according to the season. The unified street with elegant exteriors and apparent social order, as represented by ... engravers, belied the noise of construction and the incompleteness of streets for some years.

This was not just true of the Crescent and the Grange, but all over Edinburgh. There was a veritable frenzy of building.

In a typical semi-detached house of the period, the entrances would be symmetrically side-by-side, with the left house being a mirror image of the right. There would normally be a vestibule or porch leading into the hall. A door off the hall would lead into the dining room, and the stairs would lead up to the first floor. The drawing room was generally on the first floor, above the dining room. There would probably be two rooms to the back of the house; one a study, for the man of the house, and the morning room, where the wife would conduct her business and perhaps entertain close friends or relations. The kitchen would be at the back of the house, and perhaps a scullery. On the first floor, to the back would be the main bedrooms, and further bedrooms and the nursery would be on the top floor.

The houses built by George Alexander on the south side of Dalrymple Crescent were a variation of this plan. Because of the steep slope of the ground, they have a basement and two other floors. Generally the kitchen and servants' quarters would have been in the basement, the parlour and dining room on the ground floor, with the drawing room and bedrooms on the first floor.

Victorians divided their houses into private and public spaces, with the grandest rooms being those where entertaining was done. Judith Flanders says that:

> In the eighteenth century ... servants and apprentices had often slept in the same rooms as family members. Gradually ... rooms ... for receiving outsiders – the dining room, the drawing room, the morning room – [were divided from] ... rooms that were for family members only – bedrooms, the study – and ... from rooms ... for servants only.[3]

The dining room was considered a 'masculine' room. The decoration would be dark, and the furniture heavy. The Scots in the 18th century had been heavy drinkers, and although habits were more moderate in Victorian times, the ladies still withdrew to the drawing room after a meal. This was a 'feminine room', where the family could display their possessions and impress visitors. Not all houses could conform to this pattern. When we redecorated our own house, for instance, we found children's wallpaper (Plate 19) behind the shutters in a small room, which would have been a dressing room originally, but must have been a nursery at some time. A note from the Victoria and Albert Museum says that, in Victorian times:

> ... the houses of the middle-class had, for the first time, sufficient space to dedicate rooms, even whole floors, to the accommodation of children and their carers – the nursemaid (later nanny) and the governess. ... With the setting up of nurseries came the introduction of furnishings of all kinds designed specifically for children's use; these included wallpapers ... [there was a] widely held view that children were uniquely sensitive to their environment, and must therefore be surrounded by things which were beautiful, 'honest' and inspiring, ... From the 1870s onwards, many more nursery wallpapers appeared, the great majority with subjects adapted from children's books. Indeed some

were the work of artists and designers who were themselves directly involved in book illustration, though others such as Greenaway and Caldecott simply allowed their illustrations to be purchased for the purpose. Perhaps the best known artist associated with the design of nursery wallpapers was Walter Crane.[4]

We have not been able to identify our wallpaper, but it appears to be in the style of Greenaway or Caldecott.

In 1938 Jenners* published a book entitled *A Hundred Years in Princes Street*, to mark its centenary. In it, the author, Mary Grierson, imagines what the social life in Edinburgh was like in Victorian times:

> Those were the days of dinner-parties and routs and balls, of needlework and 'airings' for the ladies, of private theatricals and excursions to admire the scenery. The dinner hour tended to become later, as improved lighting made it possible to work to a later hour.[5]

A DIARY OF THE CRESCENT: 1863–71

In this section I have tried to describe the street as if I were living there at the time, giving the view of a fictitious neighbour. This has allowed me to use my imagination, more than in the other sections.

 1863

Dalrymple Crescent might be said to have come into existence on 22 March 1862, when the plots of land were put up for auction. It was in 1863, when the first residents moved in, that life in the street began.

---

* The department store in Princes Street, now part of House of Fraser.

One of the first residents was MR WILLIAM GORRIE. He is one of the owners of the tailors shop 'Gorrie and Anderson' which opened its doors in the new buildings on North Bridge last year. Mr Gorrie and his family moved into the first house in the street, approaching from the Lauder Road end. Mr and Mrs Gorrie have six children, and soon after they moved in, Mrs Gorrie was delivered of a little girl. Sadly, the baby was premature, and did not live above six weeks.

The cottage next door is to be rented out. It is owned by MISS SINCLAIR and her sister, who come from Caithness, but who now live in Stirling. Miss Sinclair, who is a single lady in her mid-forties, is at present preparing the house for her new tenants.

The next cottage along is also occupied. MR EDWARD LOTHIAN is a single gentleman who works for the Bank of Scotland. He is a quiet gentleman who lives alone, looked after by his housekeeper, Mrs Sommerville, and her daughter.

The plot next to that has not been developed yet, and beyond that another cottage is being erected by MR JAMES HUNTER His father, MR ROBERT HUNTER, has already built No 6, and is living there with his wife and four adult children. His other son, MR SAMUEL HUNTER is newly married, and he is building three houses on the other side of No 6.

Beyond Mr S. Hunter's construction work, the firm of architects, Leadbetter and Smith, have been building two detached villas. One is already sold to MR GEORGE T. BATHGATE who works for a trade association.

The house on the east corner of Dalrymple Crescent and Findhorn Place is a handsome villa belonging to MR ROBERT MIDDLEMASS, the biscuit manufacturer. Mr Middlemass and his wife have six children, the eldest being eleven and the youngest just a year old.

Only the north side of the Crescent has been put up for auction, so all the houses have a view of green fields and look towards the Grange estate to the south.

❧ *1864*

By the end of the year most of the houses in the street have now been occupied. Next door to Mr and Mrs Gorrie, MR ALEXANDER AITKEN, is renting No 2 from Miss Sinclair. Mr Aitken works for David Mason & Co, the tea and coffee dealers on South Bridge. Mrs Aitken tells me that they met when her husband came to work for her father at his distillery in Wigtown. Mrs Gorrie herself gave birth to a baby boy in April.

Mr Samuel Hunter finished building his houses this year, and frequently advertised Nos 7, 8 and 9 in *The Scotsman* newspaper. Only one of them has been sold: DR CHARLES WILSON bought No 7 early in the year. Dr Wilson has newly retired from his medical practice, and lives with his wife Mrs Elizabeth Wilson. Formerly they lived in Moray Place, but were attracted by the open aspect of the Grange estate.

In July, Mr James Hunter sold No 5 to another medical gentleman. MR HENRY NEWCOMBE is a surgeon who was working near Manchester before moving to Edinburgh. His wife, Mrs Ann Maria Newcombe, comes from Edinburgh. They are both in their forties, but they have no children.

To date the most eminent resident in the street is PROFESSOR JOHN DUNCAN who has bought No 10 from the architects Leadbetter and Smith. It will be remembered that he was one of the key figures in the Disruption in 1843, and he became the first Professor of Hebrew and Oriental Languages at the New College. He shares the house with his good friend, Miss Mary Sandeman, who moved here with him from his house in Buccleuch Place.

Mr Bathgate did not stay long in the Crescent. In May he sold his house (No 11) to MR RICHARD LISTER, who is a commercial traveller. He and his wife have a son of 15 and a baby daughter aged two. Next door to them, Mrs Middlemass gave birth to a baby boy in March.

In September the feus for the south side of the street were

put up for auction, so soon the views of green fields will disappear. It is said that the plots have been bought up by the City Architect, Mr Robert Paterson. Already a villa is being constructed on the corner of Findhorn Place, opposite Mr Middlemass's house.

1865

This year was overshadowed by the horrifying murder at No 6 on 5 October. Mr John Hunter was not known to many in the street, but apparently he has always been of unsettled disposition, and was kept within the house. The day before the tragedy he was seen in the front garden of the house, behaving wildly. The following day he came out of the house and passed into the street. His mother and sister followed him and appear to have tried to bring him back to the house, whereupon he turned on them and beat both of them to death with an iron bar he was carrying. A mason heard the commotion, although he did not observe the event. He raised the alarm, and a number of neighbours soon came on the scene. The murderer made his way to the back garden, where he remained until the police and his father and brother seized him and took him away.

His mother, Mrs Marion Hunter had been in her 68th year, and his sister, Miss Elizabeth Hunter was the eldest sister, and the only one living at home. The newspapers reported the incident in some detail, and for several days the Crescent was disturbed by the invasion of a large crowd of people who came to witness the scene of the murder.

The event was particularly distressing since the street had not long since welcomed a number of new residents. Early in the year Mr Samuel Hunter sold his remaining houses, and the greater part of the south side is now developed. The villa on the south-east corner is completed, and was advertised for sale in January. Next to it MR GEORGE ALEXANDER, who has a building yard in Fountainhall Road, is in the process of erecting ten semi-detached villas to be rented out.

No 9 has been bought by MR D. C. MUDIE, who owns the Panmure iron foundry, situated in the North Back of the Canongate. He moved into the street in January with his eight-year old daughter, Isabella. MRS CAMPBELL moved into No 8 at about the same time. She is a widow who comes from Halkirk in Caithness, the same village that is the birthplace of the Misses Sinclair of No 2; in fact they were born about the same time as Mrs Campbell's eldest daughter. Her grandson, who is about 15, lives with her.

The year also saw the first resident on the south side of the street. The villa on the corner with Findhorn Place was bought by REV. ROBERT GEMMELL. He is the minister at Arthur Street United Presbyterian Church. He and his wife already had a young son and baby daughter, and another daughter was born to them in November.

The street saw two other births this year; Mr Lister's second daughter was born in March, and Mrs Gorrie gave birth to a son in May. Sadly she lost the baby who had been born last year; he died in January, aged nine months.

1866

There was only one change of address this year; Mr Hunter and his family moved away from the scene of their tragedy. No 6 was sold to MR DAVID HENDERSON, who owns the hat shop at 46 North Bridge. He also has another establishment in Leith. Mr Henderson is not married, but lives with his two sisters, Miss Agnes and Miss Margaret. He is a keen gardener, and plans to improve the greenhouse and other outhouses at the back.

This year Professor Duncan, Miss Sandeman and Mrs Campbell all enjoyed their 70th birthdays (Professor Duncan being exactly one week older than Miss Sandeman), and Mrs

Middlemass gave birth to another son in June. In September she showed me the photograph, taken by Mr Doull, of her son John and his two young sisters, Mary and Jane. [See Plate 20a]

Work has at last started on the plot between the houses of Mr Lothian and Dr Newcombe which has been empty all this while. A cottage is being erected by the builders DAVID RUTHERFORD & SONS.

🥀 1867

This year the Gorrie children lost their playmates, as Mr and Mrs Aitken moved out of No 2. Their place was taken by MR and MRS JOHN WATT, who have two very young sons, aged one and two years.

However, in April another young family moved into No 4, which was completed early in the year. MR ROBERT SINCLAIR SMITH is a tax surveyor, and has three children. William at 15 is three years older than Daniel Gorrie; Anne is the same age as Mary Gorrie, and Robert Smith and Robert Gorrie are the same age.

On the other side of the street, the villas of Mr Alexander have almost been completed, while at the Lauder Road end there is still a large expanse that has not been developed at all.

🥀 1868

Most of Mr Alexander's villas are nearing completion now; indeed some are already occupied. The ones to be taken first were the ones in the centre of the street, opposite Mr Henderson, Dr Wilson and Mrs Campbell. The last house in the row, at the Lauder Road end is still empty, but the next one, No 22, has been rented by MRS FORSTER PRATT. She has been widowed some five years; her husband having been a solicitor in Berwick on Tweed.

Next door to her, and opposite Dr Wilson, the nephew of Sir James Young Simpson, the famous physician, is renting No 21. He is MR JOHN SIMPSON, and he works at the firm of Duncan Flockhart and Co, the firm who supplied Sir James with the chloroform for his pioneering work on anaesthetics in 1847. Mr Simpson is married, with a baby boy, Alexander, just one year old, and Mrs Simpson gave birth to another boy, Peter, in October of this year.

No 20 is taken by MRS ROSIE. She is a widow who has opened a small boarding school within the house, and has her sister, Miss Leitch, to help her. At present she has three young ladies boarding with her, all coming from Paisley.

The end of the street nearest to Findhorn Place is becoming quite an ecclesiastical community. Professor Duncan is in No 10, and Mr Gemmell in No 13, on the south corner. Now they have been joined by REV. JOHN PULSFORD and his family, who are renting No 15. Mr Pulsford has just become the minister of Albany Street Chapel, where his brother, Rev. William Pulsford ministered some years ago. It seems that the intervening minister was not to the congregation's liking, and he resigned his post. Rev. John Pulsford has published some devotional books, notably Quiet Hours, of which the critics have said 'The thought and feeling are truly and deeply Scriptural and Christian'.

Mr and Mr Gorrie quit the street this year, and their place has been taken by another minister, REV. ROBERT WILLIAM FRASER, of St John's Parish Church, in the Canongate. Mr Fraser lives with his wife, his grown-up daughter, and his sister.

Next door at No 2, Mrs Watt had a son on 4 June, and at the other end of the street, Mrs Middlemass added to her numerous offspring with a baby girl five days later.

Mr Mudie at No 9 is married again. His wife, Miss Joanna Low Anderson, is some ten years younger than him, and he has known her since he lived in Dundee. It is good to know that young Isabella will have a mother again.

1869

Mr Sinclair Smith stayed only two years in No 2, and his place was taken by MR JAMES SINCLAIR, who owns a draper's shop in Bank Street. He and his wife are quite elderly, and they are now living quite close to their daughter, Mrs Thomas Stevenson, who lives in Lauder Road. This end of the street is now quite sedate, as nearly all the families with children have moved out. No doubt the small cottages at this end of the street are somewhat small for growing families.

Another of Mr Alexander's houses was let this year. No 23 is rented by MR HENRY BROUGHAM CROUCH, who owns a jeweller's shop in Hanover Street. He was married in June, and moved into the Crescent with his young bride, Mrs Maria Jane Crouch.

Mr Gemmell's mother died at his house in February of this year. She was 78. And at No 10 Professor Duncan lost his friend Miss Sandeman, who died in May.

1870

The whole street was saddened by the death, in February, of Professor John Duncan. He was given a very moving funeral, with numerous dignitaries from the Free Church in attendance. At 1.30 on 3 March a large company of professors, students and ministers of the Free Church assembled at Grange Free Church. The company walked in procession to No 10, where a service was held. The cortège then progressed to Grange Cemetery where Professor Duncan was interred. The chief mourner was his colleague from New College, Rev. George Smeaton,* and the pall-bearers were the Revs C. J. Brown, Bonar, Davidson, Moody Stuart, and Grey, and Mr McDonald and Mr Balfour.

Soon after, trustees rented No 10 to REV. HARRY ANDERSON,

---

* George Smeaton was Professor of Exegetical Theology at New College, (appointed 1857).

who had been minister at Juniper Green Free Church, and his two sisters, Miss Helena and Miss Susan Anderson. Mr Anderson had been ill for some time, and died in the November of this year.

In May the house next door, No 11, was sold. Mr Lister left the area, and the house was bought by MR HENRY HAIG BANKS, Mr Banks is married, and has three children. He is the son of William Banks, the engraver and works at his father's establishment in North St David Street.

On the opposite side of the street, another of Mr Alexander's villas has been let for the first time. MR STEPHEN WELLSTOOD and his wife are members of the Society of Friends. Mr Wellstood was a founder member of the foundry at Bonnybridge that bears his name, but more recently he has devoted himself to Politics. Mrs Wellstood's sister also lives with them at No 14.

Further along, Mrs Forster Pratt has left No 22, and the house is rented by MRS BRAND. Like Mrs Rosie she is a widow, and has a number of young girls as boarders, although she does not teach them. In the house between Mrs Rosie and Mrs Brand, Mrs John Simpson gave birth to a baby girl in August.

At the Lauder Road end of the street, Mr John Watt has left No 2, which has been taken by MR JOHN CROSBIE PATERSON. Mr Paterson works for the Inland Revenue. He is married, with a young son aged about three.

🍂 1871

Another of Mr Alexander's houses has been rented out now, leaving only two vacant, and these still have to be completed. MR JOHN SIBBALD is the tenant at No 16. He has just been appointed as Deputy Commissioner in Lunacy, and has moved to Edinburgh from Argyllshire where he was Medical Superintendent of the District Asylum. Mrs Sibbald comes from Ireland. They have two young sons and a daughter. At present Mrs Sibbald's sister, Miss Phelan, is staying with them.

On the subject of visitors, there are quite a few in the Crescent this year. Mr Wellstood's nephew from New York, and Mrs Wellstood's niece from England are both staying at No 14. At No 20, Mrs Rosie's niece, Miss Catherine Leitch is helping out with the school.

Mr and Mrs Mudie have a young visitor from Anstruther, a young lady who is a few years older than Miss Isabella Mudie. Next door, at No 8, Mrs Campbell has a full house. As well as Mr Benjamin Campbell, who now works as a clothier's shopman, she has a grand-daughter, her daughter and son-in-law with her. Mr Henderson also has some more permanent guests. His two nephews, Mr William and Mr David Waddell are staying with him. Mr William is a Clothier's Apprentice and Mr David is an Architect's Apprentice.

THE SCOTSMAN, MONDAY 3 APRIL 1871

To round up this review of the decade, we will take a look at the copy of *The Scotsman* that was published on the morning after census day in 1871. It contained two interesting articles on the international scene, from Paris and from Madrid, covering the changes that were taking place in Europe.

This was the time of the Paris Commune, which lasted from 18 March to 26 May 1871. The Franco-Prussian war in 1870 had led to the siege of Paris, when Prussian forces besieged the capital from September 1870 to January 1871. The National Government of France had moved to Versailles, and in January 1871 signed an armistice with Prussia. However the citizens and National Guard of Paris rebelled, threw up the barricades and set up a socialist Commune. Karl Marx was to describe it as the prototype for a revolutionary government of the future. *The Scotsman*'s 'own correspondent' however, took a different view. Writing on the eve of the government's counteroffensive, he first pointed out the main problem that the Commune had – lack of finance.

> Crowds of people are leaving Paris. It is said that 200,000 have taken their departure within the last fortnight, and this flight of money-spending people has thrown many persons out of work.

He then displays his view of the Commune:

> It is suggested that the churches should be confiscated. The Commune will not object to the Catholic religion being exercised; it will simply levy a tax upon the faithful. … [they] will subscribe towards a Government which is perfectly hateful to all Christian people.

He is also contemptuous of their ability to fight:

> Half of Paris would now be glad to see the Prussians enter the city and put this hideous rabble to flight. I only hope that I shall have the pleasure of witnessing the first skedaddle of the civic heroes who have been swaggering behind their barricades for the last month.

Finally, he makes his opinion quite clear:

> These people are unfit for constitutional government. I said to a friend of mine who is on the Municipal Council. 'You must know that a Republic in France is an impossibility and you ought to be shot.'

Spain, meantime, was recovering from a coup d'état that had happened in 1868, when Queen Isabella II was deposed and a liberal constitution was instituted. A 'gentleman long resident in Spain' wrote to a friend in London. He begins:

> You say that in Spanish matters I am an optimist, ... but I
> think you good people in London are informed too exclu-
> sively of our defects and fail to recognise much that is worthy
> of encouragement in this country.

He admits that 'Madrid is a hot-bed of petty intrigue' but 'it is
necessary to bear in mind that it possesses no political education ...
Only two years ago the people were suddenly let loose from bondage.'
However, his view of the worthiness of the Spanish is somewhat
patronising.

> I do not raise my expectations very high. To me it appears
> that the Spanish people are not capable of great things; but I
> believe they will show themselves worthy of a respectable
> place among mankind, and that a fair development of the
> country's wealth will render good service to the world.

Nearer home, the Leith Ragged Industrial School was celebrating its
tenth anniversary. 'The school was tastefully decorated with
evergreens and a number of appropriate mottoes were exhibited.' It
appears that the school was doing 'a great work in preventing crime
and misery'. The rate of imprisonment of poor boys from Leith was
now one tenth of what it had been ten years ago.
    According to one of the directors:

> ragged schools were the most powerful means of elevating
> the lower classes which had yet been discovered and ...
> were well worthy of the support of all classes of the
> community.

Also on the subject of education, the Scotch Education Bill was going
through Parliament, and school masters as far apart as Arbroath and
Dunbar were petitioning Parliament with numerous resolutions. It
cannot be coincidence that the list for the two communities was very
similar:

- Current schoolmasters in parochial schools should be recognised as holding 'certificates of competency';
- Religious instruction should continue 'according to use and wont';
- There should be a minimum and maximum salary (£50 and £100); and
- There should be better provisions for retiring allowances.

CHAPTER 9
Life in the 1870s

~

THE 1870s

Education was a key issue in the 1870s. The Education Act of 1696 had aimed to establish a school and a schoolmaster in every parish in Scotland. The landlord was obliged to provide a schoolhouse and salary for a schoolmaster, supplemented by fees paid by the parents. Similarly Royal Burghs were given the authority to administer a Burgh School.

By the end of the 18th century this requirement of a school for each parish had largely been met, but was proving inadequate because of the size of some parishes and increasing population. The gap was increasingly filled by private schools funded entirely by fees per pupil. In Edinburgh there was a surge in provision around 1760, with numerous private schools opening. The council funded four supplementary 'English schools', such as the Royal High School. This remained the state of affairs until the Education Act of 1872.

This Act made education compulsory for all children aged between five and 13. Schools now came under School Boards run by local committees and many new schools were built by the new Boards. The new system was co-ordinated nationally by the Scotch Education Department* with the curriculum emphasising the teaching of reading, writing, and arithmetic (the three Rs). The churches made a crucial contribution to the new system by handing

* It was renamed the Scottish Education Department in 1918.

over their schools without charge to the School Boards.

W. M. Gilbert gives some statistics for the Edinburgh School Board (it will be recalled that Donald MacKinnon was secretary for the first ten years). In May 1875 the Board was responsible for 16 schools, and 7142 pupils. By 1900, Gilbert reports, there were 31 schools and 37,923 pupils: 22,350 boys and 15,573 girls.[1]

Other notable events in the 1870s included the repeal of the 1712 Patronage Act, which paved the way for the reunification of the main churches in Scotland, and the City of Glasgow Bank failure in 1878, which has already been described in Chapter 4. Politically, there were two elections in 1874, which resulted in a Conservative government under Disraeli. Then in 1879 came Gladstone's Midlothian campaign.

This was a series of foreign policy speeches given by William Gladstone: it is often cited as the first modern political campaign. At the beginning of 1879, he accepted an invitation to stand for Midlothian in the general election expected for 1880. In November 1879, Gladstone left Liverpool for Scotland with the intention of introducing himself to his prospective constituents through a series of speeches. These emotive but logical speeches, denouncing the government's support for the Ottoman Empire and its indifference to atrocities it had carried out, were immensely popular. He addressed 20,000 at Waverley Market, where people fainted and had to be handed out over the heads of the crowd. The following year, Gladstone won Midlothian and the Liberals won the general election. This was the context of Robert Gemmell's letter to *The Scotsman* in April 1879.

Fashion had also changed. The crinoline had disappeared before the end of the 1860s, and the bustle was in fashion in 1875, as illustrated in the Jenners book (see Plate 20b). Dresses similar to these might have been worn to the first performance of Gilbert and Sullivan's operetta, *HMS Pinafore*, which was performed in Edinburgh at the Theatre Royal, in September 1878, only six months after its debut in London.

Theatres had a habit of burning down in Victorian times. In 1857 the Adelphi in Broughton Street was burned to the ground, also destroying part of St Mary's Catholic Church. The Theatre Royal, which rose in its place, was itself burnt down in 1865, and again in 1875. After the latter incident it was rebuilt to a design by C. J. Phipps, and this was the theatre that staged *HMS Pinafore*.

A DIARY OF THE CRESCENT: 1872–81

In this section I will continue with the diary of the street written from the point of view of a fictitious resident of the Crescent.

 1872

This year is the tenth anniversary of the feuing of the Crescent, and only four plots remain undeveloped. The area on the south side, at the Lauder Road end, is still a green field. Opposite, in No 1, Rev. Robert Fraser is living with his wife and sister. Next door, Mr and Mrs Paterson have one son, John, who is five. Mr Lothian has occupied the cottage in No 3 since the street was first built. He still works in the Bank of Scotland, but keeps himself to himself. The same cannot be said of Mrs Sinclair in No 4. She is forever talking about her daughter in Lauder Road and her four grandsons.

The two doctors are still living in the centre of the street: Mr Newcombe at No 5 and Dr Wilson at No 7. Between them, Mr Henderson is still winning prizes for his fruit and flowers. Mrs Campbell and her family are still at No 8. She is now 76 years old.

There has been a great deal of change in the villas opposite them. Mrs Rosie has moved her school from No 20 to No 17, and the house is now rented by COLONEL WILLIAM TURNER, a military gentleman with connections to India. It seems that his eldest children (two daughters, aged 11 and 9) will remain here in Edinburgh, while he and his wife return to India with their young sons.

Mr and Mrs Simpson are still at No 21, while No 22 has been taken by MR RICHARD LISTER, who sold No 11 to Mr Henry Banks only a few years ago. I think he has been down in England in the intervening years.

No 23 also has a new tenant. The house is now let to MR ROBERT DICK, who is a colleague of Mr Simpson, also working at the chemists, Duncan Flockhart and Co. He is married, and his wife gave birth to a daughter in June. No 19 also has a new tenant named Dick, although I do not think they are related. The gentleman in No 19 is DOCTOR JOHN DICK, and he and his wife are considerably older than Mr and Mrs Robert Dick.

There have also been changes at the Findhorn Place end of the street. Mr D. C. Mudie has bought No 10 from the trustees of Professor Duncan, and the family has moved into the house. He has let No 9 to MR ANDREW HENDERSON, who is clerk to Lord Gifford, the judge, and has four young children. His wife was delivered of another son in July. Opposite him, MR ROBERT BEATTIE, a plumber with premises in South St David Street, has occupied No 14. No 18 was taken by MRS WEBSTER and her daughter, Miss Ann Webster, but Mrs Webster died in June, at the age of 74.

Mr Gemmell is still at No 13, Mr Pulsford at No 15, and Dr Sibbald at No 16. On the opposite corner, Mr Middlemass has been in his house since he built it in 1863. He now has nine children. His eldest son, Mr John Middlemass, is now 20.

1873

Mr Beattie did not stay long in No 14. He was soon replaced by MISS SOPHIA CLELAND and her sister, Miss Margaret Cleland, who share the house with two cousins. This was the only move in the street this year, but at No 18, Miss Webster's brother from Melbourne came to visit, and in December his wife gave birth to a baby boy.

Sadly we also had two deaths in the street. Mrs Henry Banks had a little girl in February, but she did not last the year. In October Mr Pulsford's wife also died, leaving three daughters to take care of their father and two brothers.

Colonel Walker and his wife have returned to India, leaving Miss Helen Walker and Miss Maud Walker at No 20 under the care of a governess. It seems that they are the children of the first Mrs Walker, who died when they were quite young. Their parents and three young brothers have arrived safely back in Poona.

✤ 1874

At No 23, Mr Robert Dick has had a terrible spring. On 18 April his wife gave birth to a baby son, but just three weeks later, his daughter, Johanna, not quite two, died of scarletina on 7 May. Her mother, who had not been well since the baby's birth, died two days later, and the baby caught the infection, and died on 11 May. Life is often cruel, but to lose three loved ones in a week is exceptionally hard.

Mrs Rosie has now left the Crescent. Her place at No 17 has been taken by MR ARCHIBALD MACCALMAN and his family. Mr MacCalman comes from the west, but Mrs MacCalman was born in Edinburgh. They have eight children all together, all born in Tarbert in Argyllshire. The elder girls are almost young ladies, while the younger son is only a year old.

On the other side of the street, between the two doctors, Mr Henderson sold his cottage to MR JAMES BRECHIN. Mr Brechin and his brother, Mr Malcolm Brechin, own the butcher's shop on the corner of West Newington Place and Newington Road. I think it was the garden that made the cottage so attractive, as Mr James Brechin, like Mr Henderson, is a keen gardener. The advertisement for the house featured a large garden, a greenhouse and two vineries.

Mr Fraser has moved to Lauriston Place, and No 1 is now rented by MISS MARY ANN PHILIPS. She is originally from Aberdeenshire, but has spent some time in Edinburgh.

At last there have been some developments in the green area opposite No 1. Mr Hogg the joiner bought the land, and he built on it a handsome villa, which he advertised several times in May this year. The house has been bought, and Mr Hogg is making some additional improvements for the new owners, who should take up residence soon.

We had two more births this year. Mrs Banks at No 11 had a son in July, and Mrs Henderson at No 9 had a baby daughter in September.

1875

The house I mentioned last year, No 30, has now been occupied. It is owned by MR CHARLES MORE, and his three elder sisters: Miss Camilla More, Miss Catherine More, and Miss Eliza More.

Mr John Simpson and his family have left the Crescent, but they have not gone far, as he has taken a house in Lauder Road. MRS DOWNIE and her daughter, Mrs Firmstone, took their place at No 21; but Mrs Downie, who was ailing, died in October.

Mr Sibbald has also moved away, to a house in St Margaret's Road, and MR JAMES SIME, the founder of Craigmount House School, now lives in No 16. The school is not far away, being situated in Dick Place, near to Kilgraston Road.

For some time, Dr John Dick at No 19 has been looking after Mrs Algeo of Morningside Place, who was very old and frail. She passed away peacefully in November this year.

As for the other news of the street, Mr D. C. Mudie of No 10 retired from his business at the Panmure Foundry, in February. Nearby, in No 8, Mrs Campbell's grandson, Benjamin, got married and moved to Calton Hill with his new bride. Finally, at No 7, Dr Charles Wilson, who has now lived in the street for 12 years, celebrated his 70th birthday this year.

 1876

This year was not a good year for the Crescent. No 20 had lain empty for some months before MRS WILLIAMSON, an elderly widow, took the house. She died soon after, in August of this year, at the age of 88. There were two other deaths in the street, both more unexpected. In January, Mrs Downie's daughter, Mrs Firmstone, died at the age of 35, and four months later Mr Lister at No 22 died at the age of 42.

No 21 was taken by the MISSES PLUMMER, two sisters who come from Dalkeith. The elder Miss Plummer seems to be about 60 years of age, and her sister is about ten years younger.

Mr Robert Dick has remarried. His new wife is Margaret Aitken, who used to live in No 2 when she was a girl. They have moved to St Andrews Terrace, and MR JOHN H. BANKS, his wife and youngest son now occupy No 23. Abernethy Banks is of school age, but they also have an older son who is a sea captain, and visits them occasionally.

At No 12, Mr Middlemass has considerably extended his house, and next year it is to be featured in the *Journal of Decorative Art*!

 1877

What a number of changes we have had this year – I can scarcely keep up with them. However, I will approach the matter in a precise manner. We have seen *seven* of Mr Anderson's villas change hands.

MISS JANET CLELAND and her sister, Miss Marianne Cleland, have moved into No 16. They are not related to Miss Sophia Cleland who lives at No 14.

Sadly, Mr MacCalman of No 17 died while on a visit to Perth, and his widow has had to move away. The house has now been taken by MR WILLIAM B. MCLACHLAN, a fish salesman. In December, his daughter, Miss Maggie McLachlan, married Mr Patrick Laing, a provision merchant in the city.

Miss Webster found No 18 too big for her once her brother and his wife returned to Australia. It has now been taken by MR WILLIAM RAMAGE LAWSON, who is editor of the *Edinburgh Courant*. He has three sons and a daughter, and his wife comes from Germany.

Nos 20 and 21 have been taken by two brothers, MR THOMAS OGILVY COWNIE and MR JAMES GIBB COWNIE. They are partners in the Gentleman's Outfitters on South Bridge, W. Cownie and Sons. Both brothers are married, and have a number of children; Mrs Thomas Cownie was delivered of a daughter in December.

A new church for the Free Church of Scotland is being built at the corner of Mayfield Road and West Mayfield. It has been designed by a famous architect, Mr Hippolyte Blanc. The first minister of the church, REV. JAMES T. STUART, is now renting No 22. He is married, with a son and three daughters.

At No 23 lives MR JAMES FULTON, who sadly is now a widower. He and his wife moved here earlier in the year, just after his wife had given birth to a baby girl, but Mrs Fulton took ill in November, and passed away on the 7th of the month. Mr Fulton works in the brewing industry.

Happier news comes from the north side of the street, where we had two marriages. At No 12, Mr John Middlemass – who was 11 when the family moved to the Crescent – married Miss Annie Grant, from Cupar in Fife. At No 6 Mr Malcolm Brechin married Miss Mary Jane Gray, and he and his bride moved into a house in Dalkeith Road. At No 11, Mrs Banks gave birth to a son, Alfred.

🌿 *1878*

This year the open ground between No 23 and the residence of Mr More and his sisters has been put to use. Mr Thomas Cownie has bought the land next to Mr More, and built a large villa for his family. They moved into the house in May. Next door, another villa is being constructed by the builder, Mr George Stratton.

Sadly Miss Eliza More died in July, being only in her early 40s. An even more tragic death was that of young Hannah Stuart, the daughter of Rev. James Stuart at No 22. She was only 12 years old.

Mrs James Cownie had a baby girl in April, and they moved out of No 21 soon after. It is now the home of MR ALEXANDER KEMP, the builder. He is a widower with two young daughters.

Mr Lothian put his house up for sale in February. He has lived in the Crescent since it was first built, but now he is moving to Murrayfield. The house has been bought by MR DUNCAN F. STEWART, a warehouseman, who lives there with his wife.

No 6 has also been sold. Mr James Brechin is to be married next year, and he has bought a house in Fountainhall Road. The house has been bought by three sisters, the MISSES THOMPSON, from Dunblane. Living with them they have three lodgers. Dr James Wilson is over 80, and has been lodging with them for some time. Mr Joseph Middlemiss and his sister, Miss Middlemiss, are also of an advanced age. Mr Middlemiss owns a wine business.

Mr Mudie's house at No 9 is let to MR ANDREW W. USHER, of the brewing family. Mr Usher is married, with a young son.

Miss Sophia Cleland has left the Crescent, and No 14 is taken by MR WILLIAM BRODIE, who owns a tea business in Picardy Place. Mr and Mrs McLachlan left No 17 soon after their daughter's wedding, and it is now rented by MISS ELEANOR FOWDEN. Miss Fowden comes from Manchester, and shares the house with Rev. George Fisher, a minister for the Baptist church, and his wife.

✣ 1879

There have not been quite so many changes in the Crescent this year. I will start at the Findhorn Place end, where Mr Gemmell and his family have moved out of No 13. The house is now rented to MR WILLIAM JENKINSON, who works in a brewery in Leith. He is married, and has four daughters, the youngest being born this year.

There have been three other births in the street this year. Mrs Thomas Cownie has had another son. They now have nine children, so it is no wonder they need the large house that they have built. (The house next door is completed, but not yet occupied.) Mrs Banks at No 11 gave birth to a daughter, and they now have seven children. On the other side of the road, Mrs Lawson, at No 18 had a son.

Miss Ellie Pulsford, the daughter of Rev. John Pulsford at No 15, married this year. Her husband is Mr John Mitchell, who is a cabinet-maker. Miss Agnes Middlemass also got married this year, to Mr W. H. Johnston.

MR HUGH ANDREW BROWN moved into No 16, but unfortunately he died of apoplexy in May, soon after he had moved.

Mr and Mrs Sutherland at No 8 have moved to Livingstone Place, and Mrs Sutherland's mother, Mrs Campbell, has moved to London to be with her son, Mr George Campbell. The house has been bought by MR WILLIAM BELL, a teacher of music. He is married with three children.

Opposite, at No 21, Mr Alexander Kemp died in October, and his sister-in-law, Miss Jane McGregor, is looking after his two daughters.

Mr Stuart has moved to the newly built Manse in West

Mayfield, and MISS ELEANOR FOWDEN has taken his place at No 22, with Mr Fisher and his wife. No 17 is now the home of MRS LAMB, a widow, with one daughter aged about 20, another who is still at school, and a son of 18, who works in a bank. Her husband was a coffee planter, and all the children were born in Ceylon.

 1880

We have a new tenant at No 21; MR DAVID CROUCH and his wife have moved in recently. Mr Crouch is the younger brother of Mr Henry Crouch, who lived in No 23 about ten years ago. Mr Crouch is the proprietor of W. Crouch and Son, the jeweller on North Bridge. After Mr Kemp died, his sister-in-law, Miss McGregor, decided to move to a smaller house, with her charges, Miss Jane (17) and Miss Elizabeth (15). They are now living in Gilmore Place.

Mr Stratton has found a tenant for his house, No 25: REV. JAMES GREGORY, who has come from Leeds and is now minister at the Augustine Congregational Church on George IV Bridge. He is married, and now has five children, since Mrs Gregory was delivered of a baby boy in the autumn. There is just one empty area in the street now. It seems that it belongs to the Stratton family, but there is no indication that they intend to build on it yet. In fact, it is used as a storage yard by Mr Alexander (the builder), which is most unsightly. Next door, Mrs Cownie added to her brood with another son.

Opposite, in No 3, Mr Stewart's father, who had been staying with him for some time, died in August, at the age of 79.

At the other end of the street, Mrs Usher at number 9 had a baby boy. Next door, Miss Isabella Mudie from No 10 was married. Her husband, Mr Yeaman, is a solicitor from Alyth, where the young couple will set up home.

1881

This year we had two more weddings in the street. At No 12, Miss Helen Middlemass, the third daughter of Mr Robert Middlemass, married Mr John Q. Donald. In June, at No 10 (Mr Mudie's house), Miss Margaret Thomson was given away by her father, Rev. Alexander Thomson, who resides in Bebek, just outside Istanbul. Her bridegroom was Rev. Donald Sage. He is minister at the Free Church in Keiss, between Wick and John O' Groats, and it is there that the happy couple will live. Meanwhile Mr and Mrs Mudie are staying at the family home in St Andrews.

There was one death: Dr James Wilson, who lodged with the Misses Thompson at No 6, died in April at the age of 84.

There were also quite a few changes amongst the residents in the street. Mr Banks the printer, his wife and seven children have moved to Mayfield Gardens. They had been at No 11 for ten years. The house is sold to a Mr John Anderson, but at present it is rented to MR JOHN D. GARDINER, a solicitor, who is married with three children. (Mr Gardiner was the agent for Mr Hogg when he sold number 27 to Mr More and his sisters.)

Mr Pulsford has moved to the north side of Edinburgh, to be near his daughter, Mrs John Mitchell. No 15 is now the home of MR DAVID K. B. WHYTE, who used to live in Findhorn Place. He is married with one son. His mother, two sisters and a brother also live with him.

No 16 lay vacant for some time, but it has now been taken by MRS OLIVER RUSSELL and her sister, who is considerably older. Mrs Russell has been widowed some 20 years, and has two married daughters.

No 20 had also been vacant after Mr Thomas Cownie moved to the house he built at No 26. It has now been let to another clergyman, REV. THOMAS DYMOCK who has recently retired from his ministry at the Free Middle Church in Perth.

He is accompanied by his wife, two adult daughters and his son.

At No 22, another widow, MRS JAMES HAY OWER, has moved in with two unmarried daughters: the elder is 24, and the younger is 17.

After Miss Helen Middlemass married Mr John Donald, four of the Middlemass children still live at home. The eldest, Miss Christina, is 25 and the youngest, Anne Middlemass, is 12. On the other side of the road, at No 13, Mrs Jenkinson has at last had a son.

THE SCOTSMAN, MONDAY 4 APRIL 1881

Following on from the diary, we will now look at the edition of *The Scotsman* that was published on the morning after census day 1881. In it was a column devoted to news from Ireland. Land reform was then a big issue. The 1870 Irish Land Act had given tenants some protection, but while the original bill had said that rents must not be 'excessive', the House of Lords had substituted 'exorbitant' in its place. This in practice enabled landlords to raise rents above what tenants could pay and then evict them for non-payment without giving any compensation.

In April, a second Irish Land Bill was going through Parliament; and when passed in August 1881, it gave tenants real security. However, there was considerable unrest prior to its passing, and *The Scotsman* gave several instances of it.

In Clogher, near Ballaghaderin, a large number of police were needed to protect a process-server who was serving writs. The police were attacked by 'a number of country people who made such a fierce resistance to the constabulary in their duty that the men were ordered to fire'. Two men were killed and four or five severely wounded (probably fatally), and 30 others reported to be injured. Two other evictions took place in the same area, while near Gurteen,

County Sligo, another large crowd attacked police protecting a writ-server.

In Dublin, the Land League – a political body looking for land reform – used the sale of a tenant's interest in two farms to highlight the issues. The paper reported a meeting the same evening. Referring to the events in Clogher, John Dillon, MP, said that he and Mr Parnell had told the House of Commons that if they would not stop the evictor in Ireland before the Land Bill was passed 'Irish soil would be reddened with the blood of Irish men', and now they had been proved right. In addition:

> Over 250 civil bills, ejectments and writs for rent have been issued on Colonel King Hartman's estate in Ireland. The tenants have determined to hold out.

The paper also cited other examples of unrest.

Nearer home, the same issue was being raised in the Highlands and Islands. *The Scotsman* reported an incident at the beginning of the troubles. A correspondent from Skye supported the status quo. He wrote 'certain circumstances … put a different complexion on the affair'. The township on the estate 'on which the difficulty has arisen' had ten tenants. It was estimated that it would be worth at least £120 to a single tenant, while the present tenants were paying £94. They had not paid their rent, saying that they were more highly rented than other tenants on the estate:

> There certainly does not appear to be any want of consider-ation on the part of the proprietor … I hope that good sense will prevail and that these tenants will not be induced to sacrifice their interests or lose their homes through the influence of an ill founded and thoughtless agitation.

However, this was at the beginning of the 'Crofters War'. For the next two years crofters protested very effectively, with rent strikes and land raids, about their lack of secure tenure of land and their severely reduced access to land. This resulted in the setting up of the Napier commission of enquiry, on which Donald MacKinnon served, and its findings ultimately led to the Crofters Act of 1886.

The paper also had a column headed 'From Private Correspondence' and dated 'London, Sunday night'. The topics covered were quite varied, and it was assumed that the reader had been following the events to which it referred. It can therefore be quite difficult to unpick the various strands.

The first two paragraphs refer to developments in parliament that affected Scotland: one on the legal system, and one on education. The writer then jumps to foreign affairs, when 'the Greek question continued to engage attention in political circles'.

Greece had gained independence from the Ottoman Empire in 1828, after a seven-year struggle. However, the majority of Greeks were still living under Ottoman rule, and throughout the 1870s Greece was continually trying to expand its borders. Things came to a head at the end of the Russo-Turkish War, when the 'Great Powers' (United Kingdom, France and Russia) were trying to negotiate a peace settlement. In 1880, France and Britain proposed a solution favourable to Greece, but the Turks objected, and it looked as if war would resume again. This was the 'question' that was engaging the politicians. Subsequently Britain and France fell out, and Greece was forced to accept a less favourable settlement.

Considerable space was given to experiments with street lighting. Two forms of electric light were being tested, and the novelty of having streets brightly lit at night ensured there were scenes of great activity:

> On the smooth asphalte [sic] with which the roadway is laid there were many bicyclists, and lively lads circled about on roller skates enjoying themselves to their hearts' content, regardless of the shouts of the 'bus drivers from whose vehicles they often ran great danger.

The writer then switches abruptly to HMS *Emerald*, located at the Solomon Islands 'whither she was sent to punish the natives for having murdered Lieutenant Bower, of the *Sandfly*'. A report from

the ship's captain was expected, and the correspondent was antici-
pating that it would be controversial.

Finally, there was a paragraph about a bill concerning non-
conformist marriages, and a Royal Commission had been appointed
'to settle the Transvaal question'. The tone of the whole column illus-
trates the confidence the writer has in Britain as a Great Power,
rightly influencing political decision throughout the world.

CHAPTER 10

Life in the 1880s

~

A key issue of the 1880s was that of the rights of women. In 1881 the Married Women's Property Act (Scotland) was passed, and also the Householders of Scotland Act, which allowed some women to vote locally. Until the passing of the former Act, almost all moveable property that a woman owned or subsequently acquired became her husband's on marriage and any heritable property remained hers, but was still administered by her husband. This was changed, and a husband no longer owned his wife's property. This was just one of a number of measures that made women more equal to men.

The 1872 Education Act had assured girls the same basic education as boys. Better education gave women more employment opportunities in the civil service, in post offices and in private business. The efforts of Sophia Jex-Blake led Edinburgh University to admit women graduates.

Sophia Jex-Blake was born in Hastings in 1840. Her father was a successful barrister, who believed it was wrong for middle-class women to work. However she prevailed on him to let her study, and worked as a teacher in the United States. After her father's death she decided she would rather be a doctor.

She persuaded Edinburgh University to allow her and her friend, Edith Pechy, to attend medical lectures. They both passed their examinations, but were not allowed to graduate. Her case generated a great deal of publicity and Russell Gurney MP persuaded Parliament to pass a bill that empowered all medical training bodies to educate and graduate women on the same terms as men. The first educational institution to offer this opportunity to women was the Irish College of Physicians. Sophia took up their offer and qualified as a doctor in 1877.

She later moved back to Edinburgh where she established a successful practice. While in Edinburgh, Sophia played an active role in the local Women's Suffrage Society. In 1899 she retired to Tunbridge Wells in Kent, but continued to campaign for women's suffrage until her death in 1912.

On the entertainment front, another Gilbert and Sullivan operetta, *The Pirates of Penzance* was shown at the Theatre Royal on 28 November 1882. A year later in June 1883, it was burnt down, but was subsequently rebuilt. Meanwhile the new Lyceum Theatre opened in September 1883, and the next Gilbert and Sullivan operetta, *The Mikado*, was put on there in January 1887.

Fashion (see Plate 21a) was influenced by the Arts and Crafts Movement, which began as a search for authentic and meaningful styles for the 19th century. This was largely as a reaction to the fashion for copying historical styles and to 'soulless' machine-made mass production According to W. M. Gilbert, 'The early eighties saw hatched two new dress movements: "the Rational" and "the Aesthetic"'.[1] The Aesthetics 'discarded the corset and attired themselves in soft material of a loose and flowing make'. This was the movement associated with Oscar Wilde, William Morris and Liberties, and pilloried in Gilbert and Sullivan's operetta, *Patience*.

The Rational movement had a different origin. Views on what was 'proper' for girls and women were changing, and middle-class women 'were given an altogether freer and healthier life. They were encouraged to ride, to walk, and to play lawn tennis. They skate in winter and many of them golf in summer'. The rational dress movement advocated woollen fabrics for underwear and the 'soft warm material enabled ladies to get rid of an immense amount of superfluous underskirts'.

On 6 May 1896 the International Exhibition of Science and Art was opened in the Meadows. The Exhibition was visited by Queen Victoria on 18 August 1886 and by the Prince and Princess of Wales on 14 October 1886. The exhibition included an exhibit of 'Old Edinburgh', showing replicas of several buildings that used to be part of the Old Town, but which no longer existed. They included such famous buildings as Cardinal Beaton's house and the Netherbow; and postcards of these reconstructions were produced by the Edinburgh photographer, Marshall Wane & Co.[2]

1887 was also the year of Queen Victoria's Golden Jubilee, when W. M. Gilbert says that there were 'festivities in the city from the 17th to the 21st [June] in honour of the Jubilee of the Queen's reign. The town was illuminated'. The Jubilee was celebrated throughout the country. There was even a new wallpaper produced in her honour, an example of which is now in the Victoria and Albert Museum. It was supplied by the company F. Scott and Son, and given to the V&A by the Royal Scottish Museum in Edinburgh.[3]

The Forth Rail Bridge was completed in this decade. It was started in 1883, and finished in 1890. It is the first bridge in Britain to be entirely built of steel. Two Englishmen, Sir John Fowler and Sir Benjamin Baker, designed it, and it was built by the Glasgow-based company, Sir William Arrol & Co. It was opened on 4 March 1890, when the Prince of Wales drove home the last rivet, gold-plated and suitably inscribed.

A DIARY OF THE CRESCENT: 1882–91

As before, this section is written in the form of the diary of a fictitious resident of the Crescent.

✤ 1882

It is hard to believe that the first buildings of the Crescent were erected nearly 20 years ago! The resident who has been here the longest is Mr Robert Middlemass, who occupies No 12, on the corner with Findhorn Place, on the north side. He bought the land in 1863, and was one of the first to build a house here. He is now over 60 years old, and no longer concerns himself with the everyday running of his biscuit manufacturing business. In fact he is often in the Borders, visiting his relations there.

Then in 1865, Mr D. C. Mudie moved into the street. He first lived in No 9,but now occupies No 10. He is also retired, and has been spending some time in the family home in St Andrews.

Dr Charles Wilson at No 7 has also been here almost 20 years. He is now 77 years old, but according to his wife, he is still corresponding with several colleagues on the continent – and in several languages!

His friend Dr Henry Newcombe, at No 5, is another longstanding resident. He also came to the Crescent in 1865, but is a comparative youngster, being only 69!

Between these long established households there have been some changes. Mr Gardiner, the solicitor, moved into No 11 only last year. Mr Andrew Usher, of the brewing family, has been at No 9 for four years, and Mr William Bell, the music teacher, moved into No 8 three years ago.

Miss Isabella Thompson and her sisters are still letting rooms at No 6, and Mr and Mrs James Sinclair have been at No 4 for over ten years, and are now in their seventies.

Since his father died in 1880, Mr Duncan Stewart at No 3 has given up his post at the warehouse, and is a man of leisure. Mr and Mrs John Crosbie Paterson have been at No 2 for over ten years. Their son, John George Paterson, is now 15.

Miss Philips has left the Crescent, and MR WALLACE HICKS and his elder sister, Miss Emelia Hicks, are now living in No 1. They come from the Isle of Bute, and he is an agent for a clothing manufacturer.

Opposite, on the south corner with Lauder Road, Mr Charles More still lives with his two sisters at No 27. Next door, at No 26, Mr T. O. Cownie, of W. Cownie & Sons on the Bridges, now has 11 children. The eldest, Miss Margaret, is 16 this year, and the youngest, May, was born this year.

No 25 has only been built for two or three years, and is let out to Mr Gregory of the Congregational Church on George IV Bridge, with his wife and five children. Another boy was born in April this year, and Mr Gregory lost his elderly mother in January.

There is still a gap between this house and the villas belonging to Mr George Alexander; in fact Mr Alexander is currently renting the land.

The rented houses in the middle of the street, on the south side, have naturally seen more changes of occupancy. Last year new tenants moved into Nos 15, 16, 20, and 22. This year No 18 has a new tenant, and Mr Gemmell has moved back into his own house, No 13, on the south corner with Findhorn Place.

Mr Lawson has left No 18, and moved to Fountainhall Road. His place is taken by MRS DALZIEL, who is in her seventies, and living with her daughter, Miss Charlotte Dalziel. Mrs Dalziel is the mother-in-law of Colonel Walker who rented No 20 a few years ago, when his children by his first wife were at school here.

1883

We have had a few changes in the Crescent this year. MR JOHN ANDERSON, who owns No 11, has recently married, and he is now living in his house with his wife and his father, Mr Duncan Anderson. Mr Anderson senior was, until recently, the Keeper of the Chapel Royal, and resided with his son at the Abbey in Holyrood Palace. The younger Mr Anderson deals in tea.

Mr Fulton at No 23 has married again. His new wife is Miss Eleanor Deas, who is a few years younger than him. After two years on his own, he will be glad to have someone to look after young Isabel.

Mrs and Mrs Brodie have moved to Portobello, and

PROFESSOR DONALD MACKINNON has moved into No 14 with his wife and family. Professor MacKinnon has recently been appointed as the first Professor of Celtic Studies at Edinburgh University. He has two daughters and two sons.

Speaking of the University, there was quite a to-do in June this year. Mr Hicks' nephew, Mr George Sibley Hicks, has been staying with him at No 1, as he is studying medicine here at the University. He quite disgraced himself when he was involved in a 'students' night' at the Theatre Royal. *The Scotsman* newspaper described it as a 'disturbance', and the University authorities took a very dim view of the affair. Mr G. S. Hicks was rusticated for a term because of his involvement in the affair, when the students disturbed the performance by singing and throwing peas and other missiles from the top balcony!

1884

After more than 12 years in the Crescent, Mr and Mrs John Crosbie Paterson have left No 2, and the owners, MISSES ELIZABETH and JANET SINCLAIR, are now living there.

In March, Dr Charles Wilson passed away at the aged of 79. He had been in the Crescent since the beginning, when he bought No 7 from the builder, Mr Hunter. He will be sadly missed. His widow, Mrs Elizabeth Wilson, is staying on in the house they have made so much their own.

In April, at No 23, Mr Fulton's wife gave birth to a daughter just a year after he remarried. The baby has been christened Margaret. Sadly, in July at No 14, Professor MacKinnon lost his younger son, Neil, at the tender age of 22 months. Just one month later, Mrs McKinnon gave birth to another son, whom they have named Duncan.

In December we lost Mrs Dalziel who had only lived at No 18 for two years. She was 77. Her daughter, Miss Dalziel, now wishes to move to a smaller establishment.

At No 26 Mrs Thomas Ogilvie had her twelfth child, a boy named Walter, and in May, at No 25, Mrs Gregory had another son, named Frederick.

 1885

At the beginning of the year, Dr John Dick died at the age of 71. He had been living in the Crescent since 1872. Mrs Dick (who is also 71) has moved to Bruntsfield Place, and so No 19 is currently lying vacant. Next door, No 18 has been taken by another widow, MRS MARGARET ANDERSON.

A heart-breaking death took place in February, when Rev. James Gregory of No 23 lost his young son, Aleck, to diphtheria. He was just three years and eight months old.

Mr Gemmell at No 13 has not been well, but his wife told me that he was 'cock-a-hoop' when Mr Gladstone won his seat in the Midlothian election in November.

Five people living in the Crescent reached their 80th birthday this year. Mrs Sinclair at No 2 has lived here with her husband since 1869, and Dr Wilson's widow has been here even longer – since 1864. Mrs Russell's sister, Miss Smith, at No 16 has been here six years, and Mr Dymock at No 20 moved here four years ago. Finally, Mr Middlemiss, who lodges with the Misses Thompson at No 6, has lived here for seven years.

By contrast, two babies were born this year. In October Mrs John Anderson of No 11 had her first child, a baby girl. They have named her Susan, after Mr Anderson's mother.

We have also had more building in the street. Mr Stewart of No 3 has greatly enlarged the house – raising the roof of the top floor, to make two handsome rooms and two smaller ones. He has also added a tower to the east side of the building, which has made the house quite striking [see Plate 21b]. Mr Stewart has removed to Greenock, and intends to rent out the house.

1886

The last gap in the Crescent has at last been filled. MR JOHN ROBB MATTHEW, who owns a draper's shop in the Lawnmarket, has bought the land and erected on it a fine detached house, No 24. The family has just moved in. As well as Mr and Mrs Matthew there are four adult daughters and five sons; two other daughters were recently married.

No 3 has been let to MR DAVID N. BERTRAM; who is the son of George Bertram, one of the founders of Bertrams, the big engineering works at Sciennes. His wife is the sister of Mr Crouch who lives in No 21. They have two young sons, Norman and George.

No 6 has been bought by MR JOHN MIDDLEMASS, the son of Mr Robert Middlemass at No 12. He was married about ten years ago, and he and his wife have just moved back to the Crescent. After seven years in the Crescent, the Misses Thompson have decided to give up renting rooms, and have moved to a smaller house.

No 19, where Dr John Dick used to live, has been taken by a lawyer, MR ARCHIBALD OLIVER. He is married, with four young sons. The youngest was born last year. Mrs Ower and her daughters have moved to Mayfield Road, and MR R. L. LUNDIN BROWN has rented No 22, with his wife. His brother, R. C. Lundin Brown, who died about ten years ago, was well known as a missionary to the native Indians of British Columbia.

In February, Mr Fulton's daughter, Madge, died at No 23, just short of her second birthday. Mr Gemmell has been ill for some months, and he passed away in November this year. Mrs Gemmell is considering renting out No 13 again.

On a brighter note, a second daughter was born to Mr and Mrs John Anderson at No 11. Mr Cownie has had a photographer in to take the family portrait. Mrs Cownie showed me the photograph, taken in their sitting room, with all 12 children.

The eldest, Maggie, is 20 and the youngest, Walter, is two [See Plate 22a].

 1887

I am sad to record the loss, in October, of Mrs Isabella Sinclair of No 4; She was 82. She and her husband have lived in the Crescent since 1869. Mr Sinclair has gone to live with his daughter in Lauder Road, and the house is let to MR DAVID GRAHAM, who is a commercial traveller from England. He is married, with four daughters.

At No 11, Mrs Anderson gave birth to her third baby girl, Elizabeth, born in October. Sadly, Mr Mudie lost his wife in December. She was 60 years old, and had lived in the Crescent since she came as a bride in 1868.

Mr Gemmell's house is let to MR BENJAMIN PEACH, who is working on the Geological Survey of Scotland. He is from Cornwall, and his wife comes from Sutherland. They have two daughters.

Mr John Robb Matthew, who only moved into the Crescent last year, died in November. His widow has nine children at home to comfort her. Earlier in the year, MR WILLIAM STEEL who had just moved into No 15 also died. His wife is left with three young children. He had taken the house after Mr David Whyte and his family moved to Leith.

Mr Fulton and his family left the Crescent after the death of his daughter, and the new tenant at No 23 is MR GEORGE MACKIE, an accountant. Mrs Lamb has also moved away, as her family is now grown up, and No 17 is lying empty.

At No 25, MR JAMES HAY is in residence after Mr Gregory and his family moved away. He has two working sons, and four younger children. I believe Mrs Hay is his second wife.

🌿 *1888*

In February Rev. Thomas Dymock died. He had not been well since he retired here in 1881, but we will all miss his gentle nature and friendly ways. He is buried in Perth, where he did most of his ministry. His family will stay on at No 20.

In October we lost another long-established member of the Crescent. Miss Elizabeth Sinclair, who bought No 2 in 1863, has died at the age of 70. Her sister, Miss Janet Sinclair, continues to live in the cottage.

There was another death in February this year. Mr Crouch's brother was visiting him at No 21, when he took ill and died. It was a difficult time for the family, as their mother had passed away just two weeks earlier, at the venerable age of 88.

We have had a few more changes, all on the south side of the street. Professor MacKinnon and his family have moved on, and two elderly sisters, the MISSES PATERSON, are now living at No 14. At No 17, which has been vacant for a few months, there is another Paterson, MR L. O. PATERSON, who is a retired army surgeon. He and his wife moved in earlier this year. MR GEORGE BROOK, a lecturer at the University, is now living at No 18. His wife gave birth to a little girl in November.

Mrs Russell has moved to Mayfield Road, and MRS ALICIA SUTHERLAND has moved into No 16 with four of her grandchildren. The eldest is a boy, and there are three girls. They are all the children of Lieutenant Colonel Miller, who is serving in the Indian Army.

There were two other births this year. Mrs Anderson at No 11 had a fourth daughter, and Mrs Peach at No 13 had a son. We also had a wedding. At No 24, Mrs Matthew's son, George, was married to Miss Elizabeth Hardie Cunningham.

✤ 1889

This year Mr Andrew Usher and his family moved away after renting No 9 for ten years. In his place we have MR ROBERT PATERSON, his wife and his son, who is about 30. Mr Paterson has a clothier business in South Bridge.

Mr R. L. Lundin Brown did not stay here long, and No 22 is now rented by another widow, MRS MCJERROW who comes from Annan. Four of her sons and her two daughters are living with her.

At No 24, Mrs Matthew had two weddings this year: her son Duncan, and her daughter Mary. Two doors along, Mr Cownie's eldest daughter, Margaret, married Mr Frederick Sly from London. This was a grand affair, and Mrs Cownie showed me a picture of the whole family and guests at the back of their house [see Plate 22b].

We have quite a number of young families in the Crescent just now – ten, to be precise. Mr Bertram at No 3 has two sons, aged 9 and 12, and next door at No 4, Mr Graham has four daughters between the ages of 9 and 14. Opposite, at No 26, seven of Mr Cownie's children are under 15: Bella aged 14, Annie aged 13, Ruth aged 12, Tom aged 10, Jack aged nine, May aged six and Walter aged four. Next door to them at No 25, are the Hay twins, Harriet and John, who are also four, and their elder sisters, Sarah and Grace (eight and ten). Gordon and Christopher McJerrow, who moved in this year, are 13 and 14.

At the other end of the street, Mr Anderson at No 11 has four daughters between one and four years old. Opposite at No 13 are the three Peach children: Angus, one, Elizabeth, seven, and Jeannie, 14.

Then in the middle, we have the three Steel children, Adeline, Wilhemina and Rueben, Mrs Brook's baby daughter, and the four Oliver boys: William, Archibald, Jasper and James. It is very pleasant to see so many young folk in the Crescent.

✥ 1890

This year MR C. J. SHIELLS, an accountant, has taken over No 18 from Mr George Brooks. Further along, Mr Mackie stayed only two years at No 23, and MRS EDGAR, who lost her husband last year, is now renting the house. Three of her daughters and her mother are staying with her. Mr Edgar was the Minister of Mauchline in Ayrshire. Mr Bertram has given up the rental of No 3, which is vacant, and is now living in his own house in Burgess Terrace.

This year the Forth Bridge opened, making the train journey to Fife and the north so much easier – no longer the train ferry from Granton to Burntisland,* but straight across the bridge and away! Mr and Mrs Anderson, who own a cottage up north, have been taking advantage of the new transport opportunities. The parents, the four children, and Mr Anderson's father, all went up there for their holiday.

Many of us in the Crescent have taken advantage of the new Public Library on George IV Bridge, which was opened in June by Lord Rosebery – a very handsome building with such a choice of books. Several people have commented on how useful it is to have such an amenity within walking distance.

✥ 1891

Earlier this year MR JAMES BETT from Bathgate rented No 3 with his daughter, Mrs John Willison, and her sons Campbell and Douglas. Both Mr Bett and Mrs Willison have been bereaved fairly recently, and they came to Edinburgh for Mr Bett's health and for her two boys' schooling. Sadly Mr Bett died in September, but Mrs Willison is keeping the house on, while the boys attend George Watson's College.

We also heard of the death of Mr James Sinclair, who lived

---

* The first train ferry in the world, which operated from 1849 to 1890.

in the Crescent for many years. He was living with his daughter in Lauder Road, and died at the age of 83.

There have been more changes in the villas owned by Mr George Alexander. Mrs Steel has moved away and No 15 is now occupied by MR WALTER STRANG, a teacher of music. He is living there with his two sons and his sister-in-law, Miss Logan. His wife died some time ago, and both his sons are in their thirties.

There has been one marriage, when Miss Annie Middlemass of No 12 married Mr Alfred Hilson, who comes from the Borders. On the opposite side of the street, Mrs Peach at No 13 had another son.

THE SCOTSMAN, MONDAY 6 APRIL 1891

The Scotsman on this day had a long article on the Census. It was taken on the night of Sunday 5 April, and enumerators were beginning the work of collecting the schedules.

It was reported that 'the poorer localities' had been well manned, the enumerators consisting mainly of officials connected with the Post Office 'whose familiarity with the neighbourhoods afforded them special advantage' in work 'of a rather difficult character for those unacquainted with the district'. They experienced 'a deal of good humoured banter' but the 'difficulty was not so much in convincing the occupants of the harmless character of the paper as in discovering their haunts':

> Groping along dark passages, stumbling over holes in the floors, scrambling up broken stairs, assailed by unsavoury odours, and encountering harrowing spectacles of misery in squalid homes, the enumerators pursued their labours under conditions far from pleasant or agreeable.

'Fear of the rent-collector and dread of the tax-gatherer operated in the minds of the poorer classes. When however they learned that there was "nothing to pay" there was less reticence shown'. Enumerators had to listen to the 'woes of the tenants' and their complaints against 'parochial authorities, rate-collectors and rack-renting landlords'.

There was 'the usual prejudice against the census among ladies of uncertain age'. One lady was anxious that her particulars should not 'come under the cognisance of her landlady'. The enumerator offered her a separate schedule, but 'she found an equally strong obstacle in the enumerator'. In the end the lady was appeased by enclosing her schedule in an envelope and addressing it to the registrar.

The article also refers to students in the Warrender Park district, the garrison at the Castle, the Royal Infirmary, and the 'birds of passage' who frequent the common lodgings of the Grassmarket, West Port and Canongate. The census was also taken at Calton Jail and the City Police Office, where there were 22 men and 12 women in the cells. They had been charged with breach of the peace, assault and drunkenness. 'With the exception of one Irishman, all belong to Scotland.' It was expected that it would take three weeks before the results of the census were known.

In other news *The Scotsman* reported that the Carl Rosa Opera Company had been performing *Il Trovatore* at the Lyceum theatre. It gave fulsome praise to the soloists and added that:

> The chorus did their work fairly. There was a well-filled house and the audience, who recognised the merits of the performance, were liberal in their applause.

Near home, there was a fire in the Chalmers Memorial Church, Grange Road. The fire brigade was dispatched without delay. The fire was caused by firewood catching alight, but, since the compartment was of brick and iron, the damage was 'immaterial'.

The death was announced 'at The Wisp, Liberton, near Edinburgh, of Mrs Dickson, the widow of a farmer, who had reached her 101st year'.

The railway race from London to the North between the east

coast route and the west coast was described in detail. The west coast route 'forced the journey in 12 hours 5 minutes' – only five minutes behind the North British train. There were detailed descriptions of how the trains matched up to the timetable, and why they had lost time, with strong winds, signalling and a burst tube being some of the obstacles.

For sport:

> The representatives of Scottish football received their first defeat on Saturday, when England was played, under Association rules, at Blackburn. The scores were: England two goals; Scotland, one.

The Scotsman also covered events abroad. The Court news included items announcing the appointment of Mr Nicholas John Hannen to be Chief Justice of the Supreme Court for China and Japan and Her Majesty's Consul-General at Shanghai. Mr H. H. Johnston was appointed British Resident for 'that part of the British territory north of the Zambesi'. He was to leave from Mozambique the following Sunday, and would be taking some engineering officers for surveying purposes; and would be organising an expedition to the Lake Nyasa district, 'over which he has been appointed British Consul-General'.

Another article reports the death, from diphtheria, of three people at the mission in Blantyre, East Africa. These were a Mrs Henderson, her three-year-old son, and the doctor who attended them. Blantyre in Lanarkshire was the home of David Livingstone, and the Church of Scotland set up a mission in what is now Malawi three years after his death in 1873. A memorial centre set up at Livingstone's birthplace says that:

> When Livingstone became the first European to explore large areas of Africa between 1841 and 1873, his exploits reported in his journals were as avidly followed as the first journey to the moon 100 years later – and were just as hazardous.[4]

It is evident from the extract in *The Scotsman* that the activities of the missionaries who succeeded him were similarly closely followed.

Turning to India, another article alludes to matters that were unfolding at the time. Manipur was an independent state on the north-east frontier of India. In 1886 the Raja died, and was succeeded by his eldest son. However, the second son and the head of the army (the *senapati*) dethroned the new Raja, who fled to Calcutta, the capital of British India. This second son was declared regent for the state.

The British Government decided to take a hand in the affairs, and in March 1891 the Chief Commissioner of Assam (Quinton) marched to Manipur with 400 Gurkhas. His purpose was to inform the new ruler that while he was recognised, the *senapati* must be removed. When the surrender of the *senapati* was not forthcoming, an attempt to arrest him was made, but failed. He then escaped, and the Manipuris attacked the British residency.

This was the situation when *The Scotsman* reported that 'The news from Manipur is such as to occasion some anxiety'. The British residency had been captured, and forces were on their way to attack Manipur. However, a Lieutenant Grant had been 'confronted by a large force of Manipuris, with guns', and:

> unless reinforcements speedily reach him the small detachment under his command may be annihilated. Rumours of the death of Mr Quinton are unconfirmed.

In fact, Quinton and four others had been murdered when they attempted to parley, and the British forces found Manipur deserted, captured the *senapati* and the regent, and installed a child of five as the new ruler, under British supervision.

Closer to home, we find evidence that times were changing. Issues relating to women's rights and those of the working class started to appear in the newspaper columns. The first public meeting of the Scottish Women's Liberal Federation was to be held on Monday 6 April; and the prize winners of the Edinburgh Association for the University Education of Women were listed. The results of the

School Board elections were discussed at some length. The thrust of the article was that 'working men have refused to vote for the so-called Labour candidates'. The article used the figures from the election results to highlight a number of issues: first, that the turnout for these elections was very low (less than 22%); second, that the wards that did vote were middle class, rather than working class (although the schools managed by the Board serve mainly working class children); third, that the voting procedure was too complicated. Lastly, the columnist thought very little of these 'so-called Labour candidates', and rejoices that a Mr Blaikie, who presented himself as a representative of the working class, received the fewest votes.

CHAPTER 11

Life in the 1890s

~

The opening of the Forth Bridge in 1890 greatly increased the ease of travelling north. We have seen that John Anderson advertised his cottage in St Fillans throughout the 1890s. St Fillans is a village that lies at the eastern end of Loch Earn. Until the early 1800s it was known as Port of Lochearn or Meikleport, and was a sleepy clachan of a few thatched cottages, a limekiln, a brewery and a distillery. In the 19th century it was laid out as a village by the Drummond family. It is five miles west of Comrie and twelve miles from Crieff. The journey between Comrie and St Fillans is widely regarded as one of the most scenic and truly beautiful routes in Central Scotland. The journey from Perth to St Fillans would have been made by road, since the railway did not arrive in Crieff until 1901, and was extended along Loch Earn in 1903.

The improvement of transport, both within cities and between cities, continued in the 1890s. In 1895 the London to Aberdeen railway races began, and in 1896 the Glasgow Underground was opened. In Edinburgh, the South Suburban Railway had been open to passengers from 1884. It had been feared that this would not be attractive to commuters, but when the half-hourly passenger services began, they were well patronised; several hundred journeys were made on the first day of operation. These services faced competition with other forms of public transport.

Horse-drawn trams had operated in Edinburgh since 1871, and a circle route, which ran via Marchmont and Church Hill to the West End of Princes Street, would have been very useful to the residents of Dalrymple Crescent. Cable trams were introduced in the 1880s. These employed a wire-rope cable within the road to pull the tram along its route. By the end of the century the system had 200 cars, servicing 25 miles of track; including the length of Princes Street, where it was introduced in 1899.

Improvements in transport also led to the expansion of the city. The Grange estate itself did not come under the jurisdiction of the city's administration until 1880. The 1890s saw the inclusion of Portobello (1896) and Granton and parts of Duddingston and Leith (all in 1900). A number of the city's landmarks were built in this decade: the Royal Observatory on Blackford Hill (1896), the McEwan Hall (1897) and the Scottish National Portrait Gallery (1889). Unlike Glasgow and Dundee, Edinburgh was never heavily industrialised, and publishing and brewing remained its principle industries.

As regards fashion, this was the age of the aniline dye, which allowed clothes to be much brighter than before. According to Fashion Era website,[1] Queen Victoria's influence over fashion was long gone and the real royal influence in fashion was the wife of the Prince of Wales, Princess Alexandra. The middle of the decade saw the 'leg-of-mutton' sleeve, with a tight bodice, and tiny waist (Plate 23a). It also saw the first appearance of 'bloomers' – baggy trousers which reached the ankles, and were particularly suitable for riding bicycles. They were named after an American, Mrs Amelia Jenks Bloomer (1818–94), although they did not become generally acceptable until after her death. Mrs Bloomer advocated these on the grounds that they were healthier than the voluminous heavy skirts generally worn, and she based her ideas on the dress of Turkish women.

Nearer home, 1895 saw the death of Professor Blackie, who had done so much to promote the Chair of Celtic Studies at Edinburgh University; the Chair first occupied by Donald MacKinnon. W. M. Gilbert reports that 'An imposing funeral, with an escort of pipers, took place on 6th March from St Giles' Cathedral to the Dean Cemetery'.[2]

1896 saw Queen Victoria's Diamond Jubilee, when there was 'great rejoicing' in Edinburgh, and bonfires were lit on many hills. In 1900, the Free Church and the United Presbyterian Church merged to form the United Free Church, a precursor to the final reunion of the Church of Scotland in 1929.

Finally, the decade saw the end of an era when Queen Victoria died on 22 January 1901, at the age of 81. Lady Monkwell captured the mood of the time when she wrote in her diary:

> A sad day to be remembered for the rest of our lives. Though we did not know it till afterwards, our dear Queen, who had been the background not only to all our lives, but our parents' lives, & has reigned 63½ years – on that afternoon *lay down to die*, I fear.
> I can hardly bear to write these words.[3]

A DIARY OF THE CRESCENT: 1892–1901

This section concludes the diary of the street written from the point of view of a fictitious neighbour living there at the time.

🌿 1892

I little realised when I started this diary 30 years ago, how many changes we would see in the Crescent. However, I am determined to record all the happenings as I have done since the street was first built.

At No 1, we still have Mr Wallace Hicks and his sister, Miss Emelia Hicks. They have lived there for nearly ten years now.

Miss Janet Sinclair has lived on her own at No 2 since her sister died three years ago.

Mrs Willison with her two sons is still renting No 3, after her father died last year. They have a farm in Perthshire, which her eldest son is looking after while young Douglas and Campbell are at school.

MR and MRS DAVID GRAHAM and their four daughters are at No 4. The owner, Mr James Sinclair, who had lived in the Crescent for many years, died at his daughter's house in December last year.

Opposite, Mrs John Robb Matthew and her family are still living at No 24. Mr James Hay and family are at No 25, and Mr Thomas O. Cownie at No 26. Mr More and his two sisters are at No 27.

In the centre, Mr Henry Newcombe has been at No 5 since he bought it from the builder in 1864. He is now into his seventies, but he and his wife are keeping reasonably good health.

Next door, at No 6, live Mr John Middlemass and his wife. He is the son of Mr Robert Middlemass of No 12, the biscuit manufacturer.

Mr Charles Wilson's widow still lives at No 7 – another couple that bought their house when it was new. Mr William Bell at No 8 has now lived here for 13 years. His two younger children (now in their twenties) are still living at home.

Opposite, Mr Archibald Oliver, the lawyer, and his family are renting No 19; Mrs Dymock, the widow of Mr Dymock is at No 20; Mr and Mrs David Crouch are still at No 21, after 11 years. Mrs Edgar, her mother and four children moved into No 23 last year.

Mrs McJerrow has left No 22, and it is now rented by MRS HANNAH PARRY. Her husband works in the Indian Civil Service, and she is here with her four children. The eldest is a medical student.

As I mentioned, Mr Robert Middlemass and family are still at No 12. Mr John Anderson and his family have been in No 11 since 1883. Mr D. C. Mudie is now living on his own at No 10, although his daughter visits him from time to time. She now has three children. Mr Robert Paterson has been at No 9 for three years.

After five years, Mr Peach is still renting No 13 from the Gemmell family. Misses Jane and Isabella Paterson have been at No 14 for four years. Mr Strang moved into No 15 last year, with his two sons, and his sister-in-law. Mrs Sutherland and Mr L. O. Paterson both moved here about four years ago. Mrs Sutherland is at No 16 and Mr Paterson at No 17. (What a lot of Patersons!)

MR JAMES HENRY BLACK and his family moved into No 18 this year, after Mr Shiells moved to Queens Crescent. Mr Black is a surveyor with the Post Office.

This year also saw the death of Mr George Alexander, who owns the villas on the south side of the street from No 14 to No 23. The business is now being run by his son, Mr James Alexander.

1893

Two of the original residents of the street passed away this year. Since his wife died some six years ago, Mr Mudie had been living alone at No 10. He died in April this year at the age of 76. He had lived in the Crescent since he bought No 9 in 1865.

In November of this year we also lost Mrs Charles Wilson, who had lived at No 7 for nearly 30 years. It was heart-breaking to see her effects being sold off by auction in December.

Another baby was born in the Crescent this year, at No 3. The happy parents are Mr and Mrs Alexander Inglis. Mrs Inglis is the sister of Mrs Willison, and the daughter of Mr James Bett who sadly died there in 1891. Mr and Mrs Inglis live in the Borders, and Mrs Inglis came to Edinburgh for the birth.

Mr Peach and his family have moved out of No 13 and it is currently being rented by MR DAVID HUGH WILSON He is a bachelor who previously worked for the Board of Supervision of the Poor. At the other end of the street, Mrs Edgar has moved away, and MRS HAY, the widow of Dr G. C. Hay is renting No 23. We had another bride at No 26 when Miss Helen Cownie married Mr John Philpott.

Mrs Parry and her children have moved to Nile Grove, and No 22 is vacant at present.

❧ 1894

Miss Sinclair, who has owned No 2 since it was built, has now sold it and moved to Corstorphine. The new owner is MR JOHN STEWART, who has a cloth-shrinking business in Mayfield Road. He is married, with two children.

Mr Mudie's house (No 10) has been rented to MR H. L. USHER, the brother of Mr Andrew Usher who rented No 9 some years ago. He is part of the Ushers Brewery family. He is married, and his wife had a baby daughter in August.

At No 11, Mr Anderson's father, Mr Duncan Anderson died two days before Christmas. He was 82. Mr David Wilson, who moved to the street last year also died late in the year, and No 13 is now let to MRS KINMONT. She was recently widowed, and has moved to Edinburgh with three daughters and a son. The youngest daughter, Miss Margaret Kinmont, teaches English, French and music. Her aunt, Miss Playfair, is also living with them.

Mrs Charles Wilson's house, No 7, has now been sold to MR FRANK RUTHERFORD, who is married with two daughters.

Across the road, three of Mr Alexander's villas have changed hands. No 17 is now rented by MR JOHN BRUCE, as Mr Leslie Paterson has moved away. Mr Black has left No 18, which is now rented by MR ALEXANDER MUSTARD, the solicitor. He is a widower, with a young son, and his sister lives with them.

No 22 is taken by MR GEORGE A. YOUNG, who has the bookshop on South Bridge. At No 16, Mrs Sutherland heard in

January that her grandson, Master Hugh Miller, had been elected to a Hon. Queen's India cadetship, after his examinations at Sandhurst. It is such a pity that his father did not live to see his success, but Lieutenant-Colonel Miller passed away at the end of last year.

Mr Wallace Hicks and his sister received quite a shock at the end of the year. Their nephew, Dr George Sibley Hicks, who lived with them when he studied at the University, has died of a horrible accident. It seems that he took a dose of laudanum to calm himself after a trying day at his practice in Derbyshire, but misjudged the amount. Despite the efforts of his fellow practitioners, he died as a result. He leaves behind a young widow, and baby son.

1895

The Willison boys have now finished their education, so Mrs Willison has taken them back to the farm in Perthshire. The new tenant at No 3 is MR RICHARD R. GIBSON. He got married this year, and the couple moved into the house in September.

There have been more changes in Mr Alexander's villas. Mr Strang has left No 15, and MR A. MACKILLOP is now living there, with his two unmarried daughters and his granddaughter, Miss Helen Thomson. He is retired, and used to work for the Inland Revenue.

Mr Bruce only remained in No 17 for a year, and MR GEORGE STEVENSON is now renting it. He is in the woollen business. His wife is from Glasgow, and they have five children. After staying here two years, Mrs Hay has gone to visit her son in Australia, and No 23 is now vacant.

Mr and Mrs David Crouch have moved to Mayfield Terrace. They came here over 12 years ago, soon after they had married. They have no children, having married rather late in life. MRS NICOLL is now living at No 21, with her two daughters.

She is the widow of a seafarer, and has moved here from Glasgow.

Two young ladies got married this year: Miss Jessie Bell and Miss Jane Cownie. Miss Bell is the only daughter of Mr William Bell, of No 8. He came here 16 years ago when Miss Bell was 13. When he came here he was working for a publisher, but more recently he has taught music from his house. Miss Cownie is the third daughter of Mr Thomas Cownie of No 26.

1896

There have been three changes in the street this year. Mr D. F. Stewart still lives in Greenock, and he has rented No 4 to MR W. F. BUIST, who has retired from the Argentine Republic. His wife was Miss Harriet Farnie, of the Burntisland shipbuilding family. Three of their children have returned with them. The former tenant, Mr Graham, lived there for eight years.

Mr Oliver and his family have moved to Lauder Road, and No 19 is taken by MR J. G. JOHNSTON. He is Canadian and unmarried, and shares the house with his mother. No 23 has being lying vacant, but it is rented now by MRS PATERSON, who is the widow of Mr John Paterson of Milton and Moat of Urr.

At No 11, Mrs Anderson has given birth to her fifth child, and her only son. He has been named Duncan, after Mr Anderson's father, who passed away two years ago.

Miss Helen Thomson, the granddaughter of Mr Mackillop, got married at No 15 in March of this year. Her husband is an American, Mr Samuel Ford Aitchison.

1897

We lost a number of residents this year. Mrs Dymock, the widow of Rev. Thomas Dymock, died in September at the age of 80. Her son, Mr Thomas Dymock, is staying on in the house with his two sisters. Earlier in the year, Mr Mackillop of No 15 passed away at the age of 83.

In January, Mrs Paterson, who moved into No 23 last year, also passed on. The house has been taken by REV. ALEX PATERSON (no relation). He is a minister with the United Presbyterian Church, and has a wife and two daughters living with him.

LIEUTENANT COLONEL ROBERT PENNEFATHER of the Royal Engineers, who has been widowed recently, is now living in No 21, with his stepson, Mr George Lowe. Mr Lowe is a medical student. Mrs Nicoll, who previously lived in the house, has moved back to Glasgow.

Two baby girls were born this year. Mr and Mrs Gibson of No 3 have been married about two years, and have their first baby, and Mrs Harry Usher gave birth to a second daughter at No 10.

1898

I have more sad deaths to report this year. Mrs Henry Newcombe died in April of heart failure, at the age of 70. She and her husband had lived in the Crescent for 33 years. Her poor husband was not in good health himself, and moved down to Woodhall Spa in England, but he died there in October. The house has been sold to MR J. T. GREIG. He and his wife (who is Australian) are in the middle years of their life. This leaves only one of the original inhabitants of the Crescent – Mr Robert Middlemass of No 12. He is 78 years old, but still enjoys good health.

Mr John Anderson of No 11 died in May, at the age of 48. His widow has been left with quite a handful, with four school-girls, and a son just one year old. Mr Anderson was a respected tea-merchant, and the family have lived in the Crescent since they were married in the early 1880s.

Perhaps the saddest was the death of Mr Thomas Cownie

in January. He was returning from work by tramcar, when he tripped at the top of the stairs, and fell to the ground, hitting his head on the cobbles. He died almost immediately. You can imagine the shock to the family. Mrs Cownie first put the house up for auction, but changed her mind and decided to stay on in the Crescent. Later that same year another daughter, Miss Annie Cownie, was married to Mr John Henry Morgan.

A number of houses have changed hands this year. MRS ELIZABETH RITCHIE has bought No 6 from Mr John Middlemass. Before her husband died she lived in Suffolk Place, and she has now moved in with her son and daughter. Her son works in the wholesale business.

No 9 is now being let to MR G. R. JAMIESON, from Shetland. He and his wife have four small children. Mr Jamieson owns an egg and butter business.

Mr Gemmell's family have decided to sell No 13. The new owner is MRS SCOTT, the widow of the Rev. George Scott. He used to be Secretary of the City Mission in Glasgow. Mr Gemmell and Miss Mary Gemmell are now living in Burntisland in Fife. Miss Elizabeth married a minister from Ayrshire some time ago.

Mrs Sutherland has left No 16, and is now living in Sciennes Road. MISS CRAWFORD, who comes from Cumnock in Ayrshire, is now renting No 16.

🌿 *1899*

Mrs Cownie had another marriage to arrange, when Miss Isabella married Mr George Montague Philpott, the brother of her sister's husband, Mr John Edward Philpott.

Two baby boys were born in the Crescent this year. Mr and Mrs Gibson of No 3 had their second child, whom they have called John. At No 9, Mrs George Jamieson also gave birth to a son, Thomas. They now have five children, the eldest being a girl of seven.

Rev. Alex Paterson has retired, and moved to Duddingston. No 23 was taken by MR JOHN STEWART OF ENSAY, whose grandson, a naval cadet, received an award in January. Unfortunately while he was here, Mr Stewart was taken ill, and died in March. He had a farm on Skye which breeds Highland cattle, and his remains were taken back to Harris, where he was born.

Two other 'newcomers' passed away this year. In August, at No 16, we lost Miss Crawford at the age of 69, and in December Mrs George Scott of No 13 also passed on. She was 74. Her son, Mr William Scott inherits the property.

Mr James Hay and his family have been living at No 25 for ten years now, but the house has been sold, so they had to move away. The new owner is MR JAMES HALL, who is now living there with his wife and four of his family.

🌿 1900

This year marks the beginning of a new century. I can hardly believe that I have been keeping this diary for almost 40 years! I am tempted to give up; but perhaps I will continue for just one more year. We had four deaths, one birth and two moves this year.

Miss Isabella Paterson at No 14 died in May, aged 65. She was the younger sister of Miss Jane Paterson, who, thankfully, enjoys good health for her years.

Both Mr and Mrs Buist have passed away. The house is being kept on by their children, and three of their grand-children are also staying in the house.

Lieutenant Colonel Pennefather died in March this year, at No 21, and the house is taken by MR AND MRS FRANK PEARSON. They are quite young, but have no children. Mr Pearson is a teacher of Mathematics.

MRS GIBSON, a widow from the Borders, is now renting

No 16. Her son and daughter are living with her. Her son works for an insurance company. Mr Usher moved out of No 10 last year, just before his wife had another baby, and it is now let to MR AND MRS R. S. GRACIE. Mr Gracie works in business. They are another young couple with no children.

Next door at No 9, however, Mrs George Jamieson had her sixth child, another boy, and they have named him after his father.

❧ 1901

This January saw the death of our own dear Queen. I feel we really are at the end of an era, and I will lay down my pen after this entry.

There have been quite a number of changes this year. No 6 has been sold again, and the new owner is the wife of REV. DUNCAN MACLEAN. I understand that she intends to rent out the house.

MR W. F. ROBERTSON, a medical man, moved into No 20 with his family early this year. They already had twin boys, just at the toddling stage, and Mrs Robertson had another boy in March.

After six years, Mr George Young has moved away, and number 22 is rented by MR JAMES ROBERTSON, with his wife and son. Mr Robertson is retired, and his son works in a lawyer's office.

No 23 is let to another widow, MRS BRYDEN, whose husband came from the Bryden family whose bell-hanging and window-blind-making business is in Great King Street. She has two daughters, Molly and Eva, and a son, John. He is the youngest, and is about 11 years old.

Miss Catherine More died in January this year. She was just 60, and had been living at No 27 with her brother and sister for over 25 years.

Now I have finished my *Diary for the Crescent*. So much has happened in the last 40 years. Only Mr Middlemass remains out of the original families who moved into the street in the 1860s. He is now 82, but still quite fit for his age. Mrs Cownie and Miss More have been in the Crescent since their houses were built in the 1870s, and Mr Bell has been in No 8 almost as long.

Mrs Anderson and Mrs Matthews have lived here for over ten years, and so have Mr Hicks and his sister. Miss Paterson has now rented No 14 for about the same amount of time, although she lost her sister last year.

There were quite a few changes in the early 1890s, when Mr Stewart bought No 2 from Miss Janet Sinclair, and Mr Rutherford bought No 7 after Mrs Wilson died.

Mr Mustard, Mr and Mrs Gibson, the Misses Mackillop, and Mr Buist and his family have also been in the Crescent over five years. The rest are still 'newcomers' to me, and I will leave them to the new century.

THE SCOTSMAN, MONDAY 1 APRIL 1901

On census day in 1901, *The Scotsman* reported an experiment in street lighting in Scotland. Dunfermline installed six high-pressure, incandescent gas lanterns near the Corporation Buildings. The High Street was 'brilliantly illuminated by a soft penetrating light'. The light was said to be half the price of electric lighting, while to obtain the same amount of light by 'an ordinary flat flame burner' would cost 'ten or twelve times' more. Electric light had been installed in Edinburgh in 1895, at the cost of £120,000, so it is clear that electric lighting had not yet become the accepted norm.

As well as the national census, a church census had been taken in Dundee the previous day (Sunday). There were over 90 churches in Dundee, and 33,470 people had attended. This was about 20% of the population of Dundee, and about half the capacity of the churches. 34% were male, 45% female and 21% children. The average collection at each church was £1-14s-3d. Nineteen of the churches were the Established church, 31 were United Free Church, and eight were Congregational. The article does not say what denomination the remaining 30 or so churches were. (The Free Church and the United Presbyterians had amalgamated in 1900). The average contribution per person in the Established church was 1½d, in the United Free Church it was 2½d, and in the Congregational church it was 3d.

Queen Victoria had died in January, and *The Scotsman* noted that:

> It is His Majesty's pleasure that full mourning be in use for the correspondence of public Departments for six months from the death of her late Majesty the Queen, and modified mourning for a further six months.

From London came a report on the Exhibition of the Royal Society of British Artists. It said that 'few, if any, show pictures of better quality than two young Scotsmen, Mr Hans Hansen* and Mr J. D. Fergusson'. The latter's paintings were 'more harmonious than Easter's scenes often are'.

The Second Boer War occupied a good deal of space in *The Scotsman* of the day. It was a lengthy war, involving large numbers of troops. It lasted three years and was very bloody. Boer commando units waged guerrilla warfare, blowing up trains and ambushing British troops and garrisons. The British Army was unable to defeat the Boers using conventional tactics and adopted many of the Boer methods. To flush the Boers into the open, they burnt farms and confiscated foodstuffs. Boer women and children were sent to concentration camps as 'collaborators', and the commandos were starved into submission. The last of the Boer commandos surrendered in May 1902, and the Boer Republics were converted into British colonies.

---

* Hans Hansen (1863–1942) was born in Copenhagen, but became known as a Scottish artist in his adult life. He was registered with the Royal Scottish Academy of Watercolourists (RSW). J. D. Fergusson, one of the Scottish Colourists, is now better known.

The detail in *The Scotsman* implies that its readers were well acquainted with the different aspects of the war. There were reports under various headings. THE WESTERN TRANSVAAL had subheadings entitled: 'The Peace Negotiations (a general surrender in the Marico District expected)', 'Successful work in the Utrecht District' and 'The Pursuit of Kritzinger (Extraordinary Boer mobility)'. THE SITUATION IN THE NORTHWEST had subheading entitled: 'Rebels again gaining strength', 'Guerrilla skirmishing in Orange Colony', 'Goods train derailed by Boers', 'Australian reinforcements', 'Restocking the new Colonies' and 'General Baden Powell in Cape Town'. There followed a list of casualties. There were seven deaths from disease between 26 and 29 March. Other casualties ranged from 'wounded, since dead' to 'slightly wounded, now returned to duty'. Next there were a number of items on movement of transports, and different regiments being sent to South Africa. The coverage of the war ended with a lengthy account of 'A dramatic incident of the war', when the army retired from Skion Kop, after a battle in which they had been defeated. The incident had taken place in January 1900, and *The Scotsman* chose to publish an extract from an article written in April 1900, describing the final retirement.

On a less sombre note, a decision by Lord Balfour, the Secretary for Scotland, to allow the Industrial Museum of Scotland to open on Sunday afternoons provoked a letter of complaint from Mr John Robson of Cluny Gardens. The letter quotes Lord Balfour as saying that 'The advantages will be very great as compared with the amount of labour involved'. This, says Mr Robson, admits the principle of imposing Sunday labour to facilitate Sunday recreation. If taken further, then 'the character of the day of rest will come to be altogether lost'.

This, however, is not his main complaint. He argues that since the museum is a national museum, Lord Balfour is acting 'as a servant of the nation'. The precedent that Lord Balfour quotes was a resolution in the Commons that the national museums and art galleries of London should be open on Sundays. Mr Robson goes on to say that when the administrators for Scotland take a resolution restricted to one English city and apply it to Scotland, 'many of us feel that we are not in any way called on to accept their decision. On the contrary, it seems to reveal to us a very serious defect in our system of government, which needs to be remedied'.

CHAPTER 12

Snapshots of Victorian Edinburgh

~

Edinburgh grew at a phenomenal rate in Victorian times. Dalrymple Crescent is just one street in the Grange, and the Grange is just one district forming part of the Victorian suburbs that ring Edinburgh today. The stories of the people that lived in Dalrymple Crescent, therefore, give us a good idea of what life was like for the middle class of Edinburgh during the latter half of the 19th century.

Because of the nature of the houses in Dalrymple Crescent, most of the residents only stayed a few years; we therefore also get a snapshot of their lives, and can trace where they came from and where they went.

With one or two exceptions, the houses of the Crescent were comparatively small, or they were 'built to let'. Therefore we get a greater cross-section of the population than might be the case for more prestigious streets, such as the adjacent Lauder Road. The population divides into a few broad groups. There were the large families, such as the Middlemasses or Cownies, who owned the larger houses and lived there for many years. There were young couples, the 'upwardly mobile', who would move on to larger houses when their families grew bigger. There were retired couples, such as Dr Charles Wilson and his wife, who were 'downsizing', and no doubt cherished the green space that Dalrymple Crescent offered compared with the townhouses of the New Town. Finally, there were the people who had moved to Edinburgh, and were renting in the street before they found a place of their own.

By looking at the lives of these various groups, we can gain an insight into life in Victorian Edinburgh, and perhaps appreciate that they were not very different from ourselves. In order to look at different aspects of their lives I have grouped these under four broad headings: occupations and finance, families and health, where they came from, and living in Edinburgh.

Excluding servants, there were 548 people who lived in Dalrymple Crescent between 1862 and 1901, in 131 households.* Of these, 166 were children (that is, less than 17 years old when they left the Crescent). Of the adults, 154 were men and 228 were women. These are the figures used in the discussions below.

OCCUPATIONS AND FINANCE

When we look at the occupations of the residents of the Crescent, we find that they are not much different from those of today's residents. Mainly we see a mixture of professional and business people. The professionals are much the same as today and included lawyers, doctors, teachers and academics, and workers in the financial centres. The one great difference is the predominance of the Church in Victorian times, which is reflected in the number of clergymen who lived in the Crescent. The businesses, however, were quite different. They consisted mainly of family businesses, predominately in the food and drink or clothing industries.

Of course, when we talk of occupations, we are talking mainly of the occupations of the men. In the 27 houses, over 40 years, only 11 women were working; eight of whom were teachers or governesses. Of the other three, one was a servant, one a nurse, and one (in 1901) a clerkess.

By contrast, most of the men worked, or had worked, for a living. Only one member of the street, Mr Charles More, consistently reported that he was living on interest, although in two cases 'Occupation' was left blank in the census forms.

---

* This may be a slight under-estimate. If I have failed to identify anyone, they would have been visitors or dependants of the head of the household.

The most common occupation for the men of the house was working in the clothing industry (11.5%). The financial sector and the food and drink industry come joint second (11%). These are followed by the Church (9%), the medical profession (7.5%), and government service (6%). These figures exclude the eight men whose occupation was unknown. Apart from the blank entries, the others were children when the census record was taken, but may have stayed on in the Crescent when they were adults.

As we have seen, the women of the Crescent generally did not work. Of the 131 households identified, 36 had women as head of the house, all either widowed or unmarried. In a number of other cases, a sister or widow became the head after the original head of household had died. Only one of these women worked for a living; she was a teacher, running her own school. The rest were living on 'private means', which would come from a variety of sources, mostly set up by their husbands or fathers.

There were several ways that women in Victorian times could be financially supported. A number of the residents reported to the census that they were 'annuitants', that is they were living off the proceeds of an annuity that had been set up for them. Others were living off the interest from capital, and others from the rent of property or land. Some, such as the Misses Thompson of No 6, found their income from letting rooms, or taking in boarders.

Bankruptcy

Bankruptcy was a common feature of Victorian financial life. With no limited liability, the personal property of the individual was not protected from business failure. There were three examples of bankruptcy in the Crescent. That of Henry Crouch was the least serious; on two occasions he waited until he was declared bankrupt, and then immediately settled his debts. Mr William Gorrie was not so lucky. The clothier business of Gorrie and Anderson was declared bankrupt in November 1869. The company, and also Gorrie and Anderson as individuals were examined for bankruptcy in December.

The firm had liabilities amounting to £517-2s-4d, which is equiv-alent to over £35,000 in today's money. Most of the creditors were based in London, with one in Paris. Several of the suppliers are still in business today, and their websites show that they are now very prestigious companies.[1] In addition, they owed £310 to their insurance company, and over £500 to William Gorrie's sisters-in-law.

Personally, William Gorrie had the following debts: £35 to Mr Proudfoot, the grocer in Grange Road; £18 to Mr Lawson, the baker in Newington; £12 to Mr Ballantyne, the baker in Clerk Street; £10 to the Mutual Insurance Company in George Street; £8 to Mr Stonehouse, the wine merchant in St Mary's Street and £100 to his partner, William Anderson.

At the time, Gorrie was living with his sisters-in-law, and the house was assessed for value. Most of the furniture belonged to the sisters, so his assets there were limited.

The bankruptcy procedure at that time was as follows: the creditors would appoint a trustee (normally a lawyer), who would evaluate the situation, and report back. He then administered the estate until the creditors were paid. In this case, the process (known as Sequestration) was completed in 1874. The main problem was that the company (Gorrie & Anderson) could not get their customers to pay, and it seems that the trustee was more successful in collecting the debts. Anderson went on to run another business, but Gorrie (as we have seen) emigrated to Canada.

The third example of bankruptcy concerns James Hunter who built No 5 and who went bankrupt in 1865. *The Scotsman*'s description of the examination was almost comical in the twists and turns of the evidence (see Chapter 2), but the more sober court account presents a serious picture. The trustee in this case was a Mr William Nevoy Masterton, a solicitor, at 10 George Street. He reported to Hunter's 76 creditors that 'the bankrupt having absconded and having left no Business books or State of Affairs' it was very difficult for him to assess the situation. Hunter owned a number of properties, which Masterton now administered on behalf of the creditors, sending a report of his (Masterton's) activities each year to New Register House as well as to the creditors.

In January 1886 the Account in Bankruptcy Department at New Register House received the following letter:

> Dear Sir
> I have to intimate that William Nevoy Masterton, Solicitor No 313 Leith Walk who was trustee on James Hunter's Sequestered Estate died on 18th May last & that I act for his Representatives
> Jas Gibson[2]

The debts were finally cleared in 1888, over 20 years after Hunter had been declared bankrupt.

FAMILIES AND HEALTH

Family structure

The family structure in the Crescent during these times ranged from a single bachelor to a family of 14. In addition, the number of years that families lived in the street ranged from 40 years or more to less than one year. Nevertheless, we can discern some pattern amid this diversity.

The households of families such as the Middlemasses of No 12 and the Cownies of No 26 represent the archetypal Victorian home. Large families lived in large houses for over 20 years. The children were born there, got married from there, and returned to the family home for frequent visits. At the west end of the Crescent, for about twenty years there lived two more households, representing another family structure. Wallace Hicks was a bachelor living with his unmarried sister, Emily, in No 1, and Camilla More was a spinster living with her unmarried siblings in No 27. Altogether there were ten examples of unmarried siblings living together. Of these, only the Brechin brothers of No 6 subsequently married, and moved out of the Crescent.

In the centre of the Crescent, the 'two doctors', Charles Wilson and Henry Newcombe and their spouses, represented a third type of family who stayed for many years: the retired couple. Elizabeth Wilson stayed on in No 7 after her husband died, but Ann Maria Newcombe died in the same year as her husband.

In only three cases were the houses of the Crescent used for what might loosely be called commercial purposes. Mrs Rosie ran her school for five years, the Misses Thomson let rooms in No 6 for seven years, and Mrs Brand took in lodgers between 1870 and 1871.

Mrs Campbell at No 8, and Mrs Sutherland at No 16 represent yet another type of household: both were widowed, and both had children and grandchildren living with them.

Of the three bachelors living on their own, Edward Lothian lived there for 14 years, but the other two were only there for a year; indeed David Hugh Wilson died soon after he moved in. There were 16 couples living in the Crescent without children. Of these, five were retired. Of the others, Mr and Mrs David Crouch lived there for 13 years after their marriage, but had no children, and John and Anne Middlemass were there for 11 years, with no family. For the rest, it is impossible to say whether they were childless, or whether their children had already left home when they moved into the Crescent.

The Robert Patersons lived at No 9 for eight years, and were one of six families that moved into the Crescent with unmarried adult offspring. Others included the Dymock family of No 20, who were there for 18 years, and William McLachlan of No 17, who was only there for one year.

James Fulton was one of three widowers who had young children. He lived in the Crescent with his daughter for eight years. Alexander Mustard stayed for seven, but Alexander Kemp died the year he moved in.

Altogether 21 widows moved into the Crescent: five had at least one child under the age of 15. This group stayed between four and seven years before moving on. Another group of six widows had adult children living with them, and they typically stayed for only one or two years.

There were 21 families who had young children born in the Crescent. They stayed anything from one to seven years. Another 21 families stayed less than a year, but in nine of them a family member died during that time.

I have dwelt on the various family structures at some length, because, despite the diversity, a definite pattern can be seen emerging. It is a pattern quite different from our own times. The bottom line is that the family stays together. Daughters never leave home before they get married, and sons only do so if they have to move away for a job or college. Even then, the preferred option is to stay with relatives. Unmarried children stay in the family house until the parent dies, and then continue to live together. Single women or widows share a home with their relatives or in-laws. The result is that the family home may be shared with parents, siblings, cousins, nieces and nephews, and grandchildren. Living alone is to be avoided if possible.

Life and Death

It sometimes seems that people moved into Dalrymple Crescent to die. Eleven people died when they had been in the street less than two years. Not all of them were old, the ages ranged from 49 to 86. Since the Grange was one of the healthier areas of Edinburgh, we cannot blame the environment. Perhaps they moved into Edinburgh to be near medical facilities. The case of James Bett certainly supports this theory. He was living with his wife in Mid Calder when she died in 1888. He then lived alone until after the 1891 census in April, when he moved into Edinburgh with his widowed daughter, Jessie Willison. He died on 4 September 1891, aged 66. Jessie stayed on in the house with her sons, and her sister Louisa came to Edinburgh for the birth of her son in September 1893. Soon after that Jessie moved back to her home in Perthshire.

By contrast, we can assume that David Cowan Mudie's move to Dalrymple Crescent, was motivated by concern for his daughter's health after her mother died of consumption in the unhealthy atmosphere of the Canongate.

To balance the deaths, there were 36 births in the street between 1862 and 1901. Sadly *The Scotsman* also reported nine infant deaths, a reminder of how precarious life was even in the relatively well-off parts of the city. In all there were 56 deaths in the street over the 40-year period. However, many lived to a ripe old age, with ten people living to over 80, and another eleven living to 70 or over.

The cause of death is recorded on the death certificate, and the following is a selection. William Alexander Dick died of scarletina aged 23 days; his sister succumbed to the same disease at the age of one year. Isabella Agnes Gorrie was a premature birth, and did not survive. Mary Banks died of bronchial pneumonia at the age of 11 weeks.

Amongst the adults, Jane Dick was 32 when she died of 'disease of the kidney'. David Hugh Wilson was 51, and after what sounds like high living, succumbed to a 'dilated fatty heart, valvular incompetence and cirrhosis of the liver'. Hugh Andrew Brown, at the age of 59, died of apoplexy. Harry Anderson died at the age of 60 having had a 'disease of the brain' for two or three years. John Duncan died of pneumonia at the age of 74. Jean Webster, at 77, died of 'Enlargement of left lobe of liver, frequent vomiting, renal congestion, exhaustion'. Charlotte Algeo, by contrast, had this verdict: 'Mrs Algeo had no particular disease, but died of natural decay at the age of 86.'

Lifestyle

What was everyday life like for the residents of the Grange? The men went to work, but the women stayed in the house. Most of them had servants, so how did they spend their day? We can imagine that the large families made their own entertainment. The older children would look after the younger ones, and there would be much comings and goings between friends, cousins, and other family members. What about the single women? Camilla More lived in the Crescent with her brother and sister from the age of 39 to 65 and older. Miss Emelia Hicks was 42 when she joined her brother at No 1, and was still there in 1901, aged 61. There are many other examples of single women living with their siblings or parents.

The Scotsman gives us some clues about their activities, with

references to various good works. In July 1891 the Russian Refugees'
Relief Fund announced the contributions that it had received. These
included £1-0s-0d from Miss More of 27 Dalrymple Crescent. In
October of the same year a bazaar was held to raise funds for the
'Furnishing and Completion' of a soldiers' home in Piershill. The
stall-holders included Miss Sutherland from 16 Dalrymple Crescent.
The 32 stall-holders were all women, and included the Hon Mrs
Hope, the Hon Mrs Montgomery and Lady Don Wauchope. After
these celebrities, 19 married women were listed in alphabetical order,
followed by 13 unmarried women.

Rosalind Marshall's book on the history of women in Scotland
gives some further suggestions. She says:

> In prosperous Victorian Britain, the feminine role was ...
> more passive. ... A leisured life was accepted as the norm for
> the married lady.[3]

Marshall goes on to suggest that time would be spent reading,
sewing, visiting and undertaking charitable work. However:

> Many women were left with long hours of tedium ... Unable
> to adapt satisfactorily to a life of inactivity and with too little
> to think about, they lay on couches in darkened rooms,
> prostrated by sick headaches and ... other symptoms. ... The
> *joi de vivre* of the eighteenth century was replaced by a
> gloomy sentimentality, and women turned more and more
> ... to doing good works.[4]

This tendency continued into the latter half of the 19th century.
Marshall reports that in 1887, Dr W. A. Finlay, at his inaugural
address at the opening of Leith Hospital to women medical students,
remarked:

> I would submit that much delicate health and lack of energy
> is occasioned by the want of an occupation fitted to satisfy
> the desires of the mind.[5]

Nevertheless, the fact that he was speaking at such an event shows that progress was being made in the provision of education for women. Daughters who lived in the Crescent may well have attended George Watson's Ladies' College, which was founded in the 1870s.

We cannot know how much of this gloomy lifestyle applied to ladies of the Crescent. Emelia Hicks was the same age as Catherine More, and they lived opposite each other for many years. Surely friendships were formed, with visits, and tea and gossip. When the Crescent was first built, private gardens were a novelty for Edinburgh. They provided opportunities for sitting out in the sun, and for developing artistic and horticultural interests; this would have added to the good works and crafts such as the 'netting and knotting, tambour work, tatting, beadwork, crochet and Berlin work' that Marshall mentions.

Transport

Until the 1830s there was very little public transport in Edinburgh.[6] In fact, throughout the Victorian period, the main way of getting round the city was by foot. John Inglis, who was chief clerk for an Edinburgh firm of lawyers, kept a diary from 1878 to 1881.[7] In it he regularly recorded how he walked to and from his office in the West End to his home in Stockbridge, as well as numerous other excursions. Nevertheless, by the 1860s the Edinburgh Street Tramways Company had been formed, and was running ten tramways for horsedrawn trams.[8] Line No 6 ran from the General Post Office up to Newington, and line No 8 from Churchhill, along Grange Road, to Salisbury Place. These would have been very useful for the residents of the Crescent, taking the ladies to the shops in Princes Street, and the men to their places of work in the Bridges, or the Canongate. In competition, the Edinburgh and Leith General Omnibus Co. also offered several routes, including Newington to Leith.[9]

Edinburgh is a very hilly city, and there were many places where trams could not run, and horse-drawn buses were initially the only option, However, there was a growing concern that the animals were being worked too hard, and better means of transport should be sought (not just in Edinburgh). The solution lay in cable tramways, which were first developed for San Francisco by a Scot, A. S. Hallidie.[10] Initially only the north side of the city was serviced, but by the end of the century the new form of transport was running up the Bridges.

An advertisement placed in *The Scotsman* on 31 December 1875 gives us one glimpse of the use of horse-drawn cabs:

> WALKING STICK – If the Cabman who found one in his Cab after taking three gentlemen to Dalrymple Crescent from the Edinburgh Theatre, will return it, he will be rewarded.

WHERE DID THEY COME FROM?

Of the 548 residents of the Crescent, just under half were born in Edinburgh, and half of these were children. A number were born abroad, although only two were true 'foreigners'. Ida, the wife of William Ramage Lawson, editor of the *Edinburgh Courant*, was German, and Mary, the wife of D. N. Bertram was Danish. The others give testament to the wandering nature of the Scots, being British subjects, born abroad. William Fraser Buist typifies this. His grandfather was a minister in St Andrews, and his father took up a military career. He himself was born in India, but went to South America, where he was an *estanciero* (a rancher). His children were born there, but he returned to Scotland when he retired, with his wife and some of his family. In all 13 children and 13 adults were born in India or Ceylon. Other parts of the world that were represented include Canada and the United States, Australia, South Africa and Russia.

Thirty-seven adults and nine children were born in England. There were ten adults from other parts of the United Kingdom, and eight of these were Irish. The other residents came from various parts of Scotland, and often the birthplaces of the children can show how the family moved around. For example, Archibald Mackillop worked for the Inland Revenue. He was born in Perthshire, but his first two children were born in Aberdeenshire in 1838 and 1839. By 1840 he had moved to Argyllshire, where his next two children were born. His youngest was born in Ireland, in the 1850s. By 1881 he had settled in Alloa, where he lived until he retired to Dalrymple Crescent.

Robert Sinclair Smith was another taxman who travelled throughout Scotland. He was born in Bower, Caithness, and his wife also came from Caithness, from Dunnett, where their eldest son was born. The next child was born in Inverness, and the next three in Edinburgh, in West Preston Street. They moved to 4 Dalrymple Crescent shortly after the birth of the last child, and stayed there for about two years. The youngest child was born in Aberdeen, and the family were living in Monifieth in 1881. By 1888 Sinclair Smith was serving as a volunteer in the Dundee battalion of the Black Watch, and he was living in Broughty Ferry when he died.

It is intriguing to speculate what brought them all to Edinburgh. In some cases it is obvious that their work brought them to the Capital. Earlier we considered the idea that the elderly or infirm might be attracted by the medical facilities. Schooling is another factor. But there remain a number of cases where the answer is not so evident.

Mrs McJerrow was born and married in Annan in Dumfriesshire. Her husband died in 1877, and in 1881 she was still living with her family in Annan. However she stayed in Dalrymple Crescent between 1889 and 1893. By 1901 she and most of her family were back in Annan. We can guess her reason for moving to Edinburgh by looking at her sons' records. In 1881 John McJerrow was a medical student at Edinburgh University, and ten years later he was still studying. Although she had two married sons still in Dumfriesshire, Thomas McJerrow, aged 21, was living in Edinburgh, although not with his mother. Ten years later, Gordon McJerrow, who had still been at school in 1891, was now living in Edinburgh. So it looks as if it was her sons' education and employment that brought her to Edinburgh.

Another widow, Mrs Edgar, moved to Edinburgh from the west

shortly after her husband died. She was the widow of the
Rev. Andrew Edgar, minister of the parish church in Mauchline,
Ayrshire. She moved to Edinburgh with three daughters, two of
school age, and her mother. They lived in Dalrymple Crescent in
1890 and 1891, and then moved to Fountainhall Road.

LIVING IN EDINBURGH

The Edinburgh and Leith Post Office Directories, and other sources
give us quite a few addresses associated with the residents of
Dalrymple Crescent. For instance where they worked, where they
lived before moving to the Crescent, and where they went after
leaving it. Of course this is only partial information, as not
everybody recorded their address in the Directory. Nevertheless we
can discern some trends.

Edinburgh at the end of the 19th century was much larger than
the city of 50 years earlier. To the south it had spread from the
Grange area to the foot of the Braid Hills (Plate 24a). Residents of
Dalrymple Crescent were part of this southward trend. They also, by
and large, moved into larger, grander, or more modern houses.

For our purposes, Edinburgh can be divided into three bands.
The first (north Edinburgh) covers most of 18th century Edinburgh:
the Old Town and the New Town, comprising everything north of a
line running west to east, roughly coinciding with the Cowgate. (This
includes later developments north of this line). The second (which I
will refer to as 'old south' Edinburgh) covers the area to the south
that was developed in the early 19th century, after the building of
South Bridge (1797) and George IV Bridge (1832). It comprises two
districts. The first is the area around the Meadows: Lauriston Place
to the south, Tollcross to the east, and Meadow Place to the north.
The second is the area that developed around the three main roads
to the south: Dalkeith Road, the extension of the Bridges, and
Causewayside and its extensions. This band is bounded to the south
by a line running west to east, and passing through Sciennes Road.
The third band ('new south' Edinburgh) is everything south of this

line, up to the edge of development at the end of the 19th century.

Before considering where the residents of Dalrymple Crescent lived before and after their time in the street, we can take a brief look at what we know about their place of work. Here we discern two main trends. Legal and financial people worked in the New Town, and merchants had their shops on the Bridges, and further south. Three solicitors and five accountants worked in the classical New Town of James Craig: George Street, Queen Street, Castle Street, St Andrew Square, Hanover Street and Charlotte Street. Nine merchants had their premises on the Bridges, or their continuation.*

On the Bridges, we can identify a number of shops whose owners lived in the Crescent: the jewellers W. Crouch & Son, the clothier and drapers William Cownie & Sons, the clothiers Gorrie & Anderson, the tailor and clothier R. Paterson, the hatter David Henderson, and the publisher and bookseller George Adams & Co (George Young). Continuing south, on or near Clerk Street, we find Brechin Brothers, butchers, poulterers and sausage makers, and Robert Middlemass & sons, bakers, confectionary & biscuit makers.

The pattern of movement in and out of the Crescent changed over the four decades, so it is best to consider each decade separately.

In the 1860s, 31 families moved into the street. About half came from the areas close to the new development, the 'old south' described above, mostly clustered around the main routes south: Arniston Place, Buccleuch Place, Duncan Street, East Newington Place, Lord Russell Place, Lutton Place, Rankeillor Street, South Gray Street, West Preston Street (see Plate 24b).

One person moved within the Grange area, from Dick Place, and five came from the 'north' of Edinburgh. Most of the remaining 30% came from outside Edinburgh, but there are a few for whom we have no previous address. Two of those from 'the north' bought their houses soon after they were built, and lived in the Crescent for the rest of their lives. Charles Wilson moved from Moray Place to No 7;

---

* This is a road with many names. After the North and South Bridges come Nicholson Street, then Clerk Street, Newington Road, Minto Street, Mayfield Gardens, and finally Craigmillar Park.

and David Cowan Mudie moved to No 9 from his house next to his iron foundry in the Canongate.

We can take a look at two other people who moved into the Crescent at this time. George Tod Bathgate was one of the few residents of the Crescent to be worse off in later years. He bought No 11 in 1863, but sold it within the year. By 1881 he was living in Murdoch Terrace, which, at that time, was a street of rather mean tenement buildings, where the flats, designed for artisan accommodation, consisted only of a bedroom, a living room-cum-kitchen, and a toilet.[11]

By contrast we can take Henry Haig Banks as an example of a family making moves to bigger and better accommodation. In 1868 he was living at 12 Arniston Place, now part of Newington Road (a continuation of the Bridges). He bought No 11 in 1870, and lived there until 1878, when he moved to 29 Mayfield Gardens, where he stayed. He married in 1860, and had three children by the time he moved to Dalrymple Crescent. He had three more children while he lived at No 11, and two more were born in his new house. Twenty-nine Mayfield Gardens is a substantial detached house, obviously better suited to a large family with ages (in 1881) ranging from 2 to 19. It is on the main road that extends south from the Bridges, and was (probably) built for him. Today it is divided into three flats. Currently the double upper top flat is advertised for let, with five bedrooms as well as a living room and kitchen.

In the next decade 39 families moved into the Crescent, and we have Edinburgh addresses for 19 of them. This time six were from the 'north'; three moved within the Grange area, and ten from the 'old south'. In this decade, more than half of the new residents were from outwith Edinburgh.

The 1880s saw the fewest number of new residents in the Crescent. Twenty-six families moved in, and the predominance of the 'old south' disappeared. The only interesting split is between those coming from Edinburgh addresses, and those coming from other areas; the split being roughly 50-50. In the final decade, the number of new residents rose to 34, and this time the dominance of the non-Edinburgh residents is noticeable: 70% came from outside the city.

Turning our attention to where they went after they left the Crescent, we find that 11 families left during the first decade. Of these, only one left Edinburgh. Seven moved within the 'new south', and half of these moved within the Grange area. This reflects a pattern that is repeated many times, and Alexander Aitken is a typical example. He came to Edinburgh in 1864, rented No 2 and stayed there for just over a year, before moving to Chalmers Crescent, where he lived until his death in 1900. Only one of the 11 people moved away from Edinburgh.

Over the next three decades, the 'new south' expanded until it reached the foot of Braid Hill. In each decade we have examples of the residents of the Crescent following this southward trend. In all, 83 families moved out of the Crescent, and 61 of these moved within Edinburgh. The numbers moving away from Edinburgh steadily increased, from one in the first decade to ten in the final decade. Of the rest, almost two-thirds remained in this expanding area.

At the end of the 1870s Fountainhall Road was being developed, and the 1881 Post Office Directory gives addresses for 11 houses. Of these, five have associations with Dalrymple Crescent. William Lawson, William McLachlan and James Brechin all moved from Dalrymple Crescent to Fountainhall Road, as did James Sime, who ran a day school at South Park.[12] James Brechin and his brother Malcolm had owned No 6, while Lawson and McLachlan rented houses from George Alexander, whose building yard was at No 1 Fountainhall Road. McLachlan, in fact, had two houses built for him in Fountainhall Road. The first was built in 1881 and the second in 1884.

In the 1880s the moves were very localised. Of the 12 people who moved, nine had their new homes in an area bounded by Lauder Road to the west, Cumin Place to the north, Queens Crescent to the east and Mayfield Gardens to the south.

In the 1890s another pattern emerges. Within Edinburgh, one family moved north, four moved to Marchmont,* and five moved to

---

* Marchmont was developed from the Warrender Estate in the 1880s and 1890s. Unlike the Grange it is predominately high quality tenement flats.

the new developments south and west of Fountainhall Road; to
Braid Avenue, Hermitage Drive, Hermitage Terrace, South Oswald
Road and Tipperlinn Road. Only two remained within the now
established areas of the Grange and Newington. It is noticeable that
in a time when Edinburgh was expanding in all directions, the
residents of Dalrymple Crescent remained 'southsiders'.

This review of addresses has taken us on a journey through time
and space, from the centre of Edinburgh, and the elegance of the
New Town, through the commercial heart of the Bridges, and up to
the Victorian suburbs of the Grange and beyond. We see that for the
earlier decades the residents of the Crescent are associated with older
and more central properties, while towards the end of the century
there is a move towards the new buildings on the south of the city. In
1861 a Professor of Divinity, John Duncan, was living in Buccleuch
Place, while 40 years later another Professor could aspire to the
spacious mansions of Corrennie Gardens. This, perhaps, encapsu-
lates how far spatially, and in ambition the inhabitants of Edinburgh
had travelled during this period.

AND FINALLY

The histories of the residents of Dalrymple Crescent in Victorian
times have given us an insight into how they lived and worked.
Official records tell us about their births and deaths, their family life
and their occupations. We know where they came from, and where
they lived in Edinburgh, and contemporary sources tell us what they
thought. Many things were different from our lives today. Disease
and death were more threatening. The majority of women were
dependent on men for financial support, either directly when they
were alive, or indirectly through the trusts set up when they died.
Their houses were colder and dirtier, and more cluttered, and
servants were needed to keep them clean and welcoming. However,
they had other things in common with the street as it is today. The
occupations of the residents were similar to those today, as were the
various types of households: a mixture of young households,

established families, and retired people. Quite a few residents had moved to the Crescent from within the Grange district, another trait that is still noticeable today. Finally, I like to think that the Crescent in those days was marked by the same friendliness and neighbourliness that is found in the street today (see Plate 23b).

AFTERWORD

The detective work

⌒

In researching the story of Dalrymple Crescent, I have been fortunate to be able to draw on two resources here in Edinburgh: the City of Edinburgh Library, and the National Archives of Scotland. I have also used the Internet widely, using a number of free sites in addition to Scotland's People and *The Scotsman* archives.

I had two starting points: the Sasine abstracts, which described the changes of ownership, and the census records, which showed who were living in the street at the time of the four censuses (1871, 1881, 1891 and 1901). The Sasine records are held in the National Archives of Scotland, in Registry House, at the east end of Princes Street. Initially I had to look up the Sasine records manually, but later they became digitised. Although the latter method is far more efficient, I am rather glad that I had the opportunity of handling the old volumes, and doing the research the hard way. It made me appreciate how much easier life is for researchers today, but we do lose out on the thrill of handling original documents. The Edinburgh Room of the Public Library on George IV Bridge holds microfilm copies of all the census records for Edinburgh.

There were two aspects of my research that made me decide to study the whole street, and not just my own house. I was struck by how connected the histories of the house were: the Hunter family and George Alexander owned a number of the properties. Secondly, having reached the census record for the Crescent, it was tempting to copy out all the information I had found; just recording one family seemed rather an anti-climax after I had spent the time locating the records.

Tracing the change of ownership was not easy, as the indexes for the period crucial to my research were only compiled by surname, and not by name of street. This was true for the 1860s; after 1872 it became much easier to find the records I wanted. However this early work made me aware of how much building was going on in Edinburgh, and in particular the how much the Hunter family was involved.

I was soon struck by the fact that many of the properties were rented, and consequently there was often no continuity between one census and the next. Because the owners were not living in the Crescent, I had no census information for them, so was forced to look to other sources to find out more about them. At this point I turned to Scotland's People.

The Scotland's People website allows you to purchase 'credits' worth 20 pence each, which you use to examine indexes or images. An index costs one credit, and an image costs five. The indexes to wills are available free of charge. In addition to wills, the information available covers births, marriages and deaths, and the census records for all of Scotland. Births, marriages and deaths are covered by two separate systems. Prior to 1855 the records were kept in Parish Registers, while after that date they were kept by the state in a national register. These records are referred to as OPR (Old Parish Registers) or SR (Statutory Registers). One of the anomalies of the records is that the indexes for the OPR records hold more information than those of the SR records. Since the people I was interested in could be born anytime during the 19th century, this fact influenced how easily (or cheaply) I could discover information about 'my people'.

For people born before 1855, the index supplies their full date of birth, and their parents' names, as well as the parish in which they were born. After 1855, the index to the Statuary Record shows only the year of their birth and the district and county of registration. Hence it was possible, with one search, to obtain the names and dates of birth of all the children of a marriage, provided they were born before 1855. However, to counterbalance this advantage, parish records were not as complete as the statuary records.

Another 'cheap' source of information was the 1881 census, which is held in record format as well as image form. While the image costs five credits, the text format costs only one credit.

By this time I had some interesting people accumulated on my computer, and a general trawl of the web threw up details about the more famous of them (for instance Professor John Duncan, Sir John Sibbald, etc). I also started using two free sites which provide very useful information: the International Genealogical Index provided by the Church of the Latter Day Saints, and FreeCEN, a part of FreeUKGEN, 'an initiative aimed at helping make high quality primary (or near-primary) records of relevance to UK genealogy conveniently and freely available online'. Both these sources are excellent, but the coverage is not complete, so whether a match is found is a matter of chance.

My next task was to fill in the years between the census returns, and two sources provided me with additional data. The Edinburgh Room at the Library has a set of Edinburgh and Leith Post Office Directories (ELPOD), which have been published annually since early in the 19th century. They contain a street directory, listing the residents of each street, and also an alphabetic list of all the businesses and residents. Since participation in the Directory was voluntary (and charged for), not everybody was included but they provided a rich source of additional material. In particular the occupations and business addresses of the citizens was often given. Having established that a person lived in the Crescent, if they lived in Edinburgh during a census year, I could often find the missing details and round out their story.

The Scotsman archives provided plenty of interesting background material. At first I searched on the phrase 'Dalrymple Crescent', but then realised that the scanning of the old newspapers was not always accurate, and a search on 'Dal* Crescent' yielded about 25% more extracts. Many were advertisements for servants, but some gave us the interesting stories that have been related in the main text. Some of the most intriguing leads were found in the Births, Marriages and Deaths announcements. One example will show how the various resources can be pulled together to obtain a (more) complete picture.

On the 17 December 1873 an announcement appeared in *The Scotsman* stating that a son had been borne to the wife of Mr Alexander Webster (of Melbourne) at 18 Dalrymple Crescent, the previous day. Using Scotland's People I established that 11 boys with surname Webster had been registered in Edinburgh in 1873. Two of these were in Newington (the District that contains Dalrymple Crescent). I used the IGI site to investigate these, but found no match. Then I realised that although he had been *born* in 1873, the chances were that the birth was not registered until the following year. I tried again for 1874, and this time got nine records, three being in Newington. This time the IGI site told me that Alexander John Webster had been born to Alexander Webster and Janet Margaret Brown on 16 December 1873.

Then I noticed that, according to the Post Office Directories *Mrs* Webster lived at number 18 in 1872, but *Miss* Webster lived there in 1873. A search of the Death record revealed that 17 females surnamed Webster had died in Edinburgh in 1872 and 1873. Of these the most promising match was Jean Webster, other surname Don, who had died in Newington at the age of 75. I looked at the image of the death certificate, and, sure enough, she had died on 18 June 1872 at 18 Dalrymple Crescent. Her husband was Joseph Webster, a mason. Her father was Thomas Don, and her mother was Jean Barclay. The IGI site stated that she was born on 22 March 1798 in Brechin, Angus.

The OPR records showed that nine children had been born to Joseph Webster and Jean Don, including Alexander, who was born on 3 August 1837. FreeCEN showed that the family had been living in the High Street in Brechin in 1841. Unfortunately Angus is not covered by FreeCEN for any other years, so I decided to halt my enquiries there.

I have one other resource to mention: the Valuation Rolls. These were taken every year, and recorded the ownership and tenancy of all the properties in Scotland. Until recently they were a formidable challenge, since they fill large books, and it is not easy to find one's way around them. However, they have now been digitised, and can be examined in the search room of the National Archives of Scotland in Register House. They do not provide a great deal of information, but they are complete, and confirmed that Miss Ann Webster was renting the house in 1875. Ann was another of Jean Webster's children, having been born in 1833.

The Valuation Rolls enabled me to track down another difficult case. The Post Office Directories showed that Mrs Nicholls had lived at number 21 in 1895 and 1896. This was not enough information to allow me to find out any more about her, but the Valuation Rolls told me that her Christian name was Louisa. A search of the 1881 census showed that Louisa Nicholls lived in Mochrum in Wigtownshire, and that she had been born around 1840 in Glasserton in the same county. Unfortunately her husband was not at home, so I did not have his first name. I did have the name of an aunt, Louisa Heron, who was visiting at the time, so I searched for her in the 1841 census, using FreeCEN. This told me that a Louisa Brien, aged 1, was living with Louisa Heron, aged 19, and John Heron, aged 34. Having found her maiden name, I was able to establish that Louisa Bryan married Gordon Nichol in Glasserton on 22 November 1866.

A further resource allowed me to dig deeper. The Friends of the Archives of Dumfries and Galloway have transcribed the 1851 census returns for Dumfriesshire, Kirkcudbrightshire and Wigtownshire. This enabled me to establish that Louisa was still living in Glasserton with her father, Hugh, and her mother, Stewart. At first I was a little thrown by her mother's Christian name, but was able to establish that it was the correct name, and moreover that *her* mother had also been called Stewart.

These two examples have been chosen to show how much information can be gleaned, from quite unpromising starts. Names mean a great deal in this detective work. Fortunately Louisa was a relatively uncommon name, and there were only two 'Louisa Nicholls's in the 1881 census. Some names are so common that it is impossible to be certain that the correct one has been identified. For example, Mrs Margaret Anderson lived in number 18 in 1885, but with no further details, we cannot pinpoint the correct Margaret Anderson.

Late in the day I discovered two other resources, and for which I visited West Register House. The first was the field books of the Inland Revenue survey of 1912. Although rather later than my period, they offered the most complete architectural description of the houses in the Crescent. The other resource was the detailed records of the bankruptcy proceedings against William Gorrie and James Hunter. They had a wealth of detail including minutes of all the meetings of creditors during the Sequestration Process.

The detective work has been fun, and it is addictive. No doubt I will continue to chase up loose ends well into the next decade. News of any more findings will be posted on my website www.dcedin. co.uk.

BIBLIOGRAPHY

Anderson, R. D., Lynch, M. and Phillipson, N., 'The University of Edinburgh, An
  Illustrated History', Edinburgh University Press, 2003, ISBN-10: 0-7486-1646-2
Beeton, I., 'Mrs Beeton's Book of Household Management', 1859–1861
Cant, M., 'Edinburgh: Sciennes and the Grange', John Donald Publishers, 1990,
  ISBN-10: 0-85976-253-X
Flanders, J., 'The Victorian House: Domestic life from childbirth to death', Harper
  Collins, 2003, ISBN-10: 0-00-713188-7
Fry, M., 'Edinburgh, a History of the City', Macmillan, 2009,
  ISBN-13: 978-0-230-70386-5
Gifford, J., McWilliam, C. and Walker, D. M., 'Edinburgh (The Buildings
  of Scotland)', Harmondsworth: Penguin Books Ltd, 1984,
  ISBN-10: 0-14-07106-8.
Gilbert, W. M. (ed). 'Edinburgh in the Nineteenth Century', Published by
  J&R Allan Ltd, Edinburgh, 1901
Grant, J., 'Old and New Edinburgh', Cassells, 1880,
  http://www.oldandnewedinburgh.co.uk/
Grierson, M. G., 'A Hundred Years in Princes Street 1838–1938', Published by
  Jenners, Princes Street, Edinburgh Ltd, 1938
Hunter, D. L. G., 'Edinburgh's Transport: The Early Years', Mercat Press, 1992,
  ISBN-10: 1-873644-02-7
Inglis, J. (ed Vaughan, E.), 'A Victorian Edinburgh Diary', The Ramsay Head Press,
  1984, ISBN-10: 0-902859-84-6
Lee, T. A., 'Seekers of truth: the Scottish founders of modern public accountancy',
  JAI press, 2006, ISBN-13: 978-0-7623-1298-6
Lythe, S.G.E., 'Gourlays of Dundee; The Rise and Fall of a Scottish Shipbuilding
  Firm', Abertay Historical Society Publication No. 10, 1964
Marshall, R. K., 'Virgins and Viragos: A History of women in Scotland from
  1080–1980', Collins, 8 Grafton Street, London W1, 1983,
  ISBN-10: 0-00-216039-0

Monkwell, Lady M. (ed Collier, E. C. F.), 'A Victorian Diarist: later extracts from
    the Journals of Mary, Lady Monkwell 1895-1909', John Murray, 1946
Pride. G. L., 'Dictionary of Scottish Building', Rutland Press, 1996,
    ISBN-10: 1-873190-45-X
Rodger, R., 'The Transformation of Edinburgh: Land, Property and Trust in the
    Nineteenth Century', Cambridge University Press, 2001,
    ISBN-10: 0-521-78024-1
Sheets, J. W., 'Professor Donald MacKinnon and Doctor Roger McNeill, Gaelic
    "Lads o Pairts" from Colonsay', University of Edinburgh Library Special
    Collection
Smith, C. J., 'Historic South Edinburgh', John Donald Publishers Ltd; 2nd Revised
    edition, 2003, ISBN-13: 978-0-85976-540-4
The City of Edinburgh Council, 'Grange Conservation Area Character Appraisal',
    http://download.edinburgh.gov.uk/caca/Grange_CACA.pdf

GLOSSARY OF
ARCHITECTURAL TERMS

⁓

The terms in this Glossary come from five main sources:
A. *Pride's Dictionary of Scottish Building Terms* (see Bibliography)
B. The Probert Dictionary of Architecture*:
   http://www.probertencyclopaedia.com/
C. The Dictionary of the Scots language: http://www.dsl.ac.uk/
D. Structural Wiki: http://www.structuralwiki.org/en/Main_Page
E. Historic Scotland Glossary: http://www.historic-scotland.gov.uk/
   memorandum-app3.pdf

Architrave (B): Architrave applies to the group of mouldings, above and on both
   sides of a door or other opening, the term being used especially if they are
   square in form.
Ashlar (B): Hewn or squared stone, as distinguished from that which is rough, as
   when it came from the quarry.
Bargeboards (E): Boards placed at the inclines of a gable to hide the ends of the
   roof timbers, and usually projected from the wall-face; often pierced,
   traceried or otherwise decoratively treated.
Bow window (B): A bow window is a elliptically-curved window projecting from
   the face of a wall. Bow windows originated with the late Gothic style. While a
   bay window reaches to the ground, a bow window differs in not reaching the
   ground.
Camp ceiling (B): A kind of ceiling often used in attics or garrets, in which the side
   walls are inclined inward at the top, following the slope of the rafters, to meet
   the plane surface of the upper ceiling.
Coursed rubble (A): Rubblework where the stones are rough-hewn, but laid in
   horizontal bands.

Droved dressing (D): A finish in stonework wrought with a broad chisel or hammer in parallel flutings across the face from end to end.

Quoin (B): A quoin was originally a solid exterior angle, as of a building. Now the term is commonly applied to one of the selected pieces of material by which the corner is marked. The quoins consist of blocks larger than those used in the rest of the building, and cut to dimension.

Rubble (E): Masonry which is not fully dressed; can be of boulders; or of random rubble retaining in some degree the natural shape of the stone; or of squared rubble in which the stones are roughly squared and may be either coursed or snecked; that is with variations in the coursing brought about by the use of small filler stones or snecks.

Rubblework (B): Rubblework is a coarse type of masonry that is constructed of rough, unsquared stones that are not large, but are irregular in size and shape.

Snecked (E): Form of rubble construction composed of squared stones in which the coursing is varied by small filler stones or snecks.

Splay (B): A splay (abbreviated from display) is a slope or bevel, especially of the sides of a door or window, by which the opening is made larger at one face of the wall than at the other.

Wallhead (A): The top of the wall: where the wall and roof meet.

PRINCIPAL PEOPLE ASSOCIATED WITH DALRYMPLE CRESCENT

Aitken
    Alexander, tenant of No 2 from 1864 to 1865
Alexander
    George, owner of Nos 14 to 23 from 1865 to 1901
Algeo
    Charlotte, visitor to No 19 in 1875
Anderson
    Harry, tenant of No 10 from 1870 to 1871
    John, owner of No 11 from 1883 to 1901
    Margaret, tenant of No 18 in 1895
Banks
    Henry Haig, owner of No 11 from 1870 to 1878
    John H., tenant of No 23 from 1875 to 1876
Bathgate
    George Tod, owner of No 11 in 1863
Beattie
    Robert Purves, tenant of No 14 in 1872
Bell
    William, owner of No 8 from 1879 to 1901
Bertram
    David Noble, tenant of No 3 from 1885 to 1889
Bett
    James, tenant of No 3 in 1891
Black
    James Henry, tenant of No 18 from 1892 to 1893
Brand
    Charlotte, tenant of No 22 from 1870 to 1871
Brechin
    James, owner of No 6 from 1874 to 1877

Brodie
>William, tenant of No 14 from 1878 to 1881

Brook
>George, tenant of No 18 in 1888

Brown
>Hugh Andrew, tenant of No 16 in 1879

Bruce
>John, tenant of No 17 in 1894

Bryden
>Lizza C., tenant of No 23 in 1901

Buist
>William Fraser, tenant of No 4 from 1896 to 1901

Campbell
>Ann, owner of No 8 from 1865 to 1878

Chalmers
>Alexander Henderson, land owner (No 13) in 1864

Cleland
>Janet, tenant of No 16 from 1877 to 1879
>Sophia L., tenant of No 14 from 1872 to 1877

Cousin
>George, surveyor for No 13 in 1864

Cownie
>James Gibb, tenant of No 21 in 1877
>Thomas Ogilvie, tenant of No 20 and owner of No 26 from 1877 to 1901

Crawford
>Margaret, tenant of No 16 in 1899

Crouch
>David Hugh, tenant of No 21 from 1880 to 1893
>Henry Brougham, tenant of No 23 from 1869 to 1871

Dalziel
>Charlotte, tenant of No 18 from 1882 to 1884

Dick
>John, tenant of No 19 from 1872 to 1884
>Robert, tenant of No 23 from 1872 to 1875

Downie
>Mary Amelia, tenant of No 21 from 1875 to 1876

Duncan
>John, owner of No 10 from 1864 to 1870

Dymock
>Thomas, tenant of No 20 from 1881 to 1898

Edgar
>Mary S., tenant of No 23 from 1891 to 1892

Firmstone
    Jean, tenant of No 21 from 1875 to 1876
Fisher
    George, tenant of Nos 17 and 22 from 1878 to 1880
Forster Pratt
    Frances, tenant of No 22 from 1868 to 1869
Fowden
    Eleanor, tenant of No 22 from 1878 to 1880
Fraser
    Robert William, tenant of No 1 from 1868 to 1873
Fulton
    James J., tenant of No 23 from 1877 to 1885
Gardiner
    John D., tenant of No 11 from 1881 to 1882
Gemmell
    Robert, owner of No 13 from 1865 to 1886
Gibson
    Agnes, tenant of No 16 from 1900 to 1901
    Richard R., tenant of No 3 from 1895 to 1901
Gilmour
    David, owner of No 1 from 1870 to 1893
Gorrie
    William, tenant of No 1 from 1863 to 1867
Gracie
    Robert S., tenant of No 10 from 1900 to 1901
Graham
    David, tenant of No 4 from 1887 to 1895
Gregory
    James, tenant of No 25 from 1880
Grieg
    James Thompson, owner of No 5 from 1899 to 1901
Hall
    James, owner of No 25 from 1899 to 1901
Hay
    James, tenant of No 25 from 1888 to 1898
    Marianne, tenant of No 23 from 1883 to 1884
Henderson
    Andrew, tenant of No 9 from 1872 to 1877
    David, owner of No 6 from 1866 to 1873
Hicks
    Wallace, owner of No 1 from 1882 to 1901

Hogg
>James, builder of No 27 from 1873 to 1874

Hunter
>James, builder of No 5 from 1862 to 1865
>Robert, builder and owner of No 6 from 1863 to 1865
>Samuel, builder of No 7, 8 and 9 from 1862 to 1865

Inglis
>Robert, land owner (No 4) from 1863 to 1866

Jamieson
>George R., tenant of No 9 from 1898 to 1901

Jenkinson
>William, tenant of No 13 from 1879 to 1881

Johnston
>Elizabeth, owner of No 1 from 1862 to 1869
>John G., tenant of No 19 from 1897 to 1901

Kemp
>Alexander, tenant of No 21 in 1879

Kinmont
>Anne, tenant of No 13 in 1897

Lamb
>Margaret G., tenant of No 17 from 1879 to 1886

Lawson
>William, tenant of No 18 from 1875 to 1881

Leadbetter
>Charles, land owner and architect of Nos 10 and 11 in 1862

Lister
>Richard, owner of No 11 and tenant of No 22, 1865 to 1876

Lothian
>Edward, owner of No 3 from 1863 to 1877

Lundin Brown
>R. L., tenant of No 22 in 1887

MacCalman
>Archibald, tenant of No 17 from 1874 to 1876

Mackie
>George, tenant of No 23 from 1887 to 1889

Mackillop
>Archibald, tenant of No 15 from 1891 to 1897

MacKinnon
>Donald, tenant of No 14 from 1883 to 1886

Maclean
>Isabella, owner of No 6 in 1901

Matthew
    John Robb, owner of No 24 from 1886 to 1901
McJerrow
    Jane, tenant of No 22 from 1889 to 1893
McLachlan
    William, tenant of No 17 in 1877
Middlemass
    John, owner of No 6 from 1886 to 1897
    Robert, owner of No 12 from 1863 to 1901
More
    Camilla, owner of No 27 from 1875 to 1901
Mudie
    David Cowan, owner of Nos 9 and 10 from 1865 to 1893
Mustard
    Alexander, tenant of No 18 from 1894 to 1901
Newcombe
    Henry, owner of No 5 from 1865 to 1898
Nicholls
    Louisa, tenant of No 21 from 1895 to 1896
Oliver
    Archibald, tenant of No 19 from 1886 to 1894
Ower
    Caroline L., tenant of No 22 from 1882 to 1885
Parry
    Hannah M., tenant of No 22 in 1892
Paterson
    Alex, tenant of No 23 from 1897 to 1899
    Anne, tenant of No 23 in 1896
    Jane, tenant of No 14 from 1888 to 1901
    John, land owner (No 27) from 1868 to 1872
    John Crosbie, tenant of No 2 from 1870 to 1882
    Leslie O., tenant of No 17 from 1888 to 1893
    Robert, tenant of No 9 from 1889 to 1897
    Robert (City Architect), land owner (Nos 13 to 27) in 1864
Peach
    Benjamin Neeve, tenant of No 13 from 1887 to 1891
Pearson
    Frank R. J., tenant of No 21 in 1901
Pennefather
    Robert P., tenant of No 21 from 1897 to 1900
Phillips
    Mary Ann, tenant of No 1 from 1875 to 1882

Plummer
> Margaret, tenant of No 21 in 1876

Pulsford
> John, tenant of No 15 from 1868 to 1880

Ritchie
> Elizabeth, owner of No 6 from 1898 to 1900

Robertson
> James, tenant of No 22 in 1901
> William Ford, tenant of No 20 in 1901

Rosie
> Margaret, tenant of Nos 17 and 20 from 1868 to 1873

Russell
> Jane Ann, tenant of No 16 from 1881 to 1887

Rutherford
> David, builder of No 4 from 1866 to 1867
> Frank, owner of No 7 from 1894 to 1901

Sandeman
> Mary, friend at No 10 from 1864 to 1869

Scott
> Janet, owner of No 13 from 1899 to 1901

Shiells
> Courtenay John, tenant of No 18 from 1890 to 1891

Sibbald
> John, tenant of No 16 from 1871 to 1874

Sime
> James, tenant of No 16 in 1875

Simpson
> John, tenant of No 21 from 1868 to 1873
> Peter, land owner (Nos 24, 25 and 26) from 1872 to 1877

Sinclair
> Elizabeth and Janet, owners of No 2 from 1884 to 1894
> James, owner of No 4 from 1869 to 1886

Smith
> James Wilson, land owner and architect of Nos 10 and 11 in 1862
> Robert Sinclair, owner of No 4 from 1867 to 1868

Steel
> William, tenant of No 15 from 1887 to 1890

Stevenson
> George, tenant of No 17 from 1895 to 1901

Stewart
> Duncan Francis, owner of No 3 from 1878 to 1884
> John, owner of No 2 from 1896 to 1901

John of Ensay, visitor to No 23 in 1899

Strang
　　Walter, tenant of No 15 from 1891 to 1894

Stratton
　　George, land owner (Nos 24 and 25) from 1878 to 1881

Stuart
　　James T., tenant of No 22 from 1877 to 1878

Sutherland
　　Alicia, tenant of No 16 from 1891 to 1896

Thompson
　　Isabella, owner of No 6 from 1878 to 1885

Usher
　　Andrew William, tenant of No 9 from 1878 to 1888
　　Harry Lawrence, tenant of No 10 from 1895 to 1898

Walker
　　William, tenant of No 20 from 1872 to 1874

Watt
　　John, tenant of No 2 from 1867 to 1869

Webster
　　Jean, tenant of No 18 from 1872 to 1875

Wellstood
　　Stephen, tenant of No 14 from 1870 to 1871

Whyte
　　David K. B., tenant of No 15 from 1881 to 1885

Williamson
　　Mary, tenant of No 20 in 1876

Willison
　　Jessie, tenant of No 3 from 1891 to 1894

Wilson
　　Charles, owner of No 7 from 1864 to 1893
　　David Hugh, tenant of No 13 from 1893 to 1894

Young
　　George A., tenant of No 22 from 1894 to 1900

INDEX OF STREET
NAMES IN EDINBURGH

The index refers to the streets of Edinburgh mentioned in the text. Some streets have been renamed since Victorian times, and for these the modern street name is given in brackets. The first column refers to the maps on Plate 24.

For Plate 24a, the second column uses the following abbreviations:

E – East Edinburgh
NE – North East Edinburgh, including Leith and Portobello
NT – the New Town
NW – North West Edinburgh,
OT – the Old Town
S – Edinburgh south of the Canongate, but not on Plate 41
SE – South of Edinburgh, and east of the area covered by Plate 41
W – West Edinburgh

For Plate 24b, the second column uses a three-by-three grid (for example A1, B2 etcetera).

NOTES

PREFACE
1. Scotland's People: http://www.scotlandspeople.gov.uk/
2. International Genealogical Index of the Church of the Latter Day Saints site: http://www.familysearch.org/eng/default.asp
3. Edinburgh City Library: http://www.edinburgh.gov.uk/internet/leisure/CEC_local_history_and_heritage
4. The National Archive of Scotland: http://www.nas.gov.uk/
5. *The Scotsman* Archive: http://archive.scotsman.com
6. FreeBMD: http://freebmd.rootsweb.com/
7. Wikipedia: http://en.wikipedia.org/wiki/Main_Page

CHAPTER ONE
1. Rodger, R. (see bibliography), page 14

CHAPTER TWO
1. Feu contract between Sir John Dick Lauder and Samuel Hunter for lot 182, owned by the author.
2. The MacDonald family, The Sheiling, Scourie, Sutherland, http://the-sheiling.co.uk/family%20tree.pdf
3. Astronomical Society of Edinburgh, Journal 43: http://www.astronomyedinburgh.org/publications/journals/43/publishing.html
4. *The Scotsman*, 6 October 1865
5. The trial of John Hunter is reported in National Archives of Scotland, references AD14/65/284 and JC26/1865/301.
6. The Dictionary of Scottish Architects: http://www.scottisharchitects.org.uk/architect_full.php?id=201286
7. The Dictionary of Scottish Architects: http://www.scottisharchitects.org.uk/architect_full.php?id=201289

8. The Dictionary of Scottish Architects:
   http://www.scottisharchitects.org.uk/architect_full.php?id=200864
9. Smith, C.J. (see bibliography), Volume 1, page 82.
10. The Dictionary of Scottish Architect:
    http://www.scottisharchitects.org.uk/architect_full.php?id=202840
11. The Dictionary of Scottish Architects:
    http://www.scottisharchitects.org.uk/architect_full.php?id=201287

CHAPTER THREE

1. Statistical Account of Scotland, 1834–1845,Volume 1:
   http://stat-acc-scot.edina.ac.uk/link/1834–45/Edinburgh/Edinburgh/1/665/
2. Anderson, R. D., Lynch, M. and Phillipson, N., (See bibliography), Page 145
3. Anderson, R. D., Lynch, M. and Phillipson, N., (See bibliography), Page 140
4. *British Medical Journal*, 1907 June 8; 1(2423) 1401:
   http://www.ncbi.nlm.nih.gov/pmc/articles/PMC2357603/?page=1
5. Postcard text by kind permission of Malcolm Cant
6. The Sheffield Independent, December 1894, courtesy of
   http://www.sheffieldindexers.com/
7. Robert Bain's family tree, Rootsweb: http://wc.rootsweb.ancestry.com/
8. National Library of Scotland, Scottish Book Trade Index,
   http://www.nls.uk/catalogues/resources/sbti
9. Willison family history: http://willison.org/
10. Edmunds from West Sussex family tree, Rootsweb:
    http://wc.rootsweb.ancestry.com/
11. India Office Family History Search: http://indiafamily.bl.uk/UI/Home.aspx
12. The Scots at War Trust: http://www.scotsatwar.co.uk/index.htm
13. British Settlers in Argentina and Uruguay – studies in 19th and 20th century
    emigration: http://www.argbrit.org/
14. Details from the Title Deeds, lent by the present owner
15. Who's Who in Glasgow in 1909:
    http://gdl.cdlr.strath.ac.uk/eyrwho/index.html
16. The Jester Family Tree: http://www.brianjester.us/tree3/
17. The Gifford Lectures: http://www.giffordlectures.org/biography.asp
18. Shetland Family History website: http://www.bayanne.info/Shetland/
19. John Duncan biography:
    http://www.newble.co.uk/hall/duncanj/biography.html
20. Scottish Book Trade Index at the National Library of Scotland:
    http://www.nls.uk/catalogues/resources/sbti
21. From *The Correspondence of William Henry Fox Talbot* Project which has
    prepared a comprehensive edition of the nearly 10,000 letters to and from Fox
    Talbot (1800–77): http://foxtalbot.dmu.ac.uk/

CHAPTER FOUR

1. Biography: British Geological Survey:
   http://www.bgs.ac.uk/archives/Peach/text/fulltext.html
2. Biography: Scottish Geology: http://www.scottishgeology.com/geology/
   scottish_geologists/people/benjamin_neeve_peach.html
3. Biography, Navigational Aids for the History of Science, Technology & the
   Environment: http://www.nahste.ac.uk/pers/p/GB_0237_NAHSTE_P0258/
4. Henry Littlejohn, biography: Archives Hub:
   http://www.archiveshub.org.uk/news/08082203.html
5. Poor Law and Board of Supervision: Scottish Archive Network:
   http://www.scan.org.uk/knowledgebase/topics/poorlaw2.htm
6. Scottish Ironwork:
   http://www.scottishironwork.org/showfoundrydetail.asp?fid=74
7. New York Times 22 January 1893: http://query.nytimes.com/gst/abstract.
   html?res=9C07E1DF1031E033A25751C2A9679C94629ED7CF
   &scp=2&sq=john+wellstood&st=p
8. John and William Wellstood: http://www.famousamericans.net/
   johngeikiewellstood/
9. Esse stoves: http://www.esse.com/stoves/history/1890.html
10. The Ancestors of Brian Doig, Rootsweb: http://wc.rootsweb.ancestry.com/
11. Brodie's tea and coffee: http://www.brodies1867.co.uk/
12. Isle of Colonsay genealogies: http://www.colonsay.org.uk/
13. Sheets, J.W., (see bibliography)
14. Norman Macleod: http://gdl.cdlr.strath.ac.uk/mlemen/mlemen061.htm
15. The Royal Commission of Inquiry into the Condition of Crofters and Cottars
    in the Highlands and Islands. Lochaber College, University of the Highlands
    and Islands: http://www.highland-elibrary.com/7.html
16. Glasgow Digital Library: http://gdl.cdlr.strath.ac.uk/airgli/airgli0228.htm
17. National Archives of Scotland: reference AD14/79/312
18. Grey River Argus, New Zealand: http://paperspast.natlib.govt.nz/
    cgi-bin/paperspast?a=d&cl=search&d=GRA18790127.2.17&srpos=1&e=01-
    01-1879-31-12-1879—10-PubMetaGRA-1——2%22john+pulsford%22-all
19. Obituary, British Medical Journal May 6 1905: http://www.ncbi.nlm.nih.
    gov/pmc/articles/PMC2320061/pdf/brmedj08115-0043.pdf
20. Phelan Family Album, 1891:
    http://picasaweb.google.com/devorsey/PhelanAlbum1891#
21. Royal Society of Edinburgh:
    http://www.royalsoced.org.uk/fellowship/all_fellows.pdf
22. Phelans of Clonmel, Ireland: http://dev-lady.biz.ly/Phelantree2.html
23. Cant, M. (see bibliography) page 148
24. Moray House School of Educations: http://www.education.ed.ac.uk/aboutus/
    morayhouse/history/Part3/fulton-paterson.html

25. The Dictionary of Scottish Architects:
http://www.scottisharchitects.org.uk/architect_full.php?id=100293

26. Memorial for William Lawson: http://www.findagrave.com/

27. The Ontario Vital Statistics Project:
http://homepages.rootsweb.ancestry.com/~maryc/oxford91.htm

28. Proceedings of the Linnean Society of London, May 1894:
http://www.archive.org/stream/proceedingsoflin189394linn/
proceedingsoflin189394linn_djvu.txt

29. Details of Alexander Mustard junior in The Purvis Family Tree:
http://www.purvisfamilytree.com

CHAPTER FIVE

1. Fry, M., (see bibliography), page 303

2. Biographies of James Young Simpson: http://en.wikipedia.org/wiki/
James_Young_Simpson and http://www.electricscotland.com/
history/other/simpson_james.htm

3. Dr Pritchard's trial: http://grange.interactive.co.uk/cgi-bin-grange/
scrap/pritchard?styled_outline=types%2FSTYLE and
http://www.ebooksread.com/authors-eng/edward-william-pritchard/
trial-of-dr-pritchard-tir/page-6-trial-of-dr-pritchard-tir.shtml

4. India Office Genealogies: http://indiafamily.bl.uk/UI/Home.aspx

5. The Balfours of Orkney: http://www.orkneybalfours.com/index.htm

6. Dictionary of Scottish Architects: http://www.scottisharchitects.org.uk/
architect_full.php?id=200031

7. Headstone in Grange Cemetery

8. Lee, T. A. (see bibliography) page 303

9. Genealogy of the house of Christie: http://www.archive.org/stream/
genealogicalmem06rogegoog/genealogicalmem06rogegoog_djvu.txt

10. Unsolved Mysteries of Canadian History: http://www.canadianmysteries.ca/
sites/klatsassin/murdersorwar/castofcharacters/643en.html

11. India Office Genealogies: http://indiafamily.bl.uk/UI/Home.aspx

12. Edinburgh Academy register, Edinburgh Room, Edinburgh City Library

13. Cruachan Highland Cattle: http://www.cruachan.com.au/1919.htm

14. Lunga Estates: http://www.lunga.com/html/stewartlus.html

15. Alexander-Mackenzie: A history of the Munros of Fowlis,page 40:
http://www.ebooksread.com/authors-eng/alexander-mackenzie/history-of-
the-munros-of-fowlis-with-genealogies-of-the-principal-families-of-th-
kca/page-40-history-of-the-munros-of-fowlis-with-genealogies-of-the-
principal-families-of-th-kca.shtml

16. *Evidence Taken by Her Majesty's Commissioners of Inquiry into the Conditions
of the Crofters and Cottars in the Highlands and Islands of Scotland,* 1884
(Napier Report), digitised and presented in PDF format by Lochaber Collage

Mallaig 2007: http://www.lochabercollege.co.uk/links/napier-commission

CHAPTER SIX

1. David W. Smith Family Tree: Rootsweb: http://wc.rootsweb.ancestry.com/
2. Personal communications from Thomas Cownie's great-grandson
3. Gifford, J. *et al* (see bibliography), page 598
4. West Blacket Association newsletter, November 2002: http://www.westblacket.org.uk/NEWS-11-2002.pdf
5. The kinsfolk of Alexander Cowan: Rootsweb: http://wc.rootsweb.ancestry.com/
6. Lythe, S. G. E. (see bibliography) page 3
7. Steam index Locomotive History: http://www.steamindex.com/manlocos/dundee.htm
8. Lythe, S. G. E. (see bibliography), page 3
9. Grant, J. (see bibliography), Volume III page 21
10. Grant, J. (see bibliography), Volume III page 20
11. Proceedings of the Society of Antiquaries of Scotland, 1851–1890. http://www.socantscot.org/content.asp?Page=251&Menu=237
12. A History of the Usher family in Scotland: http://freepages.genealogy.rootsweb. ancestry.com/~usher/ ushersct/files/cmusher_book_word.exe
13. The Usher Family of Scotland: Rootsweb family tree: http://wc.rootsweb.ancestry.com/

CHAPTER SEVEN

1. Flanders, J. (see bibliography), pages 103 – 108
2. Beeton, I. (see bibliography), page 446
3. Mull Genealogy: http://www.mullgenealogy.co.uk/

CHAPTER EIGHT

1. Gilbert, W. M., (see bibliography), page 257
2. Rodger, R., (See Bibliography), page 77
3. Flanders, J. (see bibliography), pages xxv
4. Victoria and Albert Museum: Wallpapers for children: http://www.vam.ac.uk/collections/prints_books/features/ Wallpaper/Wallpapers_Children/index.html
5. Grierson, M. G., (see bibliography), page [13]

CHAPTER NINE

1. Gilbert, W. M., (see bibliography), page 149

CHAPTER TEN

1. Gilbert, W. M., (see bibliography), pages 167, 265, 266
2. Edin Photos Website: http://www.edinphoto.org.uk/1_edin/1_edinburgh_history_-_dates.htm
3. Victoria and Albert Museum: http://collections.vam.ac.uk/item/O17882/wallpaper-print-queen-victorias-golden-jubilee/
4. Rampant Scotland: http://www.rampantscotland.com/visit/blvisit_livingstone.htm

CHAPTER ELEVEN

1. Fashion-Era: http://www.fashion-era.com/mid-late_victorian_fashion.htm#1890s
2. Gilbert, W. M., (See bibliography), page 175
3. Monkwell, Lady, (see bibliography), page 77

CHAPTER TWELVE

1. Dormeuil Brothers, Paris: http://www.dormeuil.com/; Holland and Sherry: http://www.hollandandsherry.com/ and Lloyd & Attree: http://www.lloydattreeandsmith.com/
2. National Archive of Scotland: CS318/33/118
3. Marshall, R., (See bibliography), page 247
4. Marshall, R., (See bibliography), page 249
5. Marshall, R., (See bibliography), page 250
6. Hunter, D. L. G., (See bibliography), page 1
7. Inglis, J, (See bibliography) page 6
8. Hunter, D. L. G. (See bibliography) page 15
9. Hunter, D. L. G. (See bibliography) page 19
10. Hunter, D. L. G. (See bibliography) page 77
11. Edin Photos Website: http://www.edinphoto.org.uk/1_edin/1_edinburgh_history_-_recollections_fountainbridge_1927-33.htm#2_liz_gatley
12. Cant, M., (See Bibliography), page 148

INDEX